☑ **W9-DCW-171**

12/09

The C...

HO...IC
RE...G
Kit

**CHECK FOR
AUDIO CD IN
FRONT OF BOOK**

Create Q... *Budget!*

800 East 96th Street, Indianapolis, Indiana 46240 USA

The Complete Home Music Recording Starter Kit: Create Quality Home Recordings on a Budget!

Copyright © 2009 by Que Publishing

All rights reserved. No part of this book shall be reproduced, stored in a retrieval system, or transmitted by any means, electronic, mechanical, photocopying, recording, or otherwise, without written permission from the publisher. No patent liability is assumed with respect to the use of the information contained herein. Although every precaution has been taken in the preparation of this book, the publisher and author assume no responsibility for errors or omissions. Nor is any liability assumed for damages resulting from the use of the information contained herein.

ISBN-13: 978-0-7897-3811-0
ISBN-10: 0-7897-3811-2

Library of Congress Cataloging-in-Publication Data:
Fayte, Buster.
  The complete home music recording starter kit / Buster Fayte.
     p. cm.
  Includes index.
  ISBN 978-0-7897-3811-0
  1. Sound—Recording and reproducing—Digital techniques—Amateurs' manuals. 2. Sound studios—Amateurs' manuals. I. Title.
  TK7881.4.F39 2008
  781.49—dc22
                         2008040863

Printed in the United States of America
First Printing: October 2008

Trademarks

All terms mentioned in this book that are known to be trademarks or service marks have been appropriately capitalized. Que Publishing cannot attest to the accuracy of this information. Use of a term in this book should not be regarded as affecting the validity of any trademark or service mark.

Warning and Disclaimer

Every effort has been made to make this book as complete and as accurate as possible, but no warranty or fitness is implied. The information provided is on an "as is" basis. The author and the publisher shall have neither liability nor responsibility to any person or entity with respect to any loss or damages arising from the information contained in this book or from the use of the DVD or programs accompanying it.

Bulk Sales

Que Publishing offers excellent discounts on this book when ordered in quantity for bulk purchases or special sales. For more information, please contact

   U.S. Corporate and Government Sales
   1-800-382-3419
   corpsales@pearsontechgroup.com

For sales outside the United States, please contact

   International Sales
   international@pearsoned.com

Associate Publisher
Greg Wiegand

Acquisitions Editor
Laura Norman

Development Editor
Kevin Howard

Managing Editor
Patrick Kanouse

Senior Project Editor
Tonya Simpson

Copy Editor
Gill Editorial Services

Indexer
Ken Johnson

Proofreader
Elizabeth Scott

Technical Editor
Heather McDonald

Publishing Coordinator
Cindy Teeters

Multimedia Developer
Dan Scherf

Book Designer
Anne Jones

Composition
Mark Shirar

CONTENTS AT A GLANCE

Table of Contents

About the Author

Buster Fayte (aka Gary Rebholz) is a musician, author, and experienced training professional. He's been recording music in a variety of home and professional studios for more than a few years now.

Buster has written a multitude of songs and recorded a fair number of them. Some of the most recent recordings are available for you to listen to at his website, www.busterfayte.com.

As the bass player for the Midwestern phenomenon of a couple decades ago, Kevin Fayte and Rocket 8, Buster also acted as the band's techie and engineered the home recording (on cassette four track!) of their album of original rockabilly, *Ridin' in a Rocket*, which won the band a contract with England's Nervous Records. In the tradition of all the true rockabilly greats, fame and riches were, alas, slow to follow.

As a training professional, Buster has tutored hundreds of people on various software applications. He creates written training materials as well as training videos, live training, web-based training, and multi-media materials. He has delivered countless presentations at training seminars, sales events, trade shows, press events, schools, and anywhere else someone wants to learn.

An accomplished author, Buster has written five books; this is his first book for Que Publishing.

When he's not writing music, books, or training materials, Buster is an avid bicyclist. He's been known to voluntarily sign up for one-day, 100-plus-mile road rides of relentless and sadistic hill climbing with nothing but his titanium LeMond Victoire and obsessive determination to pull him to the crest of each rise.

Buster lives in a quiet Midwestern USA village with his wife, Rebecca, and five wonderful children—each of whom has called him "coach" on the soccer field at one time or another.

Buster would love to receive a friend request from you at www.myspace.com/busterfayte and see you at his website at www.busterfayte.com.

Dedication

I dedicate this book to my older brother, Tom, who would have been filled with pride and happiness had he been able to see me meld my loves of music and writing.

Acknowledgments

The music seems as good a place as any to attempt an expression of my gratitude to the large group of people without whom this project could never have been completed. So I'll start with my musical heroes and work from there.

My beautiful mother, Rose Rebholz, has done so much more for me than teach me my first guitar chords. She watched with joy and pride as my ability on the instrument quickly surpassed her own, although she still humbles me on the piano and the accordion and with her angelic singing voice!

Thanks to Kevin Fayte (aka Rau) and M. Scott Young, who have been musical mentors and collaborators as well as the closest of friends for all these years. Joe Snare (aka Vosen), Matthew Berger, and Michael Bryant have each played an important role in keeping the music alive in me, and I thank them for that.

I want to thank my good friend Chandru Solraj, a gentle soul whose encouragement, enthusiasm, and wisdom have helped me view my art and my life in a completely new way.

My father, Jack Rebholz, instilled in me the kind of ethic it takes to recognize what needs to be done and stick to the task until it is. He taught me to work hard and take pride in my work. Without those skills to apply to my music and writing, there would be only silence, and this book would not have been written.

My lovely sisters, Sue, Judy, Jeanne, Barb, and Nancy, are each in her way a special inspiration to me.

There are many people to thank at Que Publishing and the Pearson Education group. Betsy Brown, with whom I've worked on past books, referred me to Que when she could not take this project on. Thank you to Laura Norman, my acquisitions editor, who with relentless enthusiasm convinced the publishers at Que to take a chance on a venture that moved in a different direction. She has been tireless in overseeing this project.

Thank you to each of my editors—Heather McDonald, Kevin Howard, Todd Brakke, and Karen Gill—for their detailed attention. Thanks to Tonya Simpson for overseeing the review process. Thanks to Pamalee Nelson, Dan Scherf, and Cindy Teeters for their help.

Thanks to Jason Gleed and Joe Vitale, Jr. I'm proud to count these talented and successful musicians among my friends, and I'm grateful for their roles in winning approval for this project.

Thanks to Peter Rebholz, who reminded me that sometimes, regardless of how busy you are, you have to take the time to study a thing beyond your first impressions to learn how it really works!

I can't thank Brian Orr enough. Not only has he encouraged me and cheered my successes, but he's been an unexpected inspiration and an ever-more trusted friend. He is an amazingly talented musician and yet has a humility about him that reveals the depth of his sincerity. He read every word of this manuscript before I submitted it to the publisher and helped me keep on track—a thankless job for which I am forever indebted.

How can I adequately thank my family? Jake, Leah, Kyri, Sam, and Max fill my life with joy and inspire me daily to be the best father this flawed human can be. I have shamefully neglected them during the book's writing, yet they understand and continue to love me. I am hopelessly proud of each of them.

Finally, I want to humbly thank Rebecca, who I love beyond love and whose love I in turn cherish as a gift from God. She not only willingly accepted the entire burden of running the household during the writing of this book, but she, too, read every word before it was sent to the publisher. A talented writer herself, Rebecca offered me suggestions that refined my all-too-often undisciplined meanderings and made this project infinitely better than it would have been if left solely up to me!

We Want to Hear from You!

As the reader of this book, *you* are our most important critic and commentator. We value your opinion and want to know what we're doing right, what we could do better, what areas you'd like to see us publish in, and any other words of wisdom you're willing to pass our way.

As an associate publisher for Que Publishing, I welcome your comments. You can email or write me directly to let me know what you did or didn't like about this book—as well as what we can do to make our books better.

Please note that I cannot help you with technical problems related to the topic of this book. We do have a User Services group, however, where I will forward specific technical questions related to the book.

When you write, please be sure to include this book's title and author as well as your name, email address, and phone number. I will carefully review your comments and share them with the author and editors who worked on the book.

Email: feedback@quepublishing.com

Mail: Greg Wiegand
　　　　Associate Publisher
　　　　Que Publishing
　　　　800 East 96th Street
　　　　Indianapolis, IN 46240 USA

Reader Services

Visit our website and register this book at informit.com/register for convenient access to any updates, downloads, or errata that might be available for this book.

Introduction

Want to set up a home studio so you can record fantastic-sounding music? Of course, you do! This book shows you how. No nonsense. No mind-numbingly technical concepts. No kidding.

But first let me step back a moment and paint a picture so you can determine whether you really need this book. Has this ever happened to you?

You want to record your music. You want to set up in your spare room or basement, so you start down the road to outfitting a home studio.

After a prolonged period of confusion during which you have no solid idea of where or how to start, you begin to look for answers. Every book you read, every website you visit, every salesperson you talk to barrages you with a dizzying array of options. And the price tag climbs. Specialized microphones (and several of them), equalizers, reverb units, fancy mixers, sound insulation, acoustical wall treatments…and the price tag climbs.

Then the technical jargon hits. Acoustical theories, signal-to-noise ratios, the logarithmic decibel scale—all of it leaves you confused and uncertain, and still the price tag climbs.

Soon the apparent complexity of what you need to learn overwhelms you, and the cost of what you're told you need to buy leaves the upper limit of your budget looking like a tiny dot in your rearview mirror. So you put your dreams on hold yet again. If you're lucky, you haven't spent much already. But probably you have. So you have a little more gear (though still not enough) and a lot less money. What you definitely do not have is a home studio capable of doing high-quality work. "Someday," you say, "someday…".

The Accessibility of Modern Recording Methods

If that story sounds sadly familiar, you've grabbed the right book! I've been there. In fact, I struggled in that frustrating cycle for years, scratching out substandard quality recordings as best I could with the gear I could beg, borrow, or (oh so rarely) buy. Don't get me wrong; I enjoyed every minute of every recording I've made over the years. But it sure would have been nice to end up with something of high enough quality that I would have felt good about releasing it. But I could never get there with the gear I had.

Well, I'm here to tell you, friend, that all this has changed in just the past few years. "Someday" has finally arrived! Suddenly, after being locked away from us mere mortals, the ability to make great-sounding home recordings without going broke—and going to college to study audio engineering—has become not only possible, but also affordable. Computers, software, and other fantastic technological advances have liberated all of us! Pretty dramatic, isn't it? Yes, as a matter of fact, it is!

Recording technique has come a long way since Édouard-Léon Scott de Martinville beat the commonly credited Edison by almost 20 years to the world's very first sound recording with his phonautogram in 1860.

EDISON REMAINS UNDIMINISHED!

Even though most people believe that Thomas Edison invented audio recording, it was actually Édouard-Léon Scott de Martinville, a French inventor/dabbler, who created the first audio recording device and the first audio recording itself. He called the machine the *phonautogram*. But if Edison happens to be your hero, don't worry! Turns out he was still a pretty smart guy.

As a twist to the bizarre story of the phonautogram, apparently Scott de Martinville, though having devised a way to record the sound onto paper as sound wave diagrams, had for some odd reason envisioned us *reading* recorded sound, not hearing it, and thus had developed no way to play it back audibly. Go figure.

Edison's recording of *Mary Had a Little Lamb* then remains by common consensus the first ever to be *heard* after it was recorded. Scott de Martinville's recording was not heard until earlier this year (2008!) when scientists devised a way to optically read the squiggles his device made and turn them into sound. The recording turned out to be of the French folk song *Au Clair de la Lune* and the audio quality was—well, let's just say you'll do far, far better with the techniques you learn in this book! But still, it was a lot easier to identify the song once we could *hear* the recording than it was when we could only *look* at it. On that score, Scott de Martinville got it wrong; Edison got it right.

We now find ourselves well into the digital age, and still it's surprising how few people have awakened to the new age of recording technology. It still isn't free to set up a home studio, but it's never been more affordable than right now. You're going to have to spend some money, but if you follow my advice, you'll be amazed at just how little we're talking about (compared to traditional recording methods) and equally amazed at the fantastic results you'll get from the gear you buy.

So prepare to be amazed, because I'm going to show you exactly how to do it. You'll be recording your music in no time.

Ten Assumptions

Throughout this book, I'm going to proceed under a certain set of assumptions. If even just a couple of these assumptions turn out to be true of you and your situation, you'll get something valuable out of this book. If you can live with most or all 10 of these assumptions, the potential exists for your recording output to explode!

As I discuss various topics throughout this book, I'll remind you of these assumptions so you have a complete understanding of why I make the recommendations that I do.

Here then I present my 10 assumptions:

1. You have a strong desire to record great-sounding music, mostly on your own, in a home studio.

2. You are not able (or willing) to set up a pro-level home studio environment. By this, I mean that it isn't practical for you to undertake a complete renovation of your basement to turn it into a state-of-the-art studio.

3. You can afford to—and are willing to—spend a reasonable amount of money on setting up your studio, but you need to make the most out of every dollar, euro, peso, or whatever it is that you spend. In other words, as we say in the United States, "You need to get the most bang for your buck."

4. You are not free to make unlimited amounts of noise during the recording process. For instance, you have roommates, parents, kids, neighbors, or others who might be less than appreciative if your power chords keep them awake at 1:23 a.m. or interrupt their viewing of *American Idol*.

5. You want the most control possible over the recording, editing, and mixing process, and you want as much flexibility as you can possibly get in how you create your projects. And, importantly, you are not afraid—or are at least willing to overcome your fear—of computers.

6. You're willing to be flexible and open minded and can set aside any purist attitudes toward gear in the interest of accomplishing great recordings in the less-than-great recording environment I mentioned in assumption 4.

7. You're willing to concede that sometimes, in the interest of getting something done given the realities of your home-studio setup and budget, it's okay to settle for techniques that the "pros" or purists might dismiss as not up to their standards. In other words, it's not the technique that obsesses you; it's the quality of the *results*.

8. You're not interested in sorting through the details of a bunch of different techniques that you might never use to find the one that might work for you. Rather, you want a clear, concise, proven path to getting your music recorded with very high quality.

9. You want to skip nonessential technical details and jargon in the interest of getting results quickly. You can—and should—learn all you can about recording technology, but I refuse to let your lack of expertise in technical areas stop you from recording music right now!

10. You're willing to record with mostly electric or electronic instruments whenever that's practical. You'll need to use a microphone for some things, but any time you can avoid a live mic, you avoid lots and lots of headaches!

Quick Guide to *The Complete Home Music Recording Starter Kit*

Throughout this book, I'll tell you exactly what you need to know to set up your home recording system. The techniques I talk about are not just theoretical; these techniques are the same proven, practical techniques that I've used to record my own musical projects. If you're interested in hearing the kind of results I get from the techniques I discuss in this book, check out my music at www.busterfayte.com. (As long as you're there, take a minute to sign onto my mailing list so I can keep you up to date with what I'm doing!)

Don't get hung up on whether or not you like my music or my singing or guitar playing. Instead, focus on the production and recording quality. Does it exhibit a level of production quality that would make a positive impression on your fans and industry contacts? Is the quality high enough to make you feel good about charging your fans $10 to buy a CD? Would you buy the music of your favorite artist if it exhibited this same recording quality? Although I know my own results will improve with every project, I'm proud to say that I think my recordings pass these tests—and my fans obviously agree! That's what we're after, and that's what this book teaches.

What We'll Discuss

The first step in the process involves basic organizational decisions and whether to go analog or digital. You've heard the arguments; here we'll discuss the realities and the logical, cut-and-dry, never-look-back, no-second-thoughts choice. The decision is really simple, and I'll show you why.

Next, we'll talk about your recording space. Remember, I'm assuming you don't have the producer's dream studio in your basement, so you have limitations. We'll talk about how you're going to not only live with, but actually thrive despite those limitations. We'll also discuss the computer gear you need and how to set all of it up.

After that, we'll lay down some guide tracks to get us started and then spend several chapters talking about the realities of recording different instruments.

We'll end with discussions of mixing, mastering, and delivery. After that, you're on your way to quality recording projects in your own studio.

Special Elements

Throughout this book, I'll sprinkle in four special elements: Notes, Tips, Cautions, and sidebars. Also, I'll end each chapter with a section called "Studio Log." The Studio Log summarizes the chapter and gives you the main points in easily reviewable form. Here's what each of these elements looks like:

NOTE

I'll use a Note when I want to give you some small piece of interesting information that doesn't really fit into the flow of the current text. It might be a resource you could look into for further understanding, a place where you can go to see or hear an example of what I'm discussing, or some other helpful tidbit.

TIP

I'll use Tips when I think I know of a way to make a task a bit easier or a way to give you better results. For instance, if I'm discussing recording a guitar, I might use a tip to remind you to make sure you're in tune.

CAUTION

I'll use Cautions when something I'm telling you to do has a potential danger toward your project, your gear, or you. For instance, if I'm telling you to play your recording back while wearing headphones, I might use a Caution to remind you to turn the volume down first so you avoid damaging your hearing.

SIDEBAR

I'll use sidebars when I have an interesting or amusing story to tell that's related to the topic I'm discussing, but not necessarily critical to the discussion. Sidebars provide a little bit of fun and color commentary. They're a lot like Notes, only longer.

You saw a sidebar earlier when I told the story of the first recording machine.

Studio Log

I'll end each chapter with a "Studio Log" section. Here I'll provide a short recap of what the chapter covered, just as you might enter a summary of what happened during a recording session into your studio log book. The Studio Log brings out the main points one more time to reinforce what you have learned in that chapter. If you want a quick summary of the entire book, you could cheat and read all the Studio Logs first.

Now that you know what this book's all about, let's get started with the details and the fun.

1

Laying the Groundwork for Recording

IN THIS CHAPTER

- Get a handle on your plan, including your budget
- Understand analog and digital options, and choose between them
- Gain historical perspective on home music recording
- Discover digital recording options
- Decide which format—analog or digital—to use

I'd like to jump right into the fun stuff of recording just as much as you would. But, naturally, you have some prep work to do and a few decisions to make. This chapter sets the stage for the rest of the book as well as the rest of your studio setup and recording procedure, so make sure to spend some time here. We'll talk about the important issues of how much money you can put into this endeavor you're about to undertake, your general options for recording format, and what format makes the most sense.

Get a Grip on Your Budget

You probably hate budget talk as much as I do. After all, we're artists, right? We want to create, not number-crunch. We have no space for digits and calculations in brains made for creativity. Numbers bog people like us down. They constrict us. Forget that number-crunching nonsense; we must be free to create beauty!

Right. Get over it. Quickly.

If you want to put together an effective home studio—and I mentioned this in the Introduction—it's going to cost you. You're going to have to spend money. How much money it costs in the end depends completely upon the decisions you make along the way. Therefore, you need to develop a clear idea of what you have in terms of financial resources, what you want to accomplish with your studio, and exactly how you can marry those two ideas to develop a system that gives you the results you're after.

If you don't think about the expenditures you need to make before you make them, you're just as likely to get your studio three-quarters put together only to find that you haven't left enough financial reserve to get you the rest of the way. And there's nothing more frustrating than *almost* having a home studio that works!

Also, you have to understand the end goal and keep that goal firmly in mind. You'll make decisions along the way that will affect decisions you'll have to make later. If you made the wrong decision early and impulsively bought gear that turns out not to be right for your setup, you've put yourself in a situation where you either have to compromise or go back and buy a different piece of gear that you should have bought in the first place.

I know you want to get started recording right now. But I urge you to read through the entire book before you buy a single piece of new gear. Once you've made it all the way through, you'll know your options. You'll understand the pieces of the puzzle as well as how they fit together. You'll know that maybe you want to spend a little less on something we discuss in Chapter 3, "Setting Up Your Computer for Music Production," because you'll need extra money to move up in quality with something that we don't touch on until Chapter 7, "Utilizing MIDI in Your Projects."

Put a budget together. Know going in how much you have available to spend on your studio. I'll make every attempt to keep the final aggregate price tag as low as possible (hopefully in the range of $1,000 to $2,500 depending on the gear you already own), and I'll give you some strategies on doing that. But you'll only be in a position to make wise purchasing decisions once you understand the options and can compare what you need with what you can afford.

Analog's Smooth Warmth or Digital's Crystal Clarity

Now that you've got your budget firmly in hand, the first fundamental decision you have to make involves the basic technology that drives your studio. You probably know that you can record onto an analog (tape-based) system or a digital system. You have likely even formed some pretty staunch opinions on the topic already.

Both camps have their pros, which they are only too glad to list for you. Both sides also have their cons, which the *other* side is happy to list. Hey, it's almost like an election!

In this book, I'll cut through all the rhetoric and finally put the argument to rest—at least for our narrow purposes anyway. First, let's meet the contestants and learn a little bit about their strengths and potential weaknesses. Here, for the first time, I invoke 2 of my 10 assumptions—numbers 8 and 9, which basically state that you don't want to get bogged down in the technical details of techniques you'll never end up using—to avoid going into discussions that hold no immediate relevance to the recommendations I'm about to make.

NOTE

You can find a wealth of good resources that will explain exactly how analog and digital recording technologies work. If you're like me, you'll find those details quite interesting, and I think it really does help to have that understanding. Still, while I urge you to add this topic to your list of further study, I see no reason for me to rewrite what other experts have already laid out. At the same time, I see no reason why a less than full understanding of the details at this point should keep you from moving ahead with setting up your recording outfit.

Analog Options

Time-tested analog recording technologies have absolutely no need to prove their merit. Any technology that turns out albums like *Revolver*, *Pet Sounds*, and *Dark Side of the Moon* has earned the right to sincere veneration. I will never cast dispersions upon this technology!

In the analog multitrack recording world, you generally have two options: reel-to-reel and cassette-based tape machines.

First are reel-to-reel tape machines. I'll be honest; I don't know too much about these machines even though I've worked with them in studios both as a musician and a recording engineer. I do know that they have been the standard in pro analog studios for many years. A great deal of absolutely fantastic music has been recorded onto countless tape reels over those years. Studios continue to record great music to them today, and they probably will for a long, long time to come.

The thing is, these types of machines hold little relevance that I can see to the type of home studio we want to set up. I say that for a couple of simple reasons.

First, after an online search at a couple of the most well-known music-related retailers (admittedly, a cursory search), I couldn't find one of these machines for sale. That seems to confirm what I already knew: These machines are specialized gear that probably sell through specialized sources and are thus quite expensive. I'm guessing they're well out of the reach of my budget and yours.

There was a time when manufacturers seemed to dabble in manufacturing machines aimed at the home recording market. Perhaps they still do. But I don't care and neither should you due to the second reason for my assertion that these machines hold no relevance for us: their inherent limitations.

Namely, reel-to-reel tape machines are incredibly limited compared to other modern methods of recording. No matter how much money you spend on a reel-to-reel multitrack recorder, that machine will always be able to record a limited number of audio tracks. It could be as many as 48 tracks or maybe more, but it's still limited. And in the budget range of the typical home studio, that limit probably looks more like maybe 8 tracks and probably only 4.

Not only that, but that machine does one thing—well, okay, two things: It records sound, and it plays sound back. Period. If you want to *do* anything to that sound, like mixing your tracks perhaps, you're going to need a lot of other gear. You'll need a mixer capable of handling all the tracks, equalizers, limiters, reverb units, patch bays, and on and on.

Frankly, if you have the budget for all that kind of gear, you're probably only reading this book because it was sitting on the table at the body shop while you were waiting for that custom paint job on your Porsche.

And if you want to actually edit the music you've recorded, you'll need to buy a razor blade and special tape. That alone should convince you. After all, it's really, really difficult to play the guitar with bandages on your fingertips!

Your other main analog option is a multitrack cassette recorder. Many of us have experience with cassette-tape-based multitrack machines. Me? I love that technology. Those machines were fantastic tools that allowed the first viable home studios to sprout up all over. My first home recordings were done on the original first-of-the-breed TEAC Portastudio 144. What a revolutionary machine that thing was! Four tracks of audio recorded onto a standard cassette tape! The ability to bounce from track to track gave me the possibility of 10 tracks with only one generation of bounce!

Two of my closest lifelong friends and musical partners each bought one of these machines (at the time, they cost around $1,000 if I remember correctly), and I'd connect them for even more recording space. You can see one of these machines in Figure 1.1. My first band (Kevin Fayte and Rocket 8) recorded an album of original rockabilly on one of those beauties, and that album was picked up by Nervous Records in England for a while. What a thrill for a bunch of kids from Hicksville, USA. And all of it was made possible by the cassette four-track. Man, those were the days!

Figure 1.1
My good friend and A-list drummer M. Scott Young still has his Portastudio 144 cassette-based multitrack recorder. We actually made a record on that thing!

Indeed, those were the days—the days of "so close and yet so far." These machines made the home studio actually possible and practical for the first time ever. But four tracks don't go far at all—even with bouncing capabilities. And although the machines had a built-in mixer, you still needed to buy outboard gear like reverb units and so on. If that machine was the best you could afford, chances were good you couldn't afford much of the outboard gear that you would need to make your recordings sound professional.

In other words, the TEAC Portastudio 144 was a tease. A regular musician could finally do multitrack recording. Initially, that was very exciting. But, the gear's limitations meant that no matter how much work you put into it, you were always going to come up short of the quality you wanted.

GOOD ENOUGH FOR THE BOSS

If you were recording with the TEAC Portastudio 144, you were in some really fine company (besides me). In the early '80s, Bruce Springsteen used one of these to record a collection of songs that were originally meant to be demos. Those recordings were eventually released as the *Nebraska* album, a bleak yet brilliant piece of work. If it's good enough for Bruce, it's good enough for you, right? Well, sort of. Don't forget that he was already a big star at that point. He had the resources in terms of both money and connections with top-notch pros that enabled him to take those rough four-track recordings and put some professional polish on them. That does make a bit of a difference. Plus, he was the Boss. He already had a huge following, and his career survived even though *Nebraska*, although critically acclaimed, was not much of a commercial success.

Still, like I said, cassette-based four-track machines were revolutionary. And the truth is, I still see a lot of value in them today. Maybe even more value than ever. The prices for modern cassette four tracks have come way down. You can get one new for less than $100 these days. At that price, it probably doesn't even pay to buy a used one. True, the same limitations as always still haunt them. But, in my opinion, these smaller, sleeker modern machines have their place in almost any home studio as a musical scratch pad. It's great to have one on hand when you want to quickly lay down a song idea. Cram a microphone into the input, arm a track, press Record, and sing away. That beats booting up the computer every time you have an idea!

Digital Options

While analog technologies hold the venerated honor of being responsible for most of the world's greatest recordings, lots of great stuff happens in the digital domain, too. Ry Cooder's *Bop 'Til You Drop* and Dire Straits' *Brothers in Arms* were the first digitally recorded, mixed, and mastered rock albums. And lots of great classical and other recordings have been recorded that way, too.

The options in the digital domain are starting to mount. You can record digitally to tape or to a hard disc. We've recently seen the advent of machines that record to writable DVD media. But hard-disc recording has really taken over the digital world—at least for now. Therefore, let's talk about hard-disc recording, which itself breaks down further into two categories that I want to focus on.

Portable Digital Studio (PDS) units, also known by several other names such as Portable Digital Workstations, owe a lot to the cassette-based multitrack machines we discussed in the previous section. In fact, they are the descendants carrying on in the home-recording tradition. These standalone recording machines work very much like those old cassette machines, only they've been souped up with all kinds of cool features that are only possible to include (in such a small package) in a digital environment.

Unlike the old Portastudio that I recoded on, PDS units typically have lots of features built in, particularly light-editing features and digital signal processing (DSP) tools like reverbs, compression, and other filters. (We'll talk about DSP later in this book.) Some even include drum machines and amp modeling, which is something we'll discuss in detail later and a key component to the type of studio we're talking about. These machines also often have built-in CD burners so you can burn your songs directly to an audio CD.

Prices have really come down for these units recently; you can get into one starting at right around $300 if you catch a sale. And you really do get a lot for your money. The built-in DSP, like the filters I mentioned, means that you don't have to spend more to buy outboard gear that does the same thing. That's huge when you're recording on a budget!

Most PDS units also offer some rudimentary editing tools. For instance, if you like the guitar riff that you played in verse one but you hate the way you muffed it in verse two, you might be able to replace the one you don't like with a copy of the one you do. That's cool.

Finally, these units offer the ultimate in portability. You can tuck the machine under your arm and take your whole project with you on vacation if you want to. Some even run optionally on batteries and therefore make great field or location recording machines.

However, the PDS world is not a utopia. These machines, like their analog ancestors, have a finite number of available tracks. Naturally, the ones on the lower end of the price scale offer fewer tracks—typically eight these days. The more you're willing to pay, the more tracks you get, but still a track limit always exists, so you're stuck back in track-bouncing land. And although track bouncing hurts less in digital than in analog since there's not tape noise to compound, it's definitely not the best way to work.

WHAT'S TRACK BOUNCING?

I've mentioned bouncing a couple of times. So what does it mean? When you're working on a system with a finite number of tracks, you soon run out of available ones. Obviously, the fewer tracks you have, the sooner you run out. One way around this is to record onto all your tracks but one and then play all those tracks while you record the output to the last remaining track. Now you have one track that holds a mix of all the other tracks, and you can erase what's on the original tracks to make room for recording something new onto them.

If you have no other option, it's a useful technique. But you can see the problems, right? Once you've mixed all the tracks together into one track and then erased what was on the original tracks, you're committed to that mix. And, by the way, it's a mono mix and will always be so. If you decide later you don't like that mix or don't like one of the parts, ouch. Live with it, or go back and redo a lot of work. Further, in the analog world, each time you bounce tracks like this, you also record the tape hiss that exists on those tracks. That's why analog bouncing has a practical limit usually considered to be one bounce. If you bounce a second time, the tape hiss starts to take over like the bass player's know-it-all spouse making the band's wardrobe decisions. Not good.

PDS units have another problem that they share with any gear really, but it needs to be kept in mind when you're making these decisions. The less expensive machines are less expensive not only because they have fewer tracks and features, but also because they typically utilize lower-quality components. That all adds up to lower-quality results in the end. Let's face it; you can't expect to turn out truly professional-sounding work on a $300 machine. But you can put together some high-quality demos.

Finally, a PDS is a one-piece unit. While there is a good aspect to this—all-in-one simplicity and porta-bility—it also means that each year that goes by sees your machine growing more and more out-dated. To update, you would have to purchase a whole new unit.

But if you're working on a slim budget, you should definitely take a serious look at your options in the PDS world.

You can also set up a Digital Audio Workstation (DAW). With a DAW you utilize multitrack software on your personal computer to record directly to your computer's hard drive. The term DAW can refer to the entire computer setup in some uses, or it can refer to the specific multitrack software. I'll use it both ways in this book and clarify which usage I mean where necessary.

I'm going to tip my hand here and tell you that, in my opinion, the DAW approach makes the most sense for your home studio. With a DAW, we're talking about using the same gear that many profes-sionals use, so you know that quality is limited only by your skills and experience.

Because we'll spend a great deal of this book exploring and using a DAW to record our music, I won't explain the DAW approach here. You'll see how it works throughout much of the remainder of this book.

The Final Analysis

All right, now that you know your options and you know where I come down, it's time for me to jus-tify my decision.

Analog Versus Digital: The Great Debate

There's just no way around it; you've simply *got* to love and respect analog recording technologies! They've given us so much great music. And I'm just as big a sucker for old-school approaches as the next guy. My wife would certainly say more so, actually.

"But isn't the future digital? It's better, right?"

"No! Analog's way better! At least that's what that expert says."

"Yeah? Well, he couldn't be more wrong according to that expert!"

This probably won't be the first place that you read about the debate that rages between the forces in the new digital vanguard and the stalwart faithful of the old analog picket. And I don't make many guarantees, but I do guarantee it won't be the last.

Some feel that analog is bad simply because it's old technology. Others hate digital simply because they've heard the bad rep it earned in the early years when even the pros were turning out less-than-stellar material because they hadn't yet learned how to work with the technology.

One argument says that analog technologies are old, outdated, and inherently noisy due to unavoidable tape hiss. On the other hand, digital technologies are cutting edge and crystal clear. They thus offer the most faithful sound reproduction possible.

A different argument asserts that analog recordings have a warmth and an indefinable charm that you feel more than hear. Those that argue this insist that you simply cannot achieve these results in the harsh, cold, sterile digital environment.

Let's solve this once and for all, shall we? The great debate over this issue is an utter and complete waste of your time and mine. (Thus, I offer my most sincere apologies for making you read the last few paragraphs.)

I've already mentioned the Beatles album *Revolver*—analog and stellar! And second to none, in my opinion. I've also mentioned *Brothers in Arms*—moody, moving, compelling, and totally digital. Let's face it; it's not about which technology was used. Rather, it's about what was done with the technology. You can have a horrible-sounding analog recording just as easily as you can have a horrible-sounding digital recording.

Take your cue from Neil Young. You probably won't find any more high-profile and adamant proponent of the superiority of analog technologies. And this guy's been in and around the studio for a whole lot of years now. To hear him talk, you might think he has no use for digital technologies.

Neil Young may be a vocal fan of analog technology, but does that mean his records are only available on vinyl? Of course not. He has released great music with both technologies and even—gasp!—with a combination of both.

So it boils down to this: You can make great-sounding recordings with digital technology. That's been proven. And, as we've discussed and as you will see more fully throughout the remainder of this book, modern digital recording equipment gives you far more flexibility and value for your limited budget than you could ever even come close to achieving with analog gear.

So can we please agree to put the great debate to rest at least for the purposes of setting up your home recording studio? In this instance, digital wins hands down. Frankly, it's not even a fair contest. But don't worry; you'll still be able to have plenty of arguments about this subject with your purist, live-analog-or-die! buddies in the dressing room during breaks between sets. But when it boils right down to it, your prolific output and quality will speak louder than their words.

PDS Versus DAW

So, you've agreed to at least consider going the digital route. It's no secret that I believe you've made a wise choice. But now you've got another decision to make. Should you go PDS or DAW? Again, I propose that the decision virtually makes itself.

I've already talked about some of the limitations of a PDS. And, yes, of course, the DAW approach has some hurdles to contend with.

A DAW is not quite as self-contained as a PDS because so much resides inside the PDS right out of the box. A DAW system is likely to cost more than a PDS. In a DAW, you have software to install, drivers to deal with, and those mystical and vexing technical issues that seem to lie in wait inside every computer I've ever touched. The computer that houses your DAW is subject to crashes, viruses, and other nasty problems that people usually turn to their IT department to solve. But in your home studio, you don't have an IT department. Well, you do, but it's a department of one, and you brush his or her teeth every morning, so you have to be pretty confident with working on computers. If you're not, you're going to have to overcome your hesitation or stick with a PDS.

We could come up with other negatives of using a DAW. For instance, unless you buy special gear, you'll be doing your mixing with clicks of a mouse instead of the satisfying tactile feel of sliders and knobs under your fingers. But I've been using a DAW for a long time now, and I've yet to come across any problem that has made me want to throw my hands up in frustration and dig out that old Portastudio. I love working in a DAW, warts and all, and you will, too, once you get comfortable with it.

You can think of a DAW setup as more of a component system. Unlike a PDS, there is not just one piece of gear that you buy to do it all. You'll have to piece together the parts, and we'll talk about a lot of options to do so. While that makes a DAW somewhat less portable, it also makes it possible to spend more money on the pieces that you feel are most important. In addition, if a piece of the system becomes outdated, you can replace it without having to replace the entire system. You'll also be able to upgrade the DAW software on a fairly regular basis and take advantage of new functionality that the manufacturer introduces with new versions.

Now, a DAW setup is going to cost you quite a bit more than a $300 PDS. But just like the component stereo system that you put together piece by piece gives you better audio quality and more control than an all-in-one unit off the department store rack, you're going to be able to achieve higher-quality, more tailored results with a DAW than with a PDS. You'll have more freedom to make the music you really want to make.

There's just no denying that nothing comes close to a DAW in terms of power and flexibility. A good DAW offers unlimited tracks, so you never *have* to bounce, although sometimes you'll *want* to, and your DAW makes that easy.

With my DAW, if I want a reverb on my vocal track, I simply apply a plug-in. If I want a different reverb on a different track, I just apply that plug-in (or a different one if I want) to the second track and change its settings. In the analog world, you'll need to buy two outboard reverb units, figure out how to patch them in, and then set up the routing to pull off that same task.

WHAT'S A PLUG-IN?

Any good DAW application can support plug-ins. Plug-ins are little applications that might be manufactured by the maker of the DAW itself or by a third-party company who's developed the plug-in to exacting software engineering standards that enable it to work inside the DAW as if it were a part of the DAW application. A plug-in brings functionality to the DAW that it doesn't have by original design.

It's sort of like the relationship between a Telecaster and an after-market whammy bar. The typical Tele works fantastically right off the showroom floor, and you can make a lot of sounds with it. But one thing you can't do is easily slacken or tighten all the strings simultaneously to temporarily change the pitch and create the cool sounds that result. So you return to the shop and have them affix a whammy bar. It costs you a little more, but when you walk outta there, it's part of your guitar and your Tele can do something it couldn't do before. For the record, most PDS units do not do plug-ins; you either live with the DSP that comes with the unit, or you patch in a piece of outboard gear.

A good DAW usually comes with multiple plug-ins built right in or bundled as a separate install. And you can use the same plug-in multiple times in the project. You can also chain many plug-ins together to get optimal control over the sound.

And when it comes to editing, signal routing, experimentation, and numerous other issues, the DAW has everything else beat by miles. With your DAW, you can do things it would take an experienced audio engineer a lot of time to pull off in the analog studio. And there are other things that a DAW handles with ease that would be just plain impossible to do on any other system. Maybe your budget dictates that you have to start with a low-end PDS, which is fine. But I suggest you work toward upgrading to a DAW at some point to take your productions to a higher level.

I'll spend a good chunk of the remainder of this book talking about the DAW in more detail. For now, we've made another decision: We're going with a DAW.

Mac Versus PC

You thought all the decisions had been made, but along comes another old debate that's getting really, really stale. What's better for the job, a Mac or a PC running Windows or some other operating system?

I've spent years working on computers. For a period of more than 10 years, I made my living working in the creative field. I worked as a graphic designer and copywriter and used the Mac exclusively. I really appreciated that Mac and made decent money with it.

"Aha! You're a Mac guy. I knew it! You have to be working on a Mac in order to be creative!"

Well, now, not so fast. One day I got a new job. On my first day I walked in, and there on my new desk, staring me in the face, sat a Windows PC. I had a choice to make in that instant. I could turn around and walk out on my new gig, or I could sit down and figure out how to use that PC. I sat down.

Now, for the past 10 years, I've been making good money on my PC. And you know what I've found? Turns out I'm cranking out creative work on my PC that's way better than the stuff I used to do on my Mac.

"I knew it! You think PCs rule!"

Uhh, that's not quite what I said.

"But you said the PC is better."

Nnno, I didn't. What I said was, the work I've turned out on my PC is better than the work I turned out on my Mac. You know why?

"Because PCs rule!"

Sigh. No. Because *my skills* have improved greatly since my days on the Mac. It's about you and your skills; it's not about your computer.

If you're loyal to the Mac, good on ya, mate! If you love your PC, right on! But look, folks, these are tools. They aren't religion. You do what you want with that information. Me? I'm going with the tool that helps me get my work done, helps me earn a living, and helps me make great musical recordings.

Today, for several reasons that don't matter here, that's the PC. If tomorrow the opportunity comes along to do better with a Mac, I'll relearn that Mac in a hurry. I have as much loyalty to one computer platform over the other as I do to my '89 Fender Telecaster or my late '60s Gibson SG. (Read that "none.") All things being equal, I may prefer one over the other. But when it comes time to lay down a lead, whichever gives me the sound I need at the time I need it, well, then, that's my favorite!

There's nothing that I will show you in this book using my PC that can't be done in a similar fashion on a Mac. If you use a Mac, this book still holds value for you despite my use of the PC. This book is about the process. The computer platform you choose will not diminish what you can learn from this book.

Now, having said that, I will say that, personally, I feel that if you're not committed to a platform yet (that is, you don't already own the computer you're going to use for recording), I recommend you tune out your friends' constant insisting that only the Mac works for creative endeavors. Look seriously at buying a Windows-based PC. The cost of entry is lower, and the selection of PCs and peripherals seems larger. That's not an endorsement of PC over Mac; it's strictly a matter of making your money stretch as far as it will go.

Besides, there's undeniable satisfaction to be gleaned from the look of confusion and disbelief on your Mac buddies' faces when they hear the quality of your music and learn that you a) made it on a PC and b) have never worn a pocket protector in your whole, entire life! And then they start asking you for advice. Now who's the lemming?

My DAW of Choice: Sony ACID Pro

I started using Sony ACID Pro back in version 1.0, and I've used it ever since. I like the intuitive interface and the no-nonsense approach the application takes. Over the years, the application has grown from a narrowly focused innovative loop-based music creation tool into a full-fledged DAW that supports looping, multitrack audio, and MIDI sequencing. I've grown with it and have become an expert user of the application, so I continue to use it as my DAW of choice.

As I said, I'm on the PC platform. If you, too, use a PC, you can obviously adopt ACID Pro as your DAW as well. But, in fact, even if you use a Mac, you can use ACID under Boot Camp or other tools that help the Mac run Windows applications. Sony doesn't test ACID Pro against the Mac and doesn't officially support it on the Mac, but I've heard good reports of people who are loyal to the Mac running ACID Pro quite successfully.

In this book, I'll focus on the pro version of the application, which you can pick up for around $400 or $500. (Look for the sales.) Sony also makes a lighter version of ACID called ACID Music Studio that you can find for more like $80 or $90. ACID Music Studio offers surprisingly robust features for a light version, and if you can't spring for the Pro version, it's a great alternative. Still, you might come out ahead with the pro version even at the higher price because of the extra software that comes bundled with it. We'll talk more about that extra software throughout this book so that by the time we're done, you'll be able to make an informed decision on the two options.

Now, you may already have decided upon a different DAW application. There are several other good ones to choose from. Some are more expensive, some less. Some are even shareware or freeware. Again, this book is still useful for you. Just like the platform discussion, it ultimately doesn't matter which DAW you choose. You can get work done in all of them. I think ACID Pro is a great tool, but if you choose to use a different one, you'll still get a lot out of the techniques we discuss in this book. That's because the book is not about ACID Pro or any other specific make or model of gear that I happen to use. It's about process. It's about establishing your home recording setup. I'll make my recommendations; you make your decisions.

I've included a trial version of ACID Pro 7 on the companion disc to this book so you can follow along with me as we discuss techniques. Install this fully functional trial and work on your own projects for 30 days while the trial period lasts.

Studio Log

You've had to make a lot of decisions in this chapter. But, having done so, you now have the basis for building your studio and putting together the gear you need. You have a handle on your financial resources and stand ready to learn how best to spend what you have available.

You've decided to shelve a few old and bitterly fought arguments and set them aside for theoretical discussions to be had sometime over coffee or a beer. In their places, you've opened your mind to making solid, practical choices—choices that will help you get the job done now.

Some of what we talk about in the remainder of the book will, quite frankly, only work on a DAW. But much of it applies with equal relevance to a PDS. In fact, many of the techniques will even work in the analog world. But if you've taken my advice, you've decided to go the DAW route.

I've made it clear that my DAW of choice is Sony ACID Pro running on a Windows PC. But hopefully you've also come away with the knowledge that you're free to run whatever software you want on either PC or Mac, and you'll still be able to follow the techniques, procedures, and advice in the remainder of this book to get your recording operation up and running.

Most of all, I hope you've learned that this book is not about the specific gear. It's about the process. To illustrate the process, I have to give you concrete examples of the gear I use. But every product I use has a competitor in the marketplace. I'm confident that if you follow each and every one of my recommendations, you'll be happy with what you purchase and you'll create great work. But if you know of a piece of gear that you prefer over my suggestion, use it. Ultimately, it's the process that's important.

Setting Up Your Recording Studio Space

Even though you made several important decisions in the previous chapter, you're still not quite ready to get to recording. First, you'll have to find someplace to serve as your studio. You don't have to have the perfect space for recording. And that's good because if you're like me, you don't have much space. But you do have to make the best of whatever space you can carve out. Hopefully you can find a place in your home or apartment that you can call your own. In this chapter we'll discuss issues related to setting up your space, no matter how limited it might seem to you now. This chapter will help you turn your space—regardless of its limitations—into a productive space for music production.

Carve Out a Space of Your Own

I work with a guy who's setting up a home studio in his basement. It's everybody's dream. He hired contractors to completely gut the basement, build new double walls with sound-baffling insulation between them and special acoustic drywall materials. They constructed separate rooms for a control room, big studio, isolation (iso) booth, and so on. The ceiling's packed with sound-insulating materials. Room dampeners sit in all the appropriate locations. A ceiling cloud kills any reflection off the ceiling. This place has got the works.

We, on the other hand, won't be doing that (recall assumption 2 from the book's introduction, which states that an extensive remodeling project is not in your future). In fact, I don't think you can really consider my coworker's studio a home studio at all. Instead, he's got a pro studio that just happens to be located in his home—big difference.

We're clearly dealing with a much smaller budget and living under a completely different reality. But that doesn't mean we can't have a decent place to work. And it certainly doesn't mean we can't produce great-sounding musical recordings.

Recall that one of the main premises of this book suggests that you don't—and won't—have the *perfect* space in which to set up your home studio. You and your fellow readers will have an endless variety of situations in your homes and apartments, so there's no way I can tell you exactly what to do.

Still, you have to have someplace where you'll work on your recordings. So let's see if we can create that space. If you follow the steps outlined in this book, the recordings you create in your space will rival—or at least hold up well when compared to—those that my friend creates in his.

Finding Your Space

For some, the future location for their home studio is as easy as spotting a heavy-metal guitar shredder on stage at a folk festival. A room that's currently just full of all the junk you should have organized long ago, a spare bedroom, basement space, and so on. Some people luckily (or not) don't have any competition in their home for those spare rooms, and they can set up basically wherever they want.

On the other hand, some find themselves in a situation where there just isn't another room to be had, no matter how you look at the place. If that's where you find yourself, you'll have to lay claim to a piece of room that's already being used for something else. That's what I had to do in the last house in which I lived. There, I had a computer desk and about two feet on each side of it. It sat in the middle of a far wall in the basement family room, directly opposite and on the other side of the couch from the TV. That was my studio. That's all I had, so that's where I recorded.

I have a different place now, and I find myself somewhere in between these two extremes. Like many others, I've had to settle for a common room in my basement. I share it with my own kids and their friends who bash in and out like a crew of sleep-deprived stage hands jacked up on Red Bull.

But luckily, it's a fairly large room, so I've set up my studio space in one corner. And, as luck would further have it, there happens to be an otherwise strangely located walk-in closet in that corner (which, of course, is why I chose that particular corner). It's not a big closet, but it's got a door and its own light and serves me quite well as a makeshift iso booth. It gets used for nothing else other than my musical endeavors. It's where I go to practice and write most of my songs. And, as I said, I can use it as a vocal and iso booth when I'm recording. It's not the B room at Abbey Road, but nonetheless it works.

The corner, along with its closet, is mine, and I've made sure everyone understands that. You may have to negotiate with your roommate to swing a similar deal for your own space, but it's important. You can see my humble space in Figure 2.1.

Figure 2.1

I call a corner of the basement my studio. I'm fortunate to have a walk-in closet in the corner to use as an iso booth.

You can see in the picture that my studio really is, as I said, just a corner in a basement room. I picked up an L-shaped desk ($50 off of craigslist.com) and have set it up to more definitely define my area.

That's what you have to do as best you can. Make a space that's yours and that you can set up exactly as you need. Make it a space where, whenever you step into it, your subconscious sends the message, "I have now stepped into my studio. This space is for serious music-making work." It might even be just the corner of a desk that you share with your roommate, but nonetheless, stake it out as yours and make it a serious work zone.

Get Comfortable

Once you've identified your space, it's important to give some real thought to how you want to utilize it and arrange it. Many times you don't really have much choice: It is what it is, and you arrange it in whatever way all the pieces fit. But whatever your space looks like, there are always little things you can do to make it a better, more productive place to work.

Get yourself a comfortable chair. Again, you don't have to spend a fortune on one; you can find lots of good chairs for great prices on craigslist.com or local yard sales. Put some nice pictures on the wall. Whatever you can do to make it seem a little nicer really helps your mental attitude toward heading to that space and working. After all, you're going to be spending hours there. Potentially you'll sit for long stretches of the day and night working on your music. If you hate the feeling of sitting there, you'll always be able to conjure up some excuse for not doing so.

Some of us need more ambiance than others. Personally, once I get into my work, it doesn't matter where I am. I can get so lost in what I'm doing that I don't think about the surroundings.

But it's not so much what you think about while you're working in your space. Once the work starts, it's easy to become absorbed and forget your surroundings. It's more about how the room shapes your attitude. If you get a bad feeling in the pit of your stomach every time you look at your space, it's likely a barrier to getting work done. There are always times when motivation wanes. I don't know about you, but during those times when my motivation is already low, I certainly don't need help from my studio space to come up with excuses not to work!

Make your space an area that facilitates your creativity. How you do that depends completely on what you can figure out about your own creative process. Try different things and see what makes a difference. Put up some pictures that evoke an emotion. Hang some colorful curtains. Maybe even shampoo the carpet once. Just try different things.

Finally, recognize that those things may change or evolve over time. Be willing to take a flexible approach to your setup. The initial layout or placement of equipment will likely shift as you learn what works best for you and what feels most comfortable.

Make the Space Work for You

Give some thought to just exactly how you're going to arrange the limited space you have. What are you going to be doing in that space most of the time? What gear do you need to access most frequently?

If you're mainly a keyboard player, will it help to create a spot where you can leave that keyboard set up all the time so you don't have to go digging for it every time you want to play? Or, if you're a guitarist, can you move something aside to make room for a guitar on a stand that you can just grab anytime the mood or inspiration strikes?

Again, it can be tough to stay motivated. The easier you can make it to get started, the better your chances of pushing through those times of low motivation.

You'll find a similar impediment if you allow your space to slide into the role of junk storage. In fact, even booting up a computer can have the same negative effect on motivation, which is why in the previous chapter I suggested that an inexpensive cassette multitrack can be a valuable tool even in the digital studio.

The last thing you need is a list of excuses for not sitting down to work on your music. You have to stay motivated, which is really hard to do sometimes. And if, because of unavoidable limitations, the space in which you work can't feed that motivation positively, at least do what you can to make sure it doesn't eat away at it negatively. Make it work *for* you, not against you.

The Special Considerations of Live Mic Recording

As I mentioned earlier, I'm going to show you every way I know to enable you to avoid recording with live microphones. Several of the assumptions I listed in the introduction to this book come into play here (at the very least, assumptions 2, 3, 4, 6, 7, and 10 apply).

Microphones are amazing things. They obviously revolutionized the recording industry when, some-time around 1925, they completely displaced clunky old technology for gathering sound. But mics also introduce some of the most frustrating, vexing, maddening, and insurmountable problems in the recording process—especially in the average home studio.

HOW DID THEY RECORD BEFORE THERE WERE MICROPHONES?

Since the microphone has become such an ingrained and integral part of the recording process, it's natural to think that the first sound recording required the first microphone, but that's not the case. A microphone gathers sound by turning sound waves into electronic signals that are then passed along to the recording device. But microphones, although they had been around for a long time (for example, in telephones), weren't developed to a level that produced sound of a quality suitable for music recording until about 1925.

Before 1925, sound was simply captured by a big acoustical horn. The horn was large on the capture end and small on the other end so that it funneled sound into a concentrated area. On the other side of the small opening was a device that contained a diaphragm and an etching needle. The sound caused the diaphragm to vibrate, which caused the device to shake in response, and in turn vibrated the needle, which sat directly on a rotating wax-coated platter. As it vibrated, the needle cut grooves in the platter. That platter became the master disc for the recording from which a mold could be made. The mold then was used to create multiple copies of the record.

Creating, or *cutting*, the master was literally like playing a vinyl record in reverse. Instead of the needle reacting to grooves that already existed in the disc and sending sound out, the sound would come in and cause the needle to cut the grooves in a smooth disc. My guess is that's how the term *cut* came to be used to refer to songs on a vinyl record.

A microphone's job is to record every sound that hits it. And a good microphone does its job very well. That's good, of course, but it's bad, too. Naturally, you want the mic to pick up the subtleties of your delicate finger-picking technique on the harp. But you've got to admit that the air conditioner rumbling in the background sort of takes away from the magic of the performance.

And, unfortunately, it works the other way, too. That is, sound doesn't only travel *to* you, but it also travels *from* you. After all, there's a reason why you have the microphone out in the first place: You want to create some kind of noise that you want the microphone to record. You want to record some-thing that you can't capture any other way than to use a microphone. If it's 2 a.m., and you're belting out that high harmony vocal you've been working so hard on, you're going to have trouble with the neighbors in the next apartment. That's not just theory; I know it from practical experience.

Technologies that have become available, even in just the past several years, greatly reduce the need for recording with a microphone. In some cases, it eliminates the need for a microphone all together. Still, even the miracles of modern technology can't enable you to eliminate microphones entirely from every process you undertake in the studio.

You'll still need a microphone to record your vocal parts. And personally, I have never found a way to get a sound that I'm happy with through my acoustic guitar's electronic pickups; thus, I need to mic my acoustic parts. No matter how you try to avoid it, for certain types of music, there's always going to be something you want to record through a mic.

With that reality in mind, you'll need to figure out how to control your environment for microphone recording.

Avoiding the Noise Makers

You have a house full of them: noise makers. The noise comes through ceilings, walls, and even floors. The heating and cooling ductwork connects the second floor with the basement as if it were designed specifically to transfer noise from one to the other. You don't notice most of these noises on a day-to-day basis. They're just a natural part of modern-day living.

But turn a microphone on, and suddenly the sweet little old neighbor lady upstairs shuffling through her living room in fuzzy slippers sounds like a road grader dragging its blade across solid concrete. For all the good it does your recording, it might as well be. You wonder in amazement at how in the world you never heard *that* before!

Your refrigerator hums. Your air conditioner whirs. Your clock ticks. Even your computer hisses as the fan works to cool down the very processor that makes your home studio so possible. Take a moment to sit in your space and just listen. Tune into all the sounds and try to figure out where they're coming from. They're everywhere.

All this noise is a bane to the home studio. And when you turn on a microphone, you pick up all of it—or at least enough of it to cause problems. And what you pick up, you record.

So your task when setting up to record with a microphone is to figure out how to minimize, if not completely eliminate, as much of this noise as possible while minimizing the impact of the noise you make on others. You do that by separating your microphone from the noise makers. That certainly sounds much, much easier than it actually is.

If you can set up your microphone in a somewhat isolated room, you've got a great advantage. The more you can physically isolate the microphone, the better off you're going to be. But some things are hard to avoid. For instance, unless you unplug that refrigerator on the other side of the wall, it's Russian roulette you're playing with whether or not it's going to kick into refrigeration mode the moment you click the Record button in your DAW. (For what it's worth, experience has taught me that the refrigerator *does not*, in fact, kick on right when you click Record. It usually waits until you're right in the middle of the most amazing recording take of your entire career.)

And you generally can't control the neighbors or the housemates in any other way than to try to find a time when they're all away—or you can move.

Audio Reflections

Even if you were to achieve a completely soundproofed environment in which to record with your microphone, you would still have other challenges to face. Sound is a tricky thing. Remember, sound is just waves floating through the air. But it doesn't merely float. It also bounces. And it can bounce a lot.

We experience bouncing audio waves all the time. As an extreme example, think about standing in the middle of your empty high-school gymnasium and dropping a heavy book flat on the floor. It sounds more like an explosion than a dropping book because the sound waves shoot out and bounce off the walls, the ceiling, the bleachers, the basketball backboards, and everything else they hit.

And almost every surface in that gym is hard, which makes it highly reflective, so the sound doesn't just bounce a little, and it doesn't just bounce once. It bounces drastically and flies through the air until it hits the next hard surface and ricochets again and again and again. Soon (all of this in a matter of milliseconds) you've got so much sound bouncing around the room that it's hitting your ears from every conceivable direction.

Not only is the sound coming at you from all over the room now, but it's coming to you at different times. It also reaches you at different volumes since the size of the waves diminishes over time (meaning the sound gets quieter over time). Some of the waves caused by the initial impact reached your ears virtually instantaneously. But some of them shot right past, bounced off the ceiling 30 feet above your head, and bounced back down to your ears. Still others took some other route back to your ears.

You perceive these differences in timing and volume as an echo, or many echoes. If the echoes are so close together that they seem indistinguishable from one another, we call the effect *reverberation*, or simply *reverb*.

Well, you're probably not recording in a gymnasium, although, for an interesting natural reverb sound, many people have recorded in cathedrals, arenas, and so on. But regardless of the size of the room in which you're recording, you must always deal with reflected audio.

GOING NATURAL

The most common examples of recordings that use natural reverberation probably exist in the classical world and in choir music. This type of music is perfect for heavy reverberation. That may be simply because that's how it's been heard for hundreds of years, so it's become as much a part of the music as the cellos, organs, and voices. Because of this and the fact that this type of music typically requires large groups of people and instruments, this music is often recorded in the natural environment of large concert halls or cathedrals, where the sounds have a long way to travel before they bounce off the high ceilings and other hard surfaces.

In the pop world, I can think of two prominent examples of music recorded in spaces that were chosen specifically for their big natural reverberation. Joe Jackson released his *Body and Soul* CD in 1984. He recorded this project (digitally, by the way!) in an old New York City Masonic Lodge that was frequently used to record classical music. A few years later, in 1988, the Cowboy Junkies released their all-time classic *The Trinity Sessions* album, which they recorded (what do you know? Digitally!) at the Church of the Holy Trinity in Toronto.

Both of these projects were recorded mostly or entirely live, and the huge, natural reverb on these albums gives them a haunting feel that's something completely different from what you get on most pop recordings these days.

You'll often hear audio engineers refer to the *sound* of the room. Or you'll hear someone say something like, "I can hear too much room in that recording." These statements refer to the reflected audio that made it back into the microphone and onto the tape (uh, I mean, onto the hard drive). While it's not always bad to hear the room in a recording, the rooms we're likely to be recording in are probably going to sound pretty ugly. So you may need to control the sound of the room—to tame it.

Generally, you do this by *dampening* or softening the surfaces in the room. You also do it by diffusing the sound waves. This means you provide an uneven surface that causes reflections to bounce off in multiple directions instead of in a specific and focused way as large, flat surfaces do. Did you ever wonder what the heck your musician friends were doing with all those empty egg cartons? They were sticking them to their walls to both soak up sound and eliminate flat surfaces. The more you make your walls, floor, ceiling, and other surfaces absorb sound instead of reflecting it, the less the sound bounces back to the microphone.

We'll talk more about controlling audio reflections in the following section.

Controlling Your Audio Environment

The pro studios spend huge amounts of money controlling the audio environment. There are companies who have as their sole purpose in life the development and sale of specialized material to aid in the accomplishment of that task. They "tune" the room first, which means they play specific audio tones inside the room and make exacting measurements to analyze the sound characteristics of the room. Then they strategically place absorption and diffusion materials throughout the room to control the sound and reflections.

Assumption 2 (listed in the introduction to the book) dictates that I proceed as if you don't have the financial wherewithal (or the willingness) to buy this type of analysis and material—or at least not much of it. The good news is that you can come up with homemade solutions that can fairly effectively solve the problems caused by a live room (that is, a room with lots of audio-reflective surfaces).

Familiarize Yourself with the Sound of Your Room

I mentioned the concept of the sound of a room a little bit ago. It's another one of those things you don't think of during the course of real life except when you walk into a room with extreme sound characteristics, like the gymnasium we discussed. But you absolutely have to take the sound of your studio room into consideration, especially when you're recording, mixing, and mastering (which is basically the entire process of making a recording!).

Of course, we're going to pass up on the expense of having the room professionally analyzed and tuned, so you'll have to train and trust your own ears to do the job.

As a first step, try to get familiar with the sound of your room so you know what you're dealing with. I already had you sit quietly and note all the sounds in your room, so hopefully you've controlled those as much as possible.

Sit or stand in a couple of different places and listen again. For instance, stand where you'll stand when you record your vocals (that is, where the microphone will be). Now listen from where you'll be sitting when you edit and mix your project.

Next, clap your hands—one sharp clap—and listen. Do you hear echoes or reverberation? You don't want the echoes, but the reverb might be okay if you like the sound of it. Do you hear any pitches coming back? For instance, the walk-in closet in my studio has a metal support post tucked away around a corner. You can't see it when you're standing in front of the microphone. I never even thought of it as anything other than a helpful pole to keep the house from falling in until I clapped my hands. I can distinctly hear a tone caused by the sound bouncing off that pole when I clap my hands.

It took me a few claps to realize what was causing the tone. Finally, I walked over to the pole and flicked it with my finger. What I heard was the exact tone I was hearing when I clapped in the mic location. If you hear a tone like that, you're going to have to find a way to kill it, or it will intrude upon your recording. If it's something like an exposed pole, you're in luck. You can easily wrap some sort of foam or other soft material around it. If it's something inside the wall (like metal studs or conduit), your job might be more difficult.

Clap again. Do you hear anything rattling? Maybe you have a loose piece of baseboard, a picture that shakes ever so slightly striking on the wall, or something rattling on your desk. You really have to listen to hear what you can hear. As you repeat the experiment, try to zero in on specific frequency ranges. Sometimes you get so focused on, say, a high pitch, that you miss a fairly prominent low tone. Think consciously about highs, clap again thinking about the mids, and once more concentrating on bass frequencies.

When you're done clapping, repeat the experiment with other sharp noises like finger snaps, tongue clicks, and so on. Don't forget to use your voice, too! Again, try it from different locations in the room. You should be getting a pretty good idea of the sounds that your room makes now and some of the things you're going to need to control or tame.

Now listen to a few familiar recordings. Find ones that you particularly like the production on—recordings that sound the way you'd like your recordings to sound. But don't just listen. Instead, listen and concentrate. Isolate various aspects of the sound you hear.

How does the bass sound? Is it clear, or does it come across like a big ball of mud?

How about the high end? Do the cymbals cut through with a pleasing crispness and sheen? Or are they harsh or "hissy"?

Listen to different aspects of the recordings to hear how they sound in your room. Then listen to the same recordings in other environments. Try your living room, a friend's house, and so on. Of course, different stereo systems affect what you hear, but if you find out you like the recording everywhere but in your studio, you know you have a problem. You might get a great education if you can listen to the recordings in a professional room.

The point is, you need to get to know your room. Get to know how it treats the sounds you make in it as well as the sounds it makes in reaction. Only when you're familiar with the room's sound characteristics can you move on in an attempt to improve them if necessary.

Attack Any Problems You Hear

Once you've identified echoes or other problems, it's time to try to eliminate them. The bouncing of sound is actually even more complicated than I've let on here, because different frequencies of sound bounce in different ways and are stopped by different things. You may not be an expert with acoustics and shaping the sound of a room, but that doesn't have to stop you from taking steps to make the room sound the best that it can on a low budget.

Start with your flat walls. Flat walls cause many problems in addition to the echoes and reverberation we've already discussed. One of these problems is a phenomenon called *standing waves*. Basically, when you have two flat surfaces directly opposite one another, you can get a buildup of certain frequencies. This might cause the room to accentuate a bass frequency, for instance.

There's much more to it than that, but the point is, you'll generally want to avoid large areas of flat, parallel surfaces in your space. By design, a room is typically a thing of flat parallel surfaces: The north and south walls, the east and west walls, and the floor and ceiling all face each other. Knowing that, you can already guess that you'll encounter some problems.

This is exactly why you've seen people tack empty egg cartons to their studio walls. The uneven shape of the egg carton breaks up the flat surface (which diffuses the sound waves that hit it), and the softer material absorbs more sound than the hard wall.

If you do have a little space in your budget, it could be well worth it to buy professional sound diffusion and absorption products. The instructions or the company's website will provide information on how to place these products for optimal benefit. Figure 2.2 shows that I've placed a bit of commercially manufactured foam absorption panels in my isolation booth/closet.

Figure 2.2

I was lucky enough to get hold of some professional sound absorption panels for the surfaces in my closet iso booth. Other sound-absorbing materials that you have around the house or can purchase inexpensively can serve the same purpose.

You can find several manufacturers of commercial sound absorption materials online (mine is made by a company called Auralex), but generally speaking the stuff doesn't come cheap. Therefore, you'll probably have to find another way to get the job done. If you're going to attack these problems with strictly guerilla tactics, some trial and error is in order.

Keep your speakers and microphones away from walls and especially corners. When the sound source is close to a wall, you experience short reflection times off that wall. That means you'll hear the reflected sound and the original sound at *almost* the same time. Almost, but not exactly, and this can result in phase problems where some frequencies are accentuated and others are cancelled out. And that obviously gives you a false sense of the sound. Adding sound-absorbing materials at the reflection point can help eliminate this phenomenon.

However, simply lining every square inch of your room with absorption is neither necessary nor ultimately the most effective approach. Absorption materials are more effective on some frequencies than others. For instance, high frequencies tend to be deadened by absorption materials to a greater extent than low frequencies. Make the room too sound-absorbent, and you could end up with a bass-heavy sound.

A Practical Approach

I feel I'm in danger of violating the assumption that states you don't want me to get too technical (assumption 9 from the introduction). Besides, like most of you, I'm no expert on sound control. But knowing these few basics helps you to improve the sound in your room. It would be helpful for you to do a lot more studying and come to understand the theories and *then* outfit your room accordingly. Or, if you have the money, hire a pro to help.

But most of us just have to deal with our situation using resources we already have or can get relatively cheaply. If you've discovered unpleasant echoes in your room or if it sounds too bright or too muddy, start experimenting. Hang a heavy blanket on a wall that seems to be causing an echo and see if that doesn't solve the problem. If you can, hang it a few inches away from the wall.

Tack up some foam and put some odd-shaped objects around the room to diffuse the sound. Just make sure those objects don't add different problems (like the pitch I get off my support post). If you have windows in your room, hang heavy curtains around them. See what it sounds like with the curtains open as well as closed. If you have a carpeted floor, you probably don't need to do anything else to it, but if your floor is a hard surface, drop a large area rug over it. You might even find that sometimes you want to remove some of your sound absorption to give the room more of a live sound while recording.

TIP

Here's a list of things that might be useful to you when you're trying to control sound reflections in your recording space:

- Blankets of varying thickness
- Foam rubber
- Packing materials
- Egg cartons
- Pipe insulation
- Fiberglass insulation (covered with cloth to keep fibers from floating)
- Curtains
- Carpet scraps
- Rugs

I'm sure you can think of more. Just find something that doesn't have a hard surface to reflect audio wave in a direct manner.

If you experiment like this, you're not likely to end up with a perfectly controlled room, but you'll probably find a way to make it sound much better than it did before. Just make sure you're happy with it. Listen to your reference recordings again, and compare them to how they sound in other environments.

In general, place absorption and diffusion at various locations throughout your room to avoid too much flat surface facing an opposite flat surface. Put some material in the corners to diffuse and absorb waves that can bounce around in there. Pay close attention as you add more absorption materials so that you don't go overboard and absorb too much of the high-frequency sounds, thus giving your room an artificially bass-heavy quality.

Studio Log

The space you call your studio deserves much more consideration and attention than many (maybe even most) home-recording enthusiasts give it. You're going to spend a lot of time in this space, so make sure it works for you. Make a space that helps feed your creativity instead of draining your motivation. Make it a place you like to be in—somewhere you want to spend a lot of time. And make it a place that everyone in your home understands belongs to you and is dedicated to your musical work.

Arrange the space in a way that works best for you. Have all your most important tools as easily at hand as possible and practical.

Listen to your room. Identify the noise makers and eliminate them as much as possible. Pay attention to audio reflections, unnaturally loud frequencies, and artificial tones created by sound bouncing off objects in the room or even inside the walls. Become intimately aware of what your room sounds like so that you can identify any audio problems it has that may color or cloud your decisions during recording and mixing.

Then attack those problems with sound diffusion and absorption materials. Listen to reference audio in your space, and compare how it sounds there to how it sounds in other environments.

All this attention to the details of your room will pay off when it comes time to record, edit, and mix your project. The more you make your room work properly for you and what you're trying to accomplish, the higher quality results you'll achieve in that room.

3

Setting Up Your Computer for Music Production

IN THIS CHAPTER

- Determining your minimum requirements for processing, memory, and storage

- Choosing your audio input/output interface (your computer audio interface)

- Assembling your audio monitoring system

In this chapter, we move into an area that doesn't have to be nearly as confusing or intimidating as many of us tend to believe it is. Here's where we'll talk about your computer and what you need to do to it to turn it into an audio-production powerhouse. When you're done with this chapter, you'll have transformed your ordinary computer into a complete Digital Audio Workstation (DAW) capable of recording great-sounding music. And it's a lot easier to do than you might think. This is an important chapter because a lack of understanding of this topic prevents far too many musicians from getting work done. That's a shame. And you're about to learn why it doesn't have to be that way.

Your Computer: Command Central

Your computer is obviously a critical component in your recording setup. As you'll see in the remainder of this book, it serves as your multitrack recorder, your storage medium, your mixer, your source for most (if not all) of your digital signal processing (DSP) work, your playback machine, your editing station, and your CD burning station. And it can even do email and your taxes! It's a wonderful thing.

Let's get down to the important details of how to make your computer serve all these important functions. The younger musicians among us have probably been using computers for most of their lives. You're most likely completely at home with the computer in general and might be tempted to skip over some of the preliminary topics in this chapter. I'd suggest you resist that urge at least enough to skim through everything to make sure you don't miss something audio specific that you haven't worked with before.

Others may very well have relatively little experience with computers in their daily lives. If that's the case, don't worry that you don't consider yourself a whiz on the computer; you *can* learn your way around. And, the truth is, you don't need to be a computer genius to make it all work for you.

In fact, computers these days are really quite reliable. Considering the complexity of what goes on inside the computer every time you push a key or click the mouse, it's amazing they work as reliably and seamlessly as they do.

Of course, that doesn't mean you won't run into problems with your machine, but hopefully you'll get comfortable enough working with it that you'll be able to overcome these issues, or more importantly, avoid them in the first place.

We discussed the Mac versus PC argument back in Chapter 1, "Laying the Groundwork for Recording," and we all agreed to put that argument to rest, so let's not rehash it here. As I mentioned, I work on the PC platform, so my examples are given on the PC. But remember, even if you use a Mac, most of what this chapter discusses applies equally to your platform too, so don't give in to the temptation to skip it.

Choosing Your Computer

There are several important considerations to keep in mind when you're choosing the computer that you're going to use for your musical projects. Understanding these issues will help you make a wise choice for what will be one of the most, if not *the* most, expensive pieces of gear you need to purchase for your studio. It's obviously also one of the most critical pieces of gear you need, so you'll want to make the right choice.

Even though you probably already own a computer, you'll be wise to consider purchasing a new one that you can dedicate solely to your recording studio. That way you can keep it clean of all the junk that everyday computing tends to pile onto your machine. It's particularly a good idea to keep your production computer away from the Internet as much as you can—totally away from it is the ideal! No one wants a virus to take down their entire production machine (and with it, the recording projects they've worked so hard on).

Minimum System Requirements

Virtually all software applications provide a list of minimum system requirements in their marketing information and packaging. The term refers to basic minimum standards in terms of storage space, random access memory (RAM), processor speed, operating system version, and so on that your computer must meet to run the software effectively.

Well, I've got great news for you: You don't need some sort of super-secret, ultra-special computer to set up your studio! In fact, if you already have a computer that you purchased within the past three years, you might just have all the computer power you need. That would obviously be great news, because you won't have the expense of a new computer to cover.

Naturally—as almost always with computers—the more powerful the machine, the better performance you'll typically get out of it. A computer that meets—but just barely—the minimum system requirements of your software may run the software, but it may not run it very effectively. You could easily become frustrated as you wait for the software to react to your commands.

If you decide that the computer you have now just won't cut it (or if you don't have a computer yet), the fact that you don't need some super tricked-out specialty machine means that you can get a great computer for a decent price. In my opinion, virtually any machine you buy new off the shelf or the website of your favorite computer retailer will make (with perhaps a few modifications that we'll discuss shortly) for a nice audio workstation. Certainly, any new machine will likely far exceed the minimum system requirements of the software you'll use to produce your music.

Obviously, a discussion of computer systems, processors, RAM, and so on can and does fill entire books, so we're not going to get too deep into that here. (Recall assumption 9 regarding technical details.) For now, suffice it to say that more power is pretty much always better. But it's also pretty much always more expensive. So, there's your trade-off!

When you're making your decision, first find out what the minimum system requirements are for all the software you'll be using. (In all likelihood, your DAW software will have the most stringent requirements.) Then make sure that the computer you're considering meets or preferably exceeds those requirements. Then buy the fastest processor you can afford (get multiple processors if you can), the most RAM you can afford, and the largest hard drive you can afford. And as long as you're at it, a second (perhaps external) hard drive is always a great idea for archiving your work.

For the record, I've done the majority of my recording on machines that I would consider standard. In fact, the machine in my studio is not nearly as beefy as anything you'll buy new today, but I'm still using it. I don't use any special high-performance audio-specific hard drives or anything like that. I've been perfectly satisfied with my basic machine. As long as your machine meets or exceeds the minimum system requirements of your software, you should be able to use it effectively for your projects, too.

The minimum requirements for the DAW I'll be using throughout this book, ACID Pro, look like this:

- **Operating system**—Microsoft Windows XP (SP2 or later) or Windows Vista
- **Processor**—1.8GHz x86
- **RAM**—1GB
- **Hard-disk space for program installation**—150MB
- **Sound device**—Windows-compatible (ASIO driver support highly recommended)

If you're using something other than ACID Pro, look for these same sets of numbers for your software. We'll talk about these requirements in more detail shortly.

Desktop and Tower Machines

Most of us think of these types of machines when we think of computers. These are the big boxes that sit either on our desks or alongside our desks on the floor. Generally, these are less expensive than laptops (discussed in the next section) yet offer more power and flexibility due to the extra space inside the box. That extra space provides room for more than one computer processor, more RAM, more than one hard drive, and computer devices that bring expanded functionality to the computer (not unlike the plug-ins we talked about earlier except that these devices are hardware instead of software).

Obviously, these systems are bulkier and not nearly as portable as a laptop. They're obviously bigger and heavier and, of course, they require an external computer monitor, keyboard, and mouse.

But the main deciding factor could be their price. You can get a nice one right off the shelf for $600 or $700 if you watch for the sales.

Laptops

Who wouldn't love to have a great laptop? The all-in-one portability they offer is absolutely fantastic. Of course, there are trade-offs for that portability.

Laptops tend to be pretty expensive (although their prices, too, are coming down). And, they're not as expandable as a tower, meaning that they provide no room inside for installing hardware devices like those I mentioned in the previous section. This may be changing, too, but generally you'll have to settle for a smaller hard drive, potentially less RAM, and a slower processor than you could get for the same money in a tower.

Still, if you want to do remote-location recordings, the new, powerful laptops can work wonderfully. More and more equipment uses fast USB and FireWire connections. This gives you a way to connect large external hard drives while easing the pain of not having room to install other hardware in your laptop. We'll talk about this in more detail a little bit later in this chapter.

Just as with tower machines, if the laptop you have (or are looking to buy) meets the minimum system requirements of your software, it passes the most critical test. I have often used a laptop to record parts of my various projects or to record live on location, and it's always worked just fine. In fact, I'll use a laptop to record the project that we'll work through in this book.

RAM, Processors, and Storage

I've mentioned processors, RAM, and storage several times already in this chapter, but what are they, and why are they important? At this point, I think it's probably safe to say that most of the people reading this book have at least some handle on these concepts, so I'm not going to go into them too deeply. There are many good resources that you can turn to for full explanations, but following are a few basic definitions for you.

The word *processor* is short for microprocessor. Another name for a processor is *central processing unit* (CPU). All three terms mean the same thing. The CPU is the brains of your computer and does all the complex calculations required by whatever it is you're doing in your software.

Therefore, processor speed is the big number everyone focuses on. The faster your processor, the more calculations it can handle in a given period of time. In other words, the faster your processor, the faster your computer does what you ask it to do. Obviously then, a fast processor makes your DAW run more efficiently, and you can get your work done faster.

You can add multiple processors to a tower machine for even more processing power, whereas a laptop typically has room for just one processor.

Fairly recently, we've seen the advent of dual-core processors, which basically means you get two processors in the space of one. This gives laptops a great source for faster processing.

Random access memory (RAM) refers to the memory available for your computer to use while it runs the operations that your software is asking it to run. For instance, when you play your project in your DAW, the application pulls from RAM memory to perform the task of transforming the computer information in your project into music that you can hear through your speakers. The more RAM you can get into your machine, the better your software should perform. For example, in ACID Pro, RAM has a direct impact on the number of audio tracks you can have playing simultaneously in your project. It also has an impact on the amount of DSP you can apply.

Think of RAM as short-term memory; whatever exists in RAM is lost when you close the application or shut down the computer.

Storage generally refers to the size of your computer's hard disc drive. This is where you store information on your computer for the long term. For instance, when you install software, the parts and pieces that make it work have to reside somewhere, and that somewhere is usually the hard drive. You also save all your files to the hard drive. For example, when you record your vocals, your DAW stores the information on the hard drive.

Drive speed can be important because you're asking your computer to pull information from the hard drive and do something with it without making you wait. For instance, when you play a file in your DAW, the computer has to read the file from the hard drive and play it in real time. Since full-resolution audio files (for example, the files that you create when you record something) can get pretty large, it's important to have the most storage space you can. A tower computer case can generally house more than one hard drive, while a laptop probably has only one. You can also connect extra hard drives to either type of computer via the USB or FireWire ports.

CAUTION

If, while you're setting up your computer, a buddy offers to do you a huge favor and "speed up the processor," just say no! Although it sounds great to think that you could get a faster computer without buying a faster processor, the extra speed comes with high risk. The technique, called *overclocking* the processor, is pretty much a jerry-rigged method of forcing your processor to run at a faster speed than that for which it was designed and tested. CPUs that have been overclocked create more heat than they were designed to handle. In turn, the extra heat might overpower the fan that cools the CPU. And excessive heat will almost certainly cause your CPU to fail. At the least, this will cause your computer to crash, and you'll lose any changes you've made to whatever you're working on. At the worst, you may destroy your CPU or other components in your computer. I know people overclock their processors all the time, but I'm not willing to take that risk, and I recommend that you avoid it, too.

Getting Sound Into and Out of Your Computer

Given the nature of what you're going to be doing in your studio, getting sound into and out of your computer could be considered a pretty critical task! Many new computers provide a method for doing this right off the shelf: the computer's *audio interface*. You might also hear the audio interface referred to as the *sound card* or the *audio device*. But whatever you call it (I'll use the term *audio interface*), many new computers have one built right onto their motherboards. Unfortunately, while that audio interface didn't cost you anything extra and it might do just fine for watching (and listening to) videos on YouTube, it's typically far from up to the task of high-quality audio work, so you're probably going to have to replace it. Let's talk about some of the issues and options involved in this decision.

Built-In Audio Interfaces

As I said, many computers have an audio interface built into them. Typically, this audio interface is actually a part of the computer's motherboard, so you can't really remove it.

Such audio interfaces are nearly without exception low-quality devices that the computer manufacturer has included simply to give you a way to hear or record audio onto the machine as soon as you unpack it.

To see if your computer has an audio interface, look for the holes (called *jacks*) into which you'd plug headphones or a microphone. The Record jack is usually red, and the headphone/speaker jack is often green or black. On a tower machine, you'll find these on either the back or the front of the machine and in some cases both. Figure 3.1 shows the jacks on the side of my laptop. Notice the little microphone and headphone icons next to the holes, which further identify their purpose.

Figure 3.1

Look for input and output jacks like the ones in this picture to see if your computer has an audio interface already.

We won't be using built-in audio interfaces, but pointing out some of their limitations helps identify important areas to consider when choosing a different one, so I'll spend a couple of paragraphs on some of those limitations.

Cheap audio devices typically have cheap components, such as their analog to digital/digital to analog (AD/DA) converters. AD/DA converters convert analog audio (such as the signal from your microphone) into digital audio that your computer can understand. Likewise they change the digital audio from your computer to analog signals that can play through your speakers.

These conversion points are absolutely critical to maintaining high quality, and that's one place inferior devices fall flat. No matter how good your microphone is or your speakers are, if you pass a great signal through low-quality AD/DA converters, your audio quality suffers.

Low-quality AD/DA converters can be very noisy, and that noise ends up in your recordings or coming out of your speakers. You'll usually hear this as a hissing sound in your recordings or the audio you play from your computer.

If you hear people talking about the *signal-to-noise ratio*, they're talking about this issue (along with other issues that cause noise). Basically, you can think of signal-to-noise ratio as how loud the noise your equipment makes is compared to the volume of the desired material. Put your headphones on and listen without playing anything through your audio interface. The amount of hiss you hear is noise that your equipment is making and noise that will end up in your recordings. Obviously, you want as little of this as possible!

To record yourself playing all the parts on a recording, the ability to listen to something that you've already recorded as you play along and record something new is critical. Most of us know this process by the term *overdubbing*. The process revolutionized music recording back in the 1940s, with the main pioneer being Les Paul. (Yes, my guitarist friends, *that* Les Paul!)

For an audio interface to pull off this simultaneous play and record magic, it must be a *full duplexing* audio interface. In terms of audio interfaces, full duplexing simply means that the device can play audio and record audio simultaneously.

Another factor, *latency*, refers to the time it takes for audio to run through the AD/DA conversions that we discussed earlier. Let's say you have your electronic keyboard's audio outputs connected to your audio interface's input jack. You press a key on the keyboard. It takes time for the audio to travel from the keyboard through the AD converter, through the software where it's being recorded, back out the DA converter, and finally to your speakers so you can hear what you're playing.

In other words, you never get instant feedback when you press that key. And if you're playing a part along with something that's already in your project, you don't hear what you play at the same time you actually play it. Obviously, you can't perform well like that!

Low-end audio interfaces will typically have unacceptably long latency; thus, even if they're full duplexing, they would still be virtually unusable for multitracking due to the latency issue. High-end audio interfaces have much lower latency.

Here's one area where you Mac users have the advantage over those of us who use the Windows operating system: The Mac operating system doesn't suffer nearly as badly from the latency problems as Windows machines do.

As you saw in Figure 3.1, built-in audio interfaces typically have 1/8-inch mini jacks. You probably know that most professional musical gear uses cannon (XLR) connections or 1/4-inch connections. Of course, you can get converters and adapters, but with all the other drawbacks for these devices, why bother?

Also, you typically get only one input and one output from these devices (although some multimedia machines will have multiple outputs so you can connect a surround-sound speaker system). That's limiting—especially on the input side—for anyone who wants to record two or more things at once. For instance, if you're recording a drum kit and want 12 microphones (not unheard of at all, but I'll show you how to avoid that nightmare later!), you're way out of luck with the built-in audio interface.

High-Quality Audio Interfaces

All right, if you can't use your computer's built-in audio interface, what can you use? Luckily, there are several great options from manufacturers who've developed audio interfaces specifically for professional music production. And you have a few different options to consider. According to assumption 8 (which I stated in the introduction to the book), you don't want me to dump a bunch of options on you and make you figure it out on your own, but there are a few times when I feel it's necessary to give you more than one option so you can pick the one that most closely fits your situation. This is one of those times. I'll try to keep the options straightforward so you can make a clear decision. Also, Appendix A, "Choosing Your Audio Interface," helps you organize your thoughts in this potentially confusing area to help you determine what type of audio interface you should purchase.

Before we start, I should note that higher-quality audio interfaces solve all the problems that I discussed earlier.

There are three common ways you can connect a new audio interface to your computer.

As I mentioned earlier, a tower-style computer has more room to expand your computer's functionality. Your computer's motherboard typically has three or more expansion slots called *Peripheral Component Interconnect (PCI) expansion slots*. These are built specifically to accept peripheral devices that use the PCI standard connection and bring some extra functionality to your computer. We talked about software plug-ins earlier. Well, these devices could be considered hardware plug-ins because they literally plug right into the PCI slots. Devices like modems, video devices, TV tuner devices, network devices, and others might use the PCI standard to connect to your computer. Audio interfaces can also use this standard.

Most of the professional-quality PCI plug-in audio interfaces have another component called a *breakout box*. The PCI device sticks out of a hole in the back of your computer that is designed specifically for it. The breakout box connects to the PCI device via some sort of cable that also comes with the package. The breakout box serves as your connection interface to the audio interface and through that to the computer. In other words, the breakout box has the input and output jacks into which you plug your input sources (microphones, mixer, and so on) and your output destinations (such as speakers, headphones, and mixer).

Figure 3.2 shows a PCI audio interface along with its breakout box. Naturally, you'll have to open your computer to install the PCI device. Make sure you follow the device's instructions carefully so that you don't damage your computer during the process.

Figure 3.2
This audio interface has three hardware components: the PCI device, the breakout box, and the cable that connects them.

Although I've had good luck with the PCI audio interfaces that I've used over the years, they've fallen out of favor with me due to a couple of factors. First, although they're not really all that difficult to install, you do have to open your computer to do it. Once you do, that device is literally part of the computer, and it's not very portable. If you want to use it on a different computer, you'll have to open the box back up, remove the device, and then open the other computer to install the device there. Also, you obviously can't install one of these into a laptop since laptops don't have room for PCI slots and devices.

Another important negative I've found with the PCI devices that I've worked with involves the connections on the breakout box. For some reason, manufacturers only seem to supply 1/4-inch jacks for analog audio connections on these devices. That means that you can't plug a standard XLR microphone cable into the device without first going through a mixer or some kind of adapter. Compared to FireWire and USB devices, these limitations were enough for me to lose my enthusiasm for PCI audio interfaces.

FireWire audio interfaces combine the audio interface and the breakout box into one unit that connects to your computer via an IEEE-1394 connection, known commonly as a *FireWire* connection. More and more new machines come with FireWire ports built in. If your computer doesn't have a built-in FireWire port, you can buy inexpensive PCI devices with FireWire ports (many with two or even three ports on a single PCI device). Figure 3.3 shows a FireWire audio interface along with the FireWire cable that connects it to the computer.

Figure 3.3

This sound device connects to the computer via a convenient FireWire connection.

In my opinion, FireWire audio interfaces offer huge advantages. First, they're completely portable. Since many computers have FireWire ports, you can easily unplug the device from one computer and plug it into a different computer. If you have a laptop with a FireWire port in it (as more and more of them do), you can easily plug the same FireWire audio interface that you use in your tower machine into your laptop.

Even more importantly in my opinion is the connectivity provided by high-quality FireWire audio interfaces. Many of these devices use handy combination input jacks that accept either a 1/4-inch plug or an XLR plug coming from a microphone. This way you can plug something like an electronic keyboard that uses 1/4-inch plugs into the audio interface when you need it but then remove it and plug a microphone directly into the device when you need that.

FireWire devices have other great features that I'll talk more about later when we actually get to recording and working with audio.

Audio interfaces that use Universal Serial Bus (USB) connections have many of the same advantages and features as the FireWire devices I just discussed. The main difference is that they connect to one of your computer's USB ports. If your computer doesn't have a FireWire port, these devices are a great alternative because virtually every computer is built with a couple of these USB ports.

There are two types of USB: USB 1.1 and USB 2.0. USB audio interfaces generally require a USB 2.0 connection since USB 1.1 connections do not provide fast enough data transfer rates. Make sure that your computer's USB ports are USB 2.0 if the audio interface you're looking at requires that standard.

NOTE

I have used several types of both PCI and FireWire audio interfaces extensively and have some (though less) experience with USB devices. My preference is for FireWire, with USB coming in close behind, and my least-favorite is the PCI device. I've never had trouble with devices I've used in any of the three formats, but I've been most happy with the FireWire devices I've used, and that's the direction I suggest you look to first.

Regardless of the type of connection you choose, the audio interface you buy will come with its own software called *drivers*. The audio interface needs this software driver to communicate with your computer and DAW software. In reality, it's the software drivers, not the hardware components that are likely to cause you the most problems with the audio interface. For that reason, it's important to make sure you have the latest versions of the drivers for your operating system.

In fact, that's true for any software you install. By the time you buy the software (or audio interface and software in this case) and unpack it at home, there have probably been a couple of updates to the driver software. Manufacturers almost without exception post these updated drivers for free download on their websites. A company puts out new drivers for good reasons; the driver update may fix bugs in the old driver, add functionality that the old driver didn't have, or support a new operating system that the old one doesn't support.

CAUTION

Before you buy an audio interface, make sure it includes drivers that will work on your operating system. If you use Windows Vista, that sound device is going to be useless to you if it only comes with Windows XP drivers. Most audio interfaces include drivers for both Windows and the Mac, but you should still verify that just to make sure.

Also, if you're running on a Windows system, make sure the audio interface includes ASIO drivers before you buy it. These drivers provide low-latency performance, which is going to be important for your work.

You need to seriously consider how many inputs and outputs you want your sound device to supply. You can find devices with 10 or more inputs and outputs (like those shown earlier in Figures 3.2 and 3.3) as well as devices with fewer. Most devices have at least two of each.

FireWire devices offer a great advantage here because, on some of them, you can string two or more devices together. For this to work, all the devices must use the same software drivers, which pretty much means they all have to be the same make and model. Stringing devices together like this gives you even more inputs. To do this, you plug the first one into the computer and the second one into a second FireWire port on the first one. The two devices strung together appear in your DAW software as if they were just one big device, and you can assign all those inputs to separate tracks in your DAW for recording simultaneously.

Give some thought to what you're going to be doing with the device so you can determine how many ins and outs you need. If you're going to record all the parts one by one, you might be perfectly happy with just one input. (Actually, most devices have a minimum of two mono audio inputs.) However, if you plan to record your whole band simultaneously with several microphones, you're going to need more inputs. And if you want to play back out of the audio interface to a surround-sound speaker system, you'll need more outputs.

Naturally, the more ins and outs your device features, the more you'll pay for the device.

Also, make sure to consider whether you need MIDI input and output. We'll talk much more about this issue in Chapter 7, "Utilizing MIDI in Your Projects." For now, just keep in mind that most higher-end devices supply MIDI input and output jacks, while lower-priced devices may not. If you don't know what MIDI is, hold off on your audio interface buying decision until you've read about it in the following chapter. Once you learn about MIDI technology, you may well want to make sure you buy an audio interface that features MIDI jacks.

Some manufacturers make audio interfaces that they combine with technology to create a multifunction piece of gear. For instance, the company Line 6 is famous for creating audio interfaces that also contain amplifier emulation technology. These devices enable you to plug directly into the audio interface and apply amplifier modeling sounds to the signal while you play or sing and record into your computer, thus eliminating the need for an actual guitar amplifier playing into a microphone or for a vocal preamp. Typically, these devices connect via USB.

Other devices combine the audio interface with a keyboard so that you always have a keyboard ready for transmitting and recording MIDI data. Still others combine the audio interface and a full hardware mixing console. In other words, there are a lot of options out there.

Such devices can provide great value, but be careful that you're not limiting yourself too much. For instance, if you need to record vocals, make sure the audio interface easily supports a microphone, not just a guitar. And make sure that the interface provides output to your speakers and that it is a full-duplexing unit.

NOTE

I've mostly used audio interfaces by three different manufacturers over the past 10 years. For a long time, I used a Delta 10-10 PCI device from M-Audio. I've also made extensive use of both PCI and FireWire devices from Echo. Finally, I've used several different FireWire audio interfaces made by Presonus. I've had great luck with each of these devices. As I mentioned earlier, I much prefer the FireWire devices over the PCI devices because of their portability and flexibility.

Setting Up an Audio Monitoring System

Obviously, you have to have some way to hear the audio that you play back from your DAW. The sound devices we just discussed are an important piece of that puzzle, but after the audio leaves the audio interface, you have to send it somewhere. There are a couple of different approaches you can take in setting up your audio monitoring system. In this section, we'll be talking specifically about monitoring through a stereo setup. If you're running some sort of surround-sound or other multiple-channel setup, the techniques will be essentially the same—you'll just have more outputs, cables, speakers, and so on to connect.

Routing Through a Hardware Audio Mixing Console

One way to get the audio signal from your sound device to your speakers is to run through a mixing console (mixer). A mixer makes it possible to control the volume and equalization of several separate audio input devices (your audio interface, a CD player, and so on) and send that signal to the same set of speakers or other device.

In a setup with a hardware mixer, the audio comes out of two output jacks on your sound device (one for the left audio signal and one for the right) and into two channels on your mixer. The audio then routes through to the mixer's outputs and from there to an amplifier. The amplifier sends an amplified signal to your speakers. The amplifier might be a separate piece of gear, or it might be built into each speaker you're using. Speakers that provide their own amplification are referred to as *self-powered* speakers.

Doing Without the Mixer

If space is an issue, or you just don't want another piece of hardware to worry about, you can do without the mixer. And, as I mentioned, if you have self-powered speakers, you can eliminate a separate amplifier, too.

This setup significantly reduces the amount of desk space you need to control your audio. In essence, your audio interface substitutes for the mixer, while the speaker's built-in amplifiers substitute for an external amplifier.

This is the way I prefer to have my studio set up because I need the extra space that the mixer takes up. If you're contemplating this type of setup, I suggest looking into an audio interface that has a few extra features that provide the control you'll be passing up by eliminating the mixer.

Choose an audio interface that has a control on its front with which you can adjust the volume of the device's main outputs. Since you don't have a mixer, you'll find this hardware control on your audio interface very valuable for easily changing the volume of the audio playback.

Since you don't have a mixer to control your audio input sources, you'll need to send those sources (like your electronic keyboard, your microphone, and so on) directly into the inputs of the audio interface. Since you'll probably be changing the devices you plug into the audio interface, it's unbelievably inconvenient to have your inputs on the back of your audio interface where you have to be a contortionist to get to them.

You'll also want to make sure that the inputs on the front of the device are universal connections that can accept either a quarter-inch plug that accepts line-level signal (from your electronic keyboard, for example) or an XLR plug that accepts a mic-level signal directly from your microphone.

It's also helpful to have at least one instrument-level jack on the front of your audio interface that can accept the signal directly from your guitar. This is especially crucial if you'll be using amplifier emulation software to achieve the sounds you want on your guitars (as opposed to playing through an actual guitar amp and recording with a microphone).

You'll really appreciate an audio interface that features *trim* controls on the front for each input channel. A trim control (usually in the form of a knob that you turn) enables you to adjust the volume level of the input source. We'll talk more about input level in Chapter 5, "Creating Your Guide Tracks," but suffice it to say for now that it's critical to set your input levels properly to achieve the best sound quality while you're recording.

You'll want a device that supplies phantom power through the XLR inputs to your microphone and an easily accessible switch to turn phantom power on and off. In a nutshell, some microphones require power to operate. The power can be supplied by a battery that you insert into the micro-phone, or often by the gear into which you plug the microphone (in this case, the audio interface) through phantom power.

You'll want a device that enables you to monitor the incoming audio signal. Again, we'll talk more about input monitoring when it comes time to record in Chapter 5, but basically this capability enables you to hear what you're sending into the audio interface. For instance, it enables you to hear yourself singing while you record your vocals. A way to control the mix between input monitoring volume and computer playback volume is a nice touch, too.

It's convenient to have a headphone jack and headphone volume control on the front of the device. In fact, this can be critical to successfully doing the type of recording we're talking about in this book—that is, the type of recording that happens at 12:30 a.m. when the neighbors, kids, or room-mates are asleep.

Deciding How You're Going to Hear the Music

Whether you decide to use a mixer or not and regardless of which audio interface you settle upon, ultimately the audio chain ends with sound coming out of a device that enables you to hear it. I've already referred to speakers and headphones, but let's talk about both of those topics in a little more detail.

Monitoring Through Speakers

Of course, you realize that a good-sounding pair of speakers is critical to making quality recordings. But it's not quite that simple. The speakers you want to use in your studio are not the same as the ones you want to use for your stereo. Home stereo speakers are designed to make the music sound as good as possible. For your studio, you want speakers that make the music sound as *accurate* as possi-ble. In other words, you don't want speakers that color the sound. Instead, you want to hear exactly what you've recorded so you can know exactly what you've got. Your studio speakers should "tell it like it is," not as you'd like it to be.

Speakers made for musical production work are called *reference monitors*. You can choose from a dizzying array of monitor options, which can be categorized in a couple of different ways.

Reference monitors fall into three general categories: near-field, mid-field, and far-field. Mid- and far-field monitors hold no real relevance to the typical home studio for a couple of reasons. First, they're bigger and more expensive. Second, they're made to be listened to from a distance—generally 5 to 10 feet away or more. You've seen the picture of my studio and can tell that I couldn't get that far away from my monitors if I wanted to!

So you're left with near-field monitors. That's not a bad thing. (In fact, for your budget and space considerations, they're a good thing.) It simply means that you need speakers that give their best sound in a range from about 3 to 5 feet away—exactly right for listening to the monitors sitting on (or preferably on stands *near*) your desk while you're sitting in your chair. When you go looking for speakers then, stick to the near-field monitor choices.

Monitors can be either active or passive. I referred to this topic earlier when I mentioned that some monitors supply their own built-in amplification. These are referred to as *active*. Monitors that require external amplification are called *passive*.

Active monitors may give more accurate sound because the amplification is obviously designed specifically for the speakers.

Each active monitor has its own amplifier that needs to be plugged into the wall, so you'll need an extra outlet.

I prefer active monitors because they eliminate the need for a separate amplifier that I would need to store at my workspace.

You should make every attempt to properly place your studio monitors. Monitor placement can have surprising effects on the quality of the sound you get, so try some different locations if you can.

I mentioned in the previous chapter that you want to avoid placing a monitor close to a wall because of the quick audio reflection that results. You might think that you're safe in putting the back of the monitor up against a wall or in a corner because the sound comes out the front of the monitor. But sound also escapes from the back of a monitor, so even if its back is against the wall, you can run into problems.

You also want to do your best to create a perfect equilateral triangle with your two monitors and your head making up the triangle points. In other words, if your two monitors are three feet apart on your desk, they should be three feet away from your head, too. This puts you right in the *sweet spot*—that area where the monitors give the most accurate sound and stereo effect.

You'll want to angle the monitors in and angle them up if you have to so that their faces point directly at yours. Better yet, if you can, raise the monitors on stands off your desk so that their *tweeters* (the smaller speaker cones in each monitor) are level with your ears. Specially designed monitor stands often don't rest flat on the floor. Instead, they stand on small spikes to minimize their contact with the floor, thus sending fewer vibrations into the floor. That's a nice touch if you can afford it.

SELECTING YOUR MONITORS

I know you can often get better prices online, but I strongly urge you not to buy studio monitors solely on reputation or recommendation. Go to your local music retailer and listen to monitors before you buy. Take a reference CD along—something with which you're intimately familiar and has production quality that you would like to achieve in your own studio. Run some blind tests where you have the salesperson switch back and forth between different speaker models without your knowing which ones you're hearing. You might be surprised which ones sound the best to you. Then, once you know exactly what you want, you can go online to find the deals.

Monitoring Through Headphones

Don't scrimp when it comes time to buy a pair of headphones. If you don't have a quality pair, make room in your budget for one. There will be times in the home studio when you want to work but you just can't make a lot of noise due to factors such as sleeping babies, grumpy neighbors, or TV-watching roommates.

If you can't afford a nice pair of studio monitors, a good pair of headphones might be within your budget. You can do most, if not all, of your work monitoring through headphones. Some would argue that you shouldn't mix or master your music in headphones because they give a different experience than monitors. That may be true, and I tend to agree that I'd rather mix in monitors, but sometimes you don't have a choice. And mixing in headphones is better than not mixing at all!

We'll talk more about the issues involved with mixing and mastering your music in Chapter 10, "Mixing Your Song," and 11, "Mastering Your Song."

There are many good headphone choices, too. I'd use the same technique in choosing the headphones as I suggested for choosing studio monitors. Your ears have to be the final judge, not the product's reputation or recommendations from friends and online forums.

You can find good headphones in both enclosed and open-air styles. Enclosed headphones cover the entire area around your ears. They keep sound from bleeding through to your ears from your environment and keep the sound they make from bleeding out the other way. That's important when you're recording with a microphone because any sound that bleeds out from your headphones may very well be picked up by the microphone and end up on your recording.

On the other hand, the open style makes it possible to keep a little more in touch with what's going on around you. This is important if, for instance, you're the one who needs to jump when the baby starts crying.

Get Familiar with Your Gear

It's important to spend some quality time with your studio monitors and headphones. Listen to a lot of music on them. Get to know their attributes and characteristics. Listen at low volumes and higher volumes, but don't damage your hearing! Get to know how the music sounds at these different levels.

The more familiar you are with the sonic attributes of your monitors and headphones, the better you'll be able to judge your music when you hear it through them. And that will help the sound of the music you produce on them.

IN A PINCH

All this information on monitoring your audio might not do you much good at the moment if you don't have room in your budget for any of the gear you need. I found myself in this same situation a while back, and I worked around it by running my audio through an old stereo system. I wouldn't recommend such a setup for mixing and mastering, but it worked adequately for me when I was in the recording stage. If it comes right down to it, you can set your system up to run through a regular consumer stereo system and use that while you save up the money for proper gear.

Studio Log

We've covered a lot of ground in this chapter. First, you learned that you don't need the newest, fanciest, most powerful computer in the world to set up your studio. As long as the machine you have meets the minimum system requirements of the software you want to use, you're in business. Of course, faster is always better, but assuming you need to watch your budget, you can probably get by with a machine that's even as old as about three years.

We also discussed many audio interface issues. Audio interfaces that come built into most computers are inadequate for the task of multitrack recording, so you need something much better. I advocated for devices that you connect to your computer via a FireWire connection because of the portability and expanded feature set of many of these devices. I also ran down several features that I look for in an audio interface. Ultimately, the most important thing to me is the convenience. Since I prefer to work without a hardware mixer, my audio interface must give me easy access to all the features I need—features that the mixer would normally supply. These features include input jacks, input trim controls, master volume control, headphone jack and volume control, and so on.

Finally, you learned about issues related to monitoring your audio. Near-field monitors make the most sense for a small studio space, and I prefer active monitors because they enable me to eliminate a separate amplifier from my workspace. I also want a quality pair of headphones for when I can't make much noise. I prefer the enclosed style partly because they prevent sound from bleeding out into the microphone when I'm recording.

4

An Introduction to ACID Pro Fundamentals

This chapter finally moves us into the fun stuff: making music! We all have to choose a Digital Audio Workstation (DAW) software package that we'll use to create our music. As I explained early on in the book, my DAW of choice happens to be ACID Pro from Sony Creative Software. I recommend that software to you because I know it's a great and stable tool. While I recognize that other great tools exist, I can't write the book without using a DAW, so I'll use the one I know best. That said, even if you're used to using something else, having a good introduction to ACID Pro will help you get the most out of what I'm discussing. When you understand what I'm doing in ACID Pro, you can figure out how to do the same or a similar task in your own software.

Once you're familiar with the interface and master a few basic techniques, you'll be ready for the following chapter, where you'll add a basic beat track that you can use as a guide to recording scratch guitar or keyboard and vocal tracks. These tracks serve as the base for the real parts that you'll lay down later.

What ACID Pro Does

Before we dive into the application, let's discuss what it does. I've called the application a DAW several times already in this book, but what exactly does a DAW do? ACID Pro works in three distinct, yet related, music production categories:

- Multitrack audio recording, editing, and mixing
- Loop-based music production
- MIDI sequencing

Other software applications may work in any or all of these same categories. Because they integrate with each other so effectively, you can create a musical project that uses any or all of these three categories and their tools. The following sections take a brief look at each of these categories.

Multitrack Audio Recording, Editing, and Mixing

This category most closely parallels working with an analog-based multitrack system. You can record multiple tracks of audio into ACID Pro, edit that audio (far more efficiently and powerfully than with an analog system), and adjust your audio tracks to create the mix you want. Then you can output that music in a variety of ways, including to CDs and MP3 files, so you can share it with your friends and fans.

MIDI Sequencing

MIDI sequencing tools enable you to record, create, and edit digital information (called *MIDI* information). ACID Pro sends the MIDI information to a sampler or synthesizer (*synth*) to instruct that device to generate audio. The sampler- or synth-generated audio is then mixed in with the other audio in your project so that it works seamlessly with audio that you recorded with your microphones or instruments. We'll talk much more about MIDI, synths, and samplers later in this chapter and even more extensively throughout the remainder of this book, so don't worry if these terms have you confused at the moment.

Loop-Based Music Production

ACID Pro is brilliant when it comes to combining music loops and creating a musical composition with them. In fact, the application popularized the practice of using loops in a software application to create music.

A music loop is a small section of music (typically from one to four measures long, but technically any number of beats is possible) that's been edited so precisely that if you play it over and over again without stopping, it plays with perfect musical timing.

ACID Pro provides tools for literally painting loops into your project, mixing them together, and thus creating an original music composition. This is a valuable tool for you because you can use loops to add instruments to your project that you don't play or can't record. For instance, I've made extensive use of drum loops in past projects to create drum tracks when I couldn't record a live drummer. I've also used drum loops to completely rebuild horribly recorded live drum tracks and transform them into great-sounding tracks that—all modesty aside—brought the project back from the brink of dis-aster. My musical collaborators were amazed!

Routing Your Playback Audio

The first time you start ACID Pro, it opens an already-finished sample project. In a few moments, we'll start a new project so that you can more easily get comfortable with the user interface. But first, let's play the sample project so you can get a taste of what you can use the software to create.

It's simple to play the project—you just click the Play button. Unfortunately, actually *hearing* what's being played in the project might not be as straightforward as that. Generally, if you can hear your computer's system sounds, you'll be able to hear the audio from your project. However, if you've made changes to your audio device according to our discussion of audio interfaces in Chapter 3, "Setting Up Your Computer for Music Production," you may have to do some *audio routing* work before you'll hear the audio.

> ## NOTE
>
> We spent a lot of time talking about audio interfaces in Chapter 3. Hopefully you have a pretty good idea of what you want. As I suggested earlier, though, I think you should read this entire book once before you buy any gear. That way you're more likely to know exactly what you need to get set up and less likely to make a purchasing mistake.
>
> I'll spend more time discussing audio interfaces throughout later chapters, and those discus-sions will help you zero in on exactly what you need to accomplish your recording goals. For now, though, I'll proceed with this chapter as if you have already made your audio interface choice, have successfully installed both the software drivers and the hardware components for that interface, have connected the outputs on your audio interface to your studio monitors (either directly or through a mixer or amplifier), and are ready to start listening to audio from your projects.
>
> So from here on out (at least in this chapter), I'll speak as if you already have your high-quality audio interface connected and ready to use.

Routing Your Windows System Sounds

As you know, your computer's operating system generates a variety of sounds. For instance, assuming you have a sound device and monitors, you hear a little tune when you first boot up your PC. You might also hear warning beeps and other sounds as you click around your screen.

If you've changed your audio device from the computer's built-in device and have plugged your stu-dio monitors into that new device rather than the built-in sound card, you may no longer hear those sounds.

If you know that you've set up all your new hardware properly and you still can't hear your system sounds, you've probably neglected to route your computer's system sounds to your new audio device. Your operating system provides a way to do that. For instance, in Windows XP, you'll find the tools you need for setting your default sound playback device on the Audio tab of the Sounds and

Audio Devices Properties dialog box, which you access through the Control Panel (found in the Start menu). Select your new audio device from the Default Device drop-down list.

Establishing Your DAW's Audio Routing

Audio routing, or the *audio signal path*, simply refers to the path that your audio takes from your project to your studio monitors. The audio doesn't know which route to take on its own, so you have to give it some help. You have to tell it where to go—tell it how to get from your project to your monitors. In theory, this is really no different from the way you may have set up routing in the past with a hardware mixer. You've already done some routing by connecting the outputs of your audio interface to your monitors through some sort of cable. That's the hardware end of the routing.

But you also have to establish routing on the software end—inside your computer. Luckily, no matter what DAW you use, it has already done much of the routing work for you, even while giving you several options for modifying that routing. For instance, when you play something from the Timeline in ACID Pro, the audio automatically goes from the track (or tracks) it's on, through various optional tools (like the DSP), and on to the *Master bus* in the mixing console (which we'll discuss in great detail in Chapter 10, "Mixing Your Song"). The Master bus in turn routes by default to the device you have set as your operating system's default audio playback device.

Think of the Master bus as a band's tour bus. If your band wants to get to the next town for a gig, everyone gets on board the bus. Someone has determined the route the bus will take to get the band to its destination. That route might go through several small towns or other stops along the way for record stores, radio appearances, and so on, but once the route has been established, the bus gets the band to the gig.

The Master bus works the same way. The audio from your project must get to your studio monitors, so it all gets on the Master bus. Now someone—namely you—just needs to determine the route that the Master bus will take to get to those monitors.

We'll talk about many of the routing options later in this book, but for now we just need to route the Master bus directly to the audio interface outputs to which you have connected your monitors. To do this, you choose the appropriate audio drivers. (Recall that audio devices require a small piece of software called *drivers* to operate properly.)

To specify the drivers you want to use, choose Options, Preferences from the ACID Pro menu bar. In the Preferences dialog, click the Audio Device tab. You use the Audio Device Type drop-down list to specify the audio drivers you want to use. By default, ACID Pro sets the Audio device type to Microsoft Sound Mapper. This setting basically picks up the settings of your system sounds and uses that same setting to play back your ACID Pro project.

Click the Audio Device Type drop-down arrow. This list shows you all the audio drivers that have been loaded on your system. Figure 4.1 shows my drop-down list.

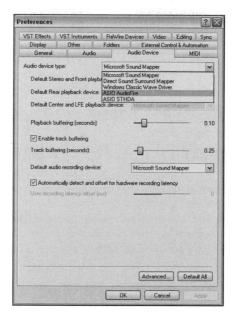

Figure 4.1

You can see that my computer has two ASIO drivers. Since I'm using my Echo AudioFire 8 audio interface, I need to select the ASIO AudioFire drivers from the list. You need to choose the ASIO drivers for your audio device.

Recall earlier that I mentioned you'll need to use the low-latency ASIO drivers for your audio device. If you've properly installed those drivers, you'll see them here in this list. Select your audio device's ASIO drivers from the list.

ACID Pro assumes that you've used analog outputs 1 and 2 from your audio device to connect to your studio monitors, so it automatically sets the Default Stereo and Front Playback device setting to those outputs. The software has also assumed that you'll most often want to use analog inputs 1 and 2 for your inputs and has set the Default audio recording device to those inputs.

Naturally, you can change all these settings on a case-by-case basis if necessary, but these settings define your default devices from now on when you start a new project (overriding the original factory default settings). In other words, once you've set them here, you won't need to worry about these settings again unless you want to override them for some reason.

You most likely won't have to worry about the other settings on the Audio Device tab, so for now, click OK to make these settings permanent.

Now you're ready to listen to the project. Figure 4.2 shows the Transport toolbar, which contains the Play and Stop buttons. Click the Play button. Assuming that you have your hardware properly set up, you should now be able to hear the project.

Play   Stop

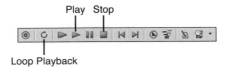

Loop Playback

Figure 4.2

The Transport toolbar contains the Play button and the Stop button, which allow you to play the project and stop play-back when you're done listening.

TIP

When the ACID Pro timeline has focus (we'll discuss that shortly), the spacebar starts playback if the project is stopped and stops playback if the project is playing.

Note that if you hover the mouse over the Play button (but don't click it), a ToolTip appears that identifies the button and tells you the keyboard shortcut for it. You can use this method to learn other keyboard shortcuts for often-used commands.

Assembling a Loop-Based ACID Pro Project

I've always appreciated the simple, clean, and intuitive look of the ACID Pro interface. As you saw in the previous section, the first time you start the application, it opens an already-finished sample project. This complete project contains various items that have already been added to it, so it tends to make the interface look more complex—and perhaps more overwhelming—than it really is, as you see in Figure 4.3. Let's start a new project so you can see what ACID Pro looks like without all the elements of a completed project.

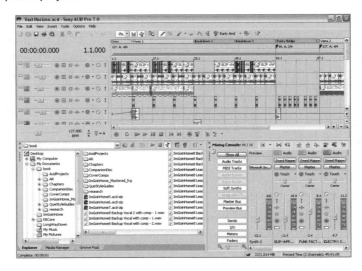

Figure 4.3

The ACID Pro interface is actually very clean and straightforward, which makes it easy to understand and use. However, the project that opens the first time you start the application makes it look more complex.

Accessing the Application Help File

You most likely know how to use menus and buttons (ACID Pro's are shown in Figure 4.4), so we don't need to spend time talking about that. If you don't know how to use these tools, you've got some studying to do before you'll be able to follow most of what I talk about in the remainder of this book. Find a good Windows basics tutorial, and you'll be able to get yourself up to speed quickly enough.

Figure 4.4

The menus and buttons in ACID Pro work just as they do in other Windows applications, and some of them should look very familiar to you.

We'll talk about many of the buttons and menus as we move along, but I do want to point out the ACID Pro help file now because it can be a valuable learning tool.

The Help menu provides a few great resources for learning more about the application and how it works. In particular, the Interactive Tutorials module under the Help menu provides an innovative and extremely useful tool for beginners. Take some time to walk through at least the basic-level wizard-based tutorials you see here, and you'll quickly get a good handle on how to use ACID Pro.

If you're looking for more specific information, the Help menu's Contents and Index option gives you detailed explanations of all the features in the application.

Starting a New Project

To start a new project, click the New button. (If you made any changes to the current project, you'll be asked if you want to save the changes.) Opening a new project simultaneously closes the existing one. Therefore, much of the information in the ACID Pro window disappears because it was related specifically to the project that you just closed. You're left looking at the basic interface, and it now looks much cleaner and simpler.

The best way to learn the different parts of the application is to work on a project, so let's get started. Instead of giving you a laundry list of all the different sections of the application window now, I'll explain them when they come into play. When we discuss various tools or techniques and you experience them in practical use, you'll learn much more quickly and effectively. And you'll have more fun learning!

Previewing Audio Files

You won't get far in your project if you don't add some audio to it. You can get audio into your project in a few different ways. For instance, you can record audio from your instruments or voice, which is, after all, the whole point of this book! But you can also bring audio that already exists as a computer file into your project. For instance, I talked earlier about creating drums using loops. Those loops are just small audio files that you can bring into your projects. You'll learn more about the loop files you'll use shortly.

The Explorer in the lower-left corner of the ACID Pro workspace works almost exactly like Windows Explorer, and it gives you a handy way to navigate through your computer drives to find the files you want to use in your project without ever leaving the ACID Pro interface.

CAUTION

Keep in mind that if you delete or rename a file in the ACID Pro Explorer window, the file is affected permanently just as if you had deleted or changed it in Windows Explorer.

Use the ACID Pro Explorer window now to navigate to a collection of loop files on your computer. If you don't have a loop collection of your own, you'll find a sample collection on the companion disc that came with this book. You can use these loops (royalty free) in any of your projects.

TIP

You can download free loops each month with the monthly *8 Packs* available at www.acidplanet.com. It's a great way to build your loop collection—for free! I'll discuss acidplanet.com in Chapter 12, "Delivering Your Music."

To access these sample loops, insert the companion disc into your computer's DVD-ROM drive. Navigate to the Sony Sound Series Sampler folder and then into the Loops folder. That folder contains several other folders. You can drill down into the various folders to find loop samples from Sony's collection of loop libraries. We'll use a few of these loops to put together a simple project.

While the ACID Pro Explorer window works much the same as the Windows Explorer, it goes beyond Windows Explorer in that it gives you the power to preview, or listen to, the audio files before you add them to your project. That functionality makes it possible to quickly audition files to determine whether you want to use them in your project.

To see how this works, find and navigate into Fleetwood Loops folder and single-click the first file in the list to select it. Assuming that the Auto Preview button is selected (which it is by default), the file begins to play. Select the next file in the list, and it begins to play. Continue selecting the rest of the files in the folder until you've listened to all of them.

Listen to these loops as many times as you need to settle on one that has a feel you might like to work with in a new song. If you don't find one you like in the Fleetwood Loops folder, navigate into some of the other folders to see what else you can find.

Adding a File to Your Project

Once you've decided on a drum loop you'd like to build upon, you can add it to your project. To do so, drag the file from the Explorer window into the dark gray area of the upper portion of the ACID Pro workspace, called the *timeline*.

When you get the file to the timeline, a rectangle appears at the location of your mouse pointer. This rectangle represents the file you're adding; you can use it to see the exact position where the file will be added when you release the mouse button. Position the rectangle at the beginning of the timeline, and release the mouse button.

This creates a new track in your project and drops the file at the beginning of the timeline in that track. Now that you have a track in your project, let's take a moment to talk a little bit about what you see here.

First, to the left of the timeline, an area called the *track list* contains a set of controls for the new track. Collectively, these controls make up the *track header* for the track. Therefore, this area is often referred to as the *track header area*. To make it easier to see all the controls in the track header, you can make it—and thus the track—taller. To do so, drag the bottom edge of the track header down. As you make the track header taller, the controls reconfigure and spread out so that you can see and work with them more effectively. You'll do this a lot throughout this book and while you're working on your own projects. Stop making the track header taller once the controls stop repositioning. You can see my track header in Figure 4.5.

Figure 4.5

When you make the track header tall enough, the controls spread out so that you can see and work with them more effectively.

We'll talk more about the various controls you see in the track header throughout the remainder of the book. For now, let's turn our attention back to the timeline.

When you drop the loop file into the timeline, the file shows up as a box with an audio waveform in it. This box, called an *event*, indicates exactly where the file will play in your project timeline.

Play the project. Depending on the length of the loop file you added, you'll hear a measure or two of drums. You can see the cursor move through the timeline as the project plays. Once the cursor passes the end of the event, the audio goes silent even though the project continues to play for a while.

Because we're dealing with an audio loop, it's purposely short. You can, however, make the music last as long as you want it to. We'll make this drum beat last for 24 measures. Stop playback.

Notice the numbers and ruler marks along the top of the timeline. This area, called the *ruler bar*, gives you a quick way to identify measures in your project so you can see how long the loop lasts. You can also use the ruler bar as a reference in making the loop last for as long as you want it to.

To make the loop event longer, drag its right edge to the right. As you drag, you'll notice that the edge of the event snaps to the ruler marks that run from the ruler bar down through the timeline.

Keep dragging the edge of the event until it snaps to 25.1 on the ruler bar, which is the start of the measure 25. You now have a full 24 measures of drum beat in your project.

Looping Your Project

When you play the project again, it will keep playing for 24 measures because you've expanded the drum event. Notice the indentations in the top and bottom of the expanded event. These indicate the loop point for the event, meaning the point at which the file actually finishes and begins instantly playing again. As you listen, notice how seamlessly this loop repeats so that the drum beat keeps perfect musical time.

Now you can add more files to your project to start developing your song. To do this, you'll want to preview loops to determine whether they sound good with the drum beat you've established. Therefore, we'll set the project to play repeatedly so you can hear it while you audition loops.

Click the Loop Playback button in the Transport bar (refer back to Figure 4.2). A dark blue bar bounded by yellow triangles appears above the ruler bar. This blue bar, called the Loop Region Indicator, defines an area of your project that will play repeatedly (again, called *looping*) until you manually stop playback. Drag the yellow triangles to make the loop region longer or shorter so that you can define the area you want to loop. We want to set the loop region to exactly match the drum event. To do that quickly and accurately, double-click the drum event. This sets the loop region to match the event.

Now play the project. When the playback cursor reaches the end of the loop region, it instantly jumps back to the beginning of the region and continues playing. As long as you've set the loop region to start at the beginning of one measure and end at the beginning of another, playback continues in perfect musical timing.

Interacting with the Time Displays

ACID Pro displays time—the location of your playback cursor—in two helpful ways in the time display area shown in Figure 4.6. On the left, you see the location of your cursor in time, and on the right, you see it in measures and beats. You'll find these displays helpful as you work in your projects.

Hours, Minutes, Seconds, and Milliseconds ——— 00:00:02.000   2.1.000 ——— Measures and Beats

Figure 4.6

The left display shows the cursor location in hours, minutes, seconds, and milliseconds, while the right display shows it in measures and beats.

Stop playback for a moment. Click on the event at measure 13.1 in your timeline. This moves the cursor instantly to that location, and the time displays update to show the position of the cursor. Click at other locations in the timeline to see these displays update according to where you click.

You can also use the time displays to jump to an exact point in your project. This is most useful with the measures and beats display. For instance, you've seen that when you click, the cursor snaps to the ruler marks. Since the ruler marks at the moment identify the beginning of measures, you can only place your cursor at the first beat of a measure. But maybe you want to place your cursor at measure 6, beat 3. You can use the time display to easily do this.

Double-click the value in the measures and beats display to highlight it. Then type 6.3.0 (measure 6, beat 3) and press the Enter key. Your cursor instantly jumps to measure 6, beat 3. You'll find this technique invaluable as you work more with the application.

Adding More Tracks

Let's get back to creating your song. You've got the loop region set to the length of your project so far, and you're in Loop Playback mode. So play the project, and just let it keep playing while you work.

Back in the ACID Pro Explorer window, navigate to find a folder that contains bass loops. You can preview the bass loops while your project continues to play. This enables you to hear exactly how the bass files sound along with the drums you've already chosen for your project. This ability to preview files while you listen to your project is a real strength of ACID Pro because you don't have to guess how things are going to sound together. You can also avoid adding files to the timeline only to find out that they don't work with your project.

Once you find a bass loop that you're happy with, drag it to the dark gray area of the timeline below the existing drum track. Once again, you see the position rectangle. This time, instead of placing the bass event at the beginning of the project, drop it in starting at beat 3.1. Then drag the right edge of the event so that it lasts for the remainder of the project as shown in Figure 4.7. Immediately, you begin to hear your drums and bass playing together.

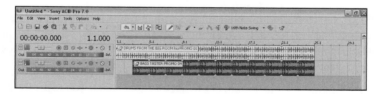

Figure 4.7
The project now has two tracks, one with drums and the other with bass.

Preview files from the other folders inside the Loops folder and add a couple more tracks to your project. Keep in mind that you can drop the new events anywhere you want in the timeline and can thus create an arrangement where one loop comes in and plays for a while, drops out, and comes back in later.

NOTE

While the scope of this book reaches far beyond creating projects based only on loops, it's worth pointing out that you can make extensive use of loops in various ways as you build your projects. I encourage you to experiment with loops and see what you can compose using them.

It's a fun exercise to build an entire song using just loops. As you work, try to envision how you might use loops to add elements to your compositions that you can't play or record yourself. For instance, it's not easy to record a horn section in your basement at 11:30 p.m. when the neighbors are asleep, but you can easily grab your collection of horn loops and experiment to see if you can find something that works.

Later you'll learn how you can work in more detail with your loops and really start to get creative. You can cut them up, change their pitches, reverse them, and much, much more. Remember to consult the help file and the interactive tutorials to learn more about what you can do.

Adjusting Tempo and Key

Part of the magic that made ACID Pro so revolutionary when it was introduced in 1998 is that the key or tempo that the loops are recorded at doesn't really matter to the application. Loops that have been designed to work in ACID Pro contain pitch and tempo information that ACID Pro can use to make everything work together.

Every ACID Pro project has a project-level tempo setting and key designation. By default, all new ACID Pro projects start out in the key of A with a tempo of 120 beats per minute (bpm). It doesn't matter what tempo or key your loops were created at; ACID Pro matches them to the project settings so that everything sounds good together.

You can adjust both the tempo and the project key. So, for instance, if you're going to be recording a song that you've written in the key of G at a tempo of about 92 bpm, you can set your project key and tempo to those values. Any loop you use in your project then conforms to those settings, regardless of how those loops were originally recorded.

Figure 4.8 shows the controls at the bottom of the track list that enable you to set the project key, tempo, and time signature. To change the tempo, adjust the Tempo slider or double-click the current bpm value and type in the tempo you want. To change the key for your project, click the Project Key button and choose the key you want from the drop-down list. Finally, to change the project time signature, click the Project Time Signature button and choose the one you want from the drop-down list.

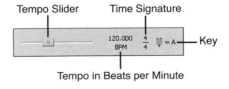

Figure 4.8

Loops you add to your project conform to the Project Tempo, Signature, and Key settings that you establish with these controls.

CHANGING YOUR PROJECT TIME SIGNATURE

Keep in mind that most loops seem to be recorded in 4/4 time since that's the most common signature for pop-based Western music (like rock, country, and folk). Of course, that doesn't mean that you'll never want to record a song in an alternate time signature. But changing your project time signature to a different setting, like 3/4 for instance, will not change the timing of the loops in your loop collection. In other words, if you're working in 3/4 time, you're going to need—and might need to buy or create—new loops that were recorded in 3/4 time.

The value of changing the project time signature lies in the ruler bar and the measures and beats time display. The information in these areas will only be accurate if you change the project signature to match the time signature of the song you're recording. So, if you're recording a song that you've written in 3/4 time, set your project signature to 3/4 time so that your measures and beats time display and your ruler bar give you accurate information.

Play the project you've created again and make adjustments to the project tempo and key settings. You'll notice that when you change the tempo of the project, all the loops you've used change their tempo to match. You may start to hear undesirable audio artifacts if you change the tempo too far from the loop's original tempo, but you actually have quite a bit of flexibility.

You'll also notice that changing the tempo has no effect on the pitch of the loops you've used in your project. That's another piece of ACID Pro innovation—you can change speed without changing pitch.

Now change the project pitch. Again, all loops are adjusted to play in the new key, and this setting has no effect on the project tempo.

Setting Up Your Desired Folder Structure

Now that you know some basics, you're ready to move into the other functional areas of ACID Pro—multitrack audio production and MIDI sequencing. Again, we'll talk in basic terms about these two areas just so you have an introduction. We'll go into much more detail later in the book.

However, before we move onto these discussions, we have to make a small side trip to talk about file management. ACID Pro gives you several ways to create new files as you're working on your projects. The most obvious (and probably most common) involve creating new files when you record audio and MIDI. If you don't have your file management under control from the start, you can end up with files scattered haphazardly across your computer. So let's make sure you know where you'll be storing the files you create.

ACID Pro gives you strong file management tools. To access them, choose Options, Preferences to open the Preferences dialog box. Click the Folders tab.

As you can see in Figure 4.9, there's a lot of information here. Essentially, you have a way to set a unique file path for every type of file creation task you can undertake in ACID Pro.

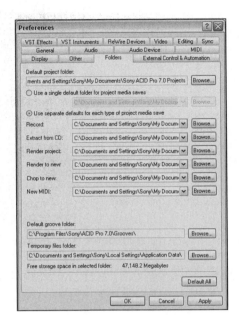

Figure 4.9

The Folders tab of the Preferences dialog box gives you tools to define unique save paths for every operation that you can use to create a new file in ACID Pro.

Although you have the flexibility to change every setting, I use just one setting here since I prefer to save all my newly created files in the same place for each project I work on.

For instance, if I'm working on a song called "I'm Goin' Home," I want every file that I create related to that song to be stored in a folder on my hard drive called (cleverly enough!) ImGoinHome. Since I want all the files saved to that same location, I don't need to specify each save location individually. Instead, I can set one global location and tell ACID Pro to drop all the files I create into that location. Let's do that now.

In the Folders tab of the Preferences dialog, select the Use a Single Default Folder for Project Media Saves radio button. This activates the Browse button for that option. Click the Browse button to open the Browse for Folder dialog box. Use the tools here to navigate to the location on your hard drive where you want to save your song. Click the Make New Folder button, name the new folder the name of your song (in this example, ImGoinHome) and click OK.

Next, click the Use a Single Default Folder for Project Media Saves drop-down list. Instead of specifying the folder you just created specifically, choose <Project> from the list. This points all of your saves to the same location into which you've saved your project (which you'll do later).

WHY NOT SPECIFY THE FOLDER SPECIFICALLY?

As you can see, you could specify the exact folder into which you want to save your files. However, I had you choose <Project> instead. Why?

Keep in mind that this setting is an application preference. Application preferences do not relate specifically to the project you happen to have open when you set those preferences. Rather, they're more global in scope.

Okay, so what does that mean? Well, if you set your save location to be the name of the song you're working on (in my example, ImGoinHome) everything will work fine *as long as you're working on that specific song*. But, when you start work on another song, you want the saves for that song to appear in a folder specifically for that song. If you've set your preferences specifically for ImGoinHome, your new song's saves will end up in the ImGoinHome folder instead of where you really want them.

On the other hand, if you set the preference to <Project>, then your saves will always go to whatever folder the file you're currently working on has been saved to. *That's* what you want!

Generally, I leave all the other settings in the Folders tab set to their defaults. I only really care that I have a logical location to save my files in. That way I can easily keep it all straight.

When you're done setting these preferences, click the OK button.

Multitrack Audio Production

Technically, you can probably consider everything you do in ACID Pro (or your DAW of choice) as falling under the general category of multitrack audio production. But here I'm making a distinction between the looping techniques we just discussed, the MIDI techniques we'll touch on in the following section, and recording your own audio tracks. I call the process of recording tracks and working with them multitrack audio production.

Think of the process of recording the audio generated by your guitar, keyboard, saxophone, voice, and so on into multiple tracks in your ACID Pro timeline. That's what I'm referring to as *multitrack audio production*. It's the part of the recording process we're discussing that most closely parallels traditional analog multitrack recording. This is the type of production that comprises the lion's share of my musical projects.

We're going to talk much more extensively about this topic as we progress through the following chapters.

MIDI Sequencing

MIDI has become an invaluable part of modern recording. Even still, when you mention the term to your musical buddies, it's surprising how often they respond with sneers and scoffs. There's a lot of negative attitude toward MIDI among musicians.

That's really unfortunate because MIDI's bad rep springs almost completely from a lack of under-standing of the technology, the potential it offers, and how to use it properly. It's true; a lot of bad-sounding music has been created with MIDI. But then, a lot of bad-sounding music has been created with traditional recording methods, too. For some reason, while musicians and producers might take the blame for bad audio recordings, as often as not MIDI itself takes the rap for bad MIDI productions. It's a bit like a guitarist blaming his axe when in reality it's his own lack of talent that makes him inca-pable of playing that blazing riff.

Well, just as a lot of really great work can be done with traditional methods, a lot of really great work can be—and has been—done with MIDI. And if you're dismissing MIDI out of hand based on negative things you've heard or your own lack of understanding, you're missing out on a key aspect to creating music in your home studio.

So, let's take a few minutes to learn some basics about MIDI now. In later chapters, we'll talk in more detail about MIDI and how you should consider using it for your projects.

What Is MIDI?

The term MIDI stands for Musical Instrument Digital Interface. In general, you can think of MIDI as a computer language. MIDI can be used for a lot of things that don't necessarily have to be related to music. But in the context of music production, you can use MIDI to generate sound. MIDI itself doesn't make sound; rather, it's the language that one device (called a MIDI controller) uses to communicate with another device (a synthesizer or sampler). It's the synth that creates the sound based on instruc-tions it receives via MIDI from the controller.

WHAT'S A SYNTHESIZER, AND WHAT'S A SAMPLER?

Synthesizers and samplers are similar beasts. They are both electronic devices designed for audio generation—they create sounds. A *synthesizer* (synth for short) generates and combines a variety of frequencies to create sound. Modern synths can generate sounds that mimic the sounds of acoustic instruments quite convincingly, although some instruments can be imitated much more accurately than others.

A *sampler* creates sound by playing back actual recordings (samples) of the instrument it's attempt-ing to imitate. These samples can be altered according to the parameters that the sampler feeds them through (that is, pitch information and any special effect information you've applied to them).

Both synths and samplers can generate an amazing variety of sounds. While some sounds mimic acoustic instruments, others sound completely artificial and create interesting special effects.

Synthesizers and samplers can be hardware devices that may or may not have a controller inte-grated into them. They can also be software that you simply load onto your computer. Software syn-thesizers and samplers are commonly referred to as *Soft Synths*, and we'll make good use of those in our project when we get to Chapter 7, "Utilizing MIDI in Your Projects."

Throughout this book, I'll mostly use the term synth because it's a lot easier to write than synthesizer or sampler. Just keep in mind that when I say synth, I could be using the term to refer to either a syn-thesizer or a sampler.

Now let's put it in more concrete terms. The most common MIDI controller for musicians is arguably a piano-style keyboard. When you press a key, the keyboard generates MIDI information that describes the musical pitch associated with that key, the force or velocity with which you've pressed the key, the length of time for which you held the key down, and many other pieces of information about the key and how you pressed it. That MIDI information is then sent to the synthesizer, which translates the MIDI information about pitch, volume, and so on into sound.

In some cases, all this happens within the same device. For instance, many synths have a built-in keyboard controller, and the synth can output both audio (from its line out jacks or built-in speakers) and MIDI through its MIDI out jacks.

Alternatively, you can buy keyboard-style controllers (and other controller devices) that serve only the controller and MIDI transmission function. They can make no music on their own. The MIDI must be sent from this type of controller to a synth that can create sound based on the instructions it receives (and that synth may or may not have a built-in controller of its own).

How Your DAW Uses MIDI

Although the main use for MIDI in ACID Pro is to help you create and control audio, your DAW is probably capable of using MIDI in more ways than one.

You could simply plug your synth's line audio outputs into your computer's audio interface inputs and record that audio into the ACID Pro timeline as you play on the MIDI controller. It's a perfectly acceptable way to work, but you open up a huge array of possibilities if you record the MIDI data from the controller instead of recording audio from the synth.

When you do this, you end up with MIDI data on your ACID Pro timeline. It's just a bunch of instructions about what pitch to play, when to play it, how long to play it for, how loud to play it, and so on. Figure 4.10 shows what MIDI information looks like in an ACID Pro track.

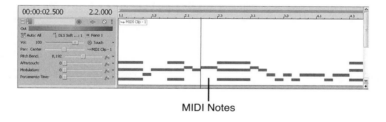

MIDI Notes

Figure 4.10

MIDI information on the ACID Pro timeline does not appear as audio waveforms because MIDI is not audio—it's purely a set of instructions.

The beauty of recording MIDI information is the flexibility it gives you to shape the audio that will eventually be generated by a synth according to these MIDI instructions. As you'll see later, you can intricately edit the MIDI information in a variety of ways. For instance, if you pressed the wrong key on the MIDI controller (for instance, you pressed the C key on your controller when you should have pressed C#), the MIDI faithfully records that wrong note information and passes it on to the synth, which then generates a note of the wrong pitch. But you can easily edit the MIDI information so that it instructs the synth to play the correct note instead.

Another huge advantage of recording MIDI is that the MIDI information doesn't care—in fact, it doesn't even know—what sound you intend to generate from that information. That decision is made at the synth well after the MIDI information has already been generated. This means that you can set the synth to generate any sound that it's capable of generating in response to the MIDI information that it receives.

What does all that mean in more practical terms? Well, you might be a monster piano player, but you couldn't toot a clean note on the trumpet even if you actually owned one. With MIDI, you can use your piano-keyboard-style controller to play a passage and document what you played with the appropriate MIDI information. You can then send that MIDI to your synth and set your synth to generate the sound of a trumpet based on the MIDI it receives. And all of this can happen virtually instantaneously so that, while you're playing the passage on the keyboard controller, you hear the sound of the trumpet through your studio monitors. As synth and sampler technology has improved, this process has become more convincing than ever.

The process of recording MIDI information and then altering that information in ACID Pro is called *sequencing*. ACID Pro contains a fairly robust MIDI sequencing module.

NOTE

As I mentioned, the most common MIDI controller format for music production takes the form of a piano keyboard. But, you can find MIDI controllers in a wide array of styles: drum pads, guitars, wind-based controllers, and on and on.

If you don't own a MIDI controller, you can still take advantage of the power that MIDI offers because you can manually draw in your own MIDI information with something like a pencil tool. It might take some time, but you can create complex MIDI sequences without ever actually touching a MIDI controller.

Studio Log

This chapter has given you a basic but solid overview of Sony ACID Pro. You've learned that the software handles audio projects in three general categories: loop based, multitrack audio, and MIDI.

You've learned how to route your audio from the ACID Pro timeline, through the Master bus, to your audio device, and finally onto your studio monitors. You also now know how to put together a loop-based project, and you understand the basic concepts of multitrack audio and MIDI.

5

Creating Your Guide Tracks

Now that you have a basic understanding of how to get around in your DAW software, we can really get down to recording a song. I'm going to walk you through the process I typically go through to record. In all likelihood, you're going to develop a process that works for you, and it will just as likely be somewhat different from mine. However, I know my process works, so it'll be a good place for you to start because you'll learn various techniques as you follow me through recording a song. Once you know those techniques, you can certainly put your own spin on the process and adjust it here and there to make it your own.

In this chapter then, you'll put together tracks that you can use as guides when it comes time to build your final tracks. Basically, you'll add a couple of tracks to your project that give the critical essence of how it will sound in the end. Typically (for songs with vocals in them), this means a scratch vocal track and an accompanying guitar or keyboard track. Here's where you establish the feel of the song as well as the arrangement. This is like your scratch pad where you'll sketch out ideas, some of which you'll end up refining for your final recording and others which you'll discard outright.

Laying Down Your Song's Basic Beat

I do my song writing with a guitar in hand. Typically, I write with my acoustic guitar. This works well because it's convenient; I can just pick it up and start working out an idea. On the other hand, sometimes writing on the acoustic pushes me toward a certain style and feel that maybe I'd like to move away from once in a while. Certainly, if I wrote while holding an electric and playing through an amp with heavy distortion, I'd come up with different ideas and different feels. But in the end, the convenience of just picking up a guitar that sounds good without any work setting up electronics usually wins out.

But that doesn't mean I always want to record my songs as acoustic works. More to the point, I realize that you may have a totally different style in mind for your music. But sometimes you may not have a fully formed vision of the final song at the start. For that reason, it's helpful to experiment with different feels and beats that might work. And this early stage of the recording process is a great time for that experimentation. Try different things and eventually you'll settle upon a beat that you'll lay down on a track so that you can build upon and work out your ideas.

Regardless of whether you write with an acoustic guitar, an electric, on a piano, or with a ukulele, you need to establish the feel for your song. The logical place to start is with the beat, and that typically translates into deciding what feel you want the drums to create. There are several methods you can use to establish the beat and tempo of your song.

Using the ACID Pro Metronome

If the music you're recording won't have a drum or percussion track, you may simply need the metronome to help you keep proper time while you record your tracks. This can be especially important if you're going to be multitracking, because if your timing is erratic on the first track, it's going to be difficult to play along with that first track while you're attempting to record subsequent tracks.

Even if you will be using drums and percussion, the metronome is useful in many different situations, so it'll be helpful to learn how to use it now.

Start a new ACID Pro project. (Don't forget to set your folder preferences as we discussed in Chapter 4, "An Introduction to ACID Pro Fundamentals.") If ACID Pro is still in Loop Playback mode from when you were building a basic project, click the Loop Playback button to turn Loop Playback mode off.

As I mentioned earlier, new projects always start with a default tempo of 120 beats per minute (bpm), in 4/4 time, and in the key of A. You know what key your song is in (after all, you wrote it or at least have been playing it for some time now), so change your new project's key to the key of your song. You also probably know your song's time signature, so set that, too. Those are easy.

> **NOTE**
>
> You'll notice that ACID Pro only gives you the choice of major keys in the Project Key drop-down list. Does that mean that you can only record songs in a major key? Naturally not. Think of the project key more as the project root note. You can set your project to F and then play in F minor if you want to.

In fact, you don't really need to set your project key (or tempo) at all if you don't want to. You can record completely independently of those settings. But as long as you can, you might as well set them to match your song. That way you'll be able to use all of ACID Pro's functionality, including adding loops to your project if you want to. Furthermore, setting the tempo and time signature properly ensures that your time displays and the ruler bar will actually be useful to you throughout the recording and editing process.

It'll take a little more experimenting to figure out your song's tempo. Even if you're eventually going to add drums to your song, the metronome helps you establish the tempo. You might already have a fairly good feel of how the speed at which you're playing and singing translates to beats per minute. If so, go ahead and take your best guess at the tempo of your song and set the ACID Pro project tempo to that.

My song, "I'm Goin' Home," is in 4/4 time, so I can leave the project signature setting at the default. I play this song in the key of A, so I set my project key to A. I don't have a good guess at the tempo, so I'll leave it at 120 bpm for the moment.

Now that you've taken a guess at the appropriate tempo setting—or even if, like me, you have no idea what the setting should be—you can dial in on an exact setting. First, in the Transport bar, click the Metronome button to engage the metronome. Figure 5.1 shows the Transport bar with the metronome-related buttons in it.

Metronome

Metronome Countoff

Figure 5.1

The Transport toolbar holds two metronome-related buttons: the Metronome button and the Metronome Countoff button.

Play the project. Even though there is nothing to play, you can hear the metronome clicking away. Start to play or sing along with the metronome. You'll immediately be able to feel whether the tempo setting isn't right. Adjust the Tempo slider. The metronome reacts to the adjustment instantly. Play along again and see if the new setting feels better. Keep working at it; eventually you'll find the tempo setting that feels right for your song.

TIP

An empty ACID Pro project plays for a long time, but it won't go on forever. Eventually it'll stop. If it does stop and you haven't yet decided on a tempo, just start playback again and keep working.

Or, you can also establish a loop region of a few measures, put your project into Loop Playback mode, and let it loop endlessly until you've dialed in your tempo.

Now that you've set a custom tempo, key, and perhaps signature for your song, it's a good time to save your project. Click the Save button. Recall that in Chapter 4, you created a folder to store all the files you create while you work on this song. It makes sense to save your project file to the same location, so set the Save In location to the folder you created. Give your file a name in the File Name field.

You have a couple of options in the Save As type drop-down list. I like to choose ACID Project with Embedded Media (*.acd-zip) from this list. This creates a file that contains the ACID Pro project file along with all the media you've used in the project, such as any loops you've used or files you've recorded. Of course, at the moment, you haven't used any media in the project, but as you begin to add and record files, you'll start to accumulate more and more of them. When you save the project as an .acd-zip file, you keep all the project's assets saved neatly in one file. That makes it easy to transfer your project to a different machine if you need to or to archive it when you're done with it.

An .acd-zip file can also be valuable if you have pulled loops from several locations while you were building your project, especially if some of those loops came directly off the loop library CD or DVD. If you don't copy those loop files to your hard drive, and you remove the disc that holds those files from your computer drive, ACID Pro won't be able to open your project properly because it won't be able to find the files it needs. When you save all the loops along with the project file in an .acd-zip file, you avoid that problem.

On the downside, the more files you associate with the project, the longer it can take to open the project file that's been zipped. Large files can take a half minute or more to open. Still, to me it's worth the wait knowing that my complete project exists in this one convenient file.

So choose ACID Project with Embedded Media (*.acd-zip) from the Save As type drop-down list, and click the Save button.

TIP

You can also save your project as an .acd file. If you do so, you will not be embedding the loops and support files you used in the project file. There's nothing wrong with that; it just means you'll have to pay a little more attention to your file management so you can always find the support files for the project later.

Establishing a Beat with ACID Pro Drum Loops

Setting the tempo is an important step and, as I mentioned, if you don't plan to record drums or percussion on your song, the metronome may be all you need as a guide while recording. But if you will be adding drums, it can be helpful to add a scratch drum track to your project before you play your scratch guitar, piano, or other rhythm part and scratch vocals. Even if it's not the final drum beat (which it isn't likely to be at this point), adding something that has the right feel and attitude can help give life to your other scratch tracks. This is important because lifeless scratch tracks could very well set the tone for the project and inspire lifeless final tracks.

As you can see, it might be a good investment to obtain a versatile drum loop library. You'll want something that has a variety of beats and patterns in the style of music you want to record. Sony Creative Software sells several great drum libraries, including titles by such drumming luminaries as

Mick Fleetwood (Fleetwood Mac), Steve Farrone (The Average White Band, Tom Petty and the Heartbreakers), and others. Other vendors also sell great drum loop libraries.

Use the techniques you learned in Chapter 4 when we discussed the ACID Pro fundamentals to navigate to and preview various drum loops. As the drum loops preview, you can play and sing along to get a feel for whether the loop comes close to the feel you want for the song.

As you're previewing your drum loops, you may find that the tempo you set with the metronome doesn't feel quite right now that the drums are playing along. You may have noticed that the preview function follows the project's tempo setting, so you can easily adjust the tempo further (even while you're previewing files) until it feels right to you.

Once you find a drum loop that has the right feel for your song, add it to your project. You probably don't know exactly how long the song will turn out to be, but you should be able to make a fairly general guess. For instance, my song is a pop/rock tune, and I know that typically this type of song isn't going to be over six minutes long. I'll assume that your song falls into that same general time range.

Drag the right edge of the drum event to the right. When you get to the end of the visible timeline, ACID Pro begins to scroll, and the event continues to expand. After a few moments, release the mouse button. If you need to scroll over to see the end of the event, use the scrollbar below the timeline. When you can see the end of the event, click at the end to place your cursor there. You can now see in the time display area how long your project is. If your project fell short of or overshot your target length, as in Figure 5.2, just keep adjusting it until it's where you want it to be.

Figure 5.2
After my initial resizing of the drum event, it lasts for about 4 minutes, 16 seconds, so I need to make it a bit longer to get to approximately six minutes.

Now that your scratch drum event is so long, you can't see the entire event on the timeline. You can zoom your timeline view in and out to see more or less of the timeline. To zoom all the way out so that you can see the entire project, roll the scroll wheel on your mouse (the one between the two mouse buttons) toward you. If you don't have a scroll wheel on your mouse, press the down-arrow key on your keyboard. Both of these methods zoom your view of the timeline out so that you can see the entire project. (To zoom in, roll the mouse scroll wheel away from you, or press the up-arrow key.)

Then click the Metronome button to turn the metronome off and play your project so you can listen to your drum beat. To listen to my project so far, open the ImGoinHome.wav file from the Chapter 05 folder on the companion disc.

Establishing a Beat with a Drum Machine

If you have a drum machine that you like, you can also use it to lay down your scratch drum track. If yours is a hardware device, it has audio output jacks and possibly MIDI output jacks. Once you've programmed your drum beat into the machine, you'll play it while recording either the audio or the MIDI into the ACID Pro timeline. We'll talk more about recording audio in the following section and more about recording MIDI in Chapter 7, "Utilizing MIDI in Your Projects."

Laying Down Scratch Rhythm and Vocal Tracks

With your scratch drum groove in place, you can start adding scratch rhythm tracks (like a guitar or piano) and scratch vocals. To do this, you'll need to learn how to record in ACID Pro. What you record here doesn't have to be your best work. Remember: These tracks are only for reference. You'll use them to work out your arrangement and guide you when it comes time to add the real drums and other instruments.

DAW: THE TOOL THAT GIVES YOU WHAT YOU NEED

This exercise of laying in scratch tracks is an interesting process. It's almost like the chicken-and-egg conundrum. To get a drum beat that really fits the song, I have to have scratch rhythm tracks (for me, guitar) and scratch vocals to guide me when it comes time to build in drum fills, rests, and so on. But to have scratch guitar and vocal tracks that have some spark of life to them, I need a scratch drum track that can give me the feel I want.

I find it fascinating to watch my projects evolve as I go through this process. Sometimes it's really just a matter of throwing things into my project to get a starting point and then refining it from there. I'm often surprised at how different my projects turn out compared to the vision I originally had in my head. (I don't know if that's a sign of my creative genius or of my inability to translate my visions into a final product, but let's leave that discussion for another time!)

You, on the other hand, may be bored to tears with all this creating of tracks you know you're not going to use. Maybe you'd rather jump right into creating the final tracks. Sometimes I work that way, too. There will be times when you'll already have a solid idea of what you want to create, and you can just get right to creating it.

That's the beauty of a great DAW; it gives you the flexibility to work in whatever manner sparks your creativity and gives you the best results. If you need a scratch pad on which to experiment and work things out, you've got it. If you just need a place to document your already fully formed creative vision, you've got that, too—and, in the same tool. That's one reason I love working in digital audio on my DAW. I've got complete flexibility to work the way I need to work on every project.

To lay down these scratch tracks, you're going to have to learn a little bit about recording new tracks in your DAW. Since these are merely scratch tracks, I usually use the quickest, most down-and-dirty methods of recording them. That's what we'll go over here. Even though these aren't the most optimal methods for recording, they'll teach you some techniques that you'll have to know to record in ACID Pro. (If you use a different DAW, this discussion will also point out techniques that you'll need to learn in your application.) We'll talk in much more detail about the "proper" methods of recording in the chapters that follow when we lay down our final tracks.

Setting Up to Record Your Scratch Tracks

There are a couple of different approaches you can take to recording your scratch tracks. I like to get the process done quickly, so when possible I record my scratch guitar and vocals simultaneously. Still, I want them to be on separate tracks, and I want as little bleed from one track to the other as possible. That's all more easily said than done, but it's a good thing to strive for. (You'll see why a little bit later.) First, though, I'll walk you through my setup. Although I'm using a guitar and you may want to use a keyboard for your scratch rhythm track, the techniques I'll talk about are easily transferable to your instrument of choice.

NOTE

While I find that recording my guitar and vocals simultaneously gives me a better groove for the recording, you don't have to do it this way. It's perfectly legitimate to record first one track and then another.

Recording the two tracks one at a time does achieve total separation, avoiding any bleed between the two tracks. You might also find that if you're not singing and playing simultaneously, you can concentrate on both parts individually and thus give a better performance on each, which may or may not be important to you at this point in your project.

I'm going to create my scratch guitar track with my acoustic guitar. Thankfully, my guitar has a pickup in it so that I can record direct without a microphone. As I mentioned early on, avoiding microphones is one of the keys to this type of recording setup. Because I can record direct, I know that my guitar track will be completely isolated and not contain bleed from my vocals. That's half the battle already!

If you don't have a pickup in your acoustic, you can use an electric guitar. Or, use a microphone to record your acoustic. If you use a microphone, you'll have to decide whether to record it simultaneously with the vocals or record them separately to achieve better separation.

This is also where an audio device that has easily accessible input jacks on it comes in handy. I simply plug the output of my guitar directly into one of my audio device's inputs, and I'm ready to go.

It's critical for you to pay close attention to your recording levels to achieve good recording quality. You want the level to be as hot (loud) as possible, but you have to take care to *never* get too hot. And you must be aware of those levels at several different points along the recording signal path, so you really have to pay attention.

If you let your audio get too hot, you'll experience a phenomenon of digital audio recording called *clipping*. Clipping destroys audio quality, so take extra care to never let it happen!

What is clipping? Basically, clipping occurs when your digital audio is too hot to be reproduced faithfully. There are only so many bits of computer information that are available to describe audio digitally. If the audio level gets too hot, you may run out of bits with which to describe the audio. When this happens, anything that can't be reproduced is discarded. It's like getting your band to the gig. A van can only hold so many musicians and so much gear. If you have too much stuff, some of it isn't going to make it, and the gig will definitely suffer. (I've known a musician or two over the years that I would have been fine with leaving behind!)

In the case of digital audio, if clipping occurs, you'll hear it as distortion. And not cool, gritty, useful distortion like you get from your guitar pedals either. No; the distortion that clipping causes sounds really ugly. I've heard recordings that use it for special effect, but in general, you don't want that noise on your recordings. So you're going to want to avoid clipping.

Turning back to recording your guitar, the first stage at which you'll need to avoid clipping occurs at the point that the analog signal from your instrument is converted to digital signal for your computer. That happens at your audio device's input.

Thankfully, since clipping is such a nasty problem, most gear gives you the tools you need to avoid it. My Echo AudioFire 8 has 2 of its 10 inputs on the front. These inputs have *Trim* controls—knobs that I can use to raise or attenuate (lower) the level of signal coming into the input. The inputs also have clip indicator LED lights. If ever I play my guitar and see a red LED light up, I know I'm clipping and need to attenuate the record level.

Remember: This is not like analog recording where pushing a little bit into the red can actually be a technique to make your recordings sound nice and warm. This is digital, and going into the red means clipping. Going into the red means you've gone instantly from good recording sound to bad.

Once you've got your input level trimmed out properly at the audio interface input jack, you'll have to move along the signal path and check once again for clipping. Many higher-quality audio interfaces include a software mixer that you can use to monitor and control your audio levels.

Figure 5.3 shows the mixer interface for my AudioFire 8. Here I have control over input levels as well as output levels. If you've plugged into input 1 on the audio interface, you'll need to monitor the level here on input channel 1. Again, if you see the meter popping into the red, you're clipping, and you'll have to back off on the recording level. For that, go back to the trim control on the face of the hardware unit.

Figure 5.3

My Echo AudioFire 8 audio interface comes with a software mixer component that enables me to monitor and adjust various levels.

Once you're satisfied that you're not clipping in either of these two locations, you're ready to go back into your DAW and make sure no clipping occurs there either. We'll do that shortly, but first you'll need to set up a track onto which you'll record your rhythm track.

From the ACID Pro menu bar, select Insert, Audio Track. This adds a new empty track to your timeline below the existing scratch drum track.

You're starting to build up tracks in your project, and you're certainly going to end up with more than just these two. Therefore, it's a good idea to start organizing your project. You should name your tracks so you can identify them quickly later.

Each track has an area called the *scribble strip*. The term comes from the area at the bottom of a hardware mixer's channel strip where the engineer writes in the name of the track (snare, lead guitar, and so on). You might need to make your tracks taller (as you learned to do in Chapter 4) to see the scribble strip.

Notice that the scribble strip for your scratch drum track already has a name. When you create a new track by adding a file to your project, ACID Pro gives the new track the name of that file. If you'd rather have this track called Scratch Drums, double-click the scribble strip to highlight the current name and type the new name; then press the Enter key.

The track you just inserted does not currently have a name, so double-click the scribble strip and name it (Scratch Guitar, Scratch Piano, and so on). Press the Enter key again to finalize the name change.

You might want to make the drum track header shorter again to conserve space. Drag the bottom edge of the track header up. You can make it quite short if you want to, which you'll appreciate as you start adding more tracks to your project.

On the other hand, make the scratch guitar track tall enough to see all of its controls. You may have noticed when you played your project earlier that the track header has an output signal level meter. You can watch this meter while you're playing your project to make sure that none of your tracks are clipping at output. (Yes, you have to worry about clipping when you're playing your project back as well as when you're recording!)

Now click the Arm for Recording button in the track header for the scratch guitar track. A new meter—the In meter—appears above the Out meter. This indicates that this track is armed and ready for recording.

ACID Pro looks to the inputs that you've specified in the Audio Device tab of the Preferences dialog box (which you set back in Chapter 4) for an input source. Figure 5.4 shows my Audio Device preferences. You can see that when I selected my AudioFire ASIO drivers, the default audio recording device was set to Analog in 1/Analog in 2.

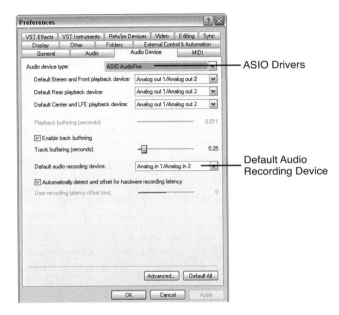

Figure 5.4
My default audio recording device has been set to Analog in 1/Analog in 2.

Play your instrument. If, as in my case, the track is looking to both inputs 1 and 2 of your sound card, you'll see only half of the input meter react to the signal from your instrument. That's because you've only connected to input 1. If you have an electronic keyboard or other instrument with stereo outputs, you could connect those outputs to both inputs 1 and 2. In that case, you'll see both halves of the meter react to your instrument, and you'll be recording to this track in stereo.

I'll assume that, like me, you've got a mono signal going into only input 1 on your audio device. Since you have only a mono signal, there's no use in recording in stereo, so you'll need to override the default audio recording device for this track.

You might need to make the track header for this track a little taller again to see all of its controls since the new meter was added. When it's tall enough, you see your input and output routing switches. The input routing button indicates the current routing. You can see my routing in Figure 5.5.

To override the default routing that you set back in the Audio Device preferences, click the Record Input button. Then select your audio device from the bottom of the pop-up menu. Since you want to record from just one input, select Mono from the cascading menu and choose Analog in 1 from the next cascading menu, as I have in Figure 5.6.

Figure 5.5

My input routing button shows that currently I'm routing Analog in 1/Analog in 2 to this track.

Routing Button

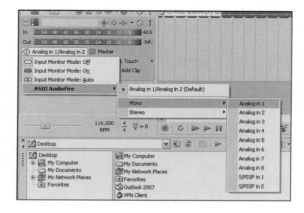

Figure 5.6

Use the cascading menus under the Record Input button to select the input you want to assign to this track.

Now when you play your instrument, the input meter is no longer split in half. This indicates that you are feeding this track a mono input source (just as you wanted to).

The input meter is the final place you need to check for clipping in the record signal path. Make sure the meter does not clip. If it does, you'll see a red box appear to the right of the meter. The number in the box indicates the maximum peak level of the audio. If the input is too hot, go back to your audio interface and attenuate the trim knob again until the clipping stops. Click the red clipping indicator box to reset it, and keep doing so until the box no longer lights up as you play.

You've almost got this track ready for recording. But before you get started, you'll have to make sure your *input monitoring* is set. That's just a fancy way of saying that you need to hear what you're playing and singing. You're going to be listening to the scratch drum track as you play and sing along, and it will be helpful to be able to hear your performance mixed in with the drums.

At this point, you should be wearing headphones. (Otherwise, the playback from your studio monitors will be picked up by your live vocal mic and end up on your recording. It could also cause a nasty feedback loop.) If you're using closed headphones that prevent outside sounds from getting to your ears, you're not going to be able to hear yourself sing and play. So you'll need to route both the existing drum track and your performance through the headphones so you can hear both. The drum track is already routed to the headphones, so now you just need to set it up so you can hear your guitar and vocals, too.

Many high-quality audio devices have built-in *input monitoring*. Input monitoring enables you to hear what you're recording through your studio monitors or headphones. If your audio device does have built-in input monitoring, it's likely that you can already hear your vocals and guitar in the headphones so that's obviously the easy way to go.

If your card does not have input monitoring, you can use your DAW's input monitoring system. In ACID Pro, you turn input monitoring on individually for each track that's armed for recording. To do so, click the Record Input button. From the pop-up menu, choose Input Monitor Mode: On. You can now hear your guitar when you play it.

WHICH INPUT MONITORING SHOULD YOU USE?

If your audio interface includes its own input monitoring, you have to decide which system to use: the audio interface's or your DAW's.

An argument for using the DAW input monitoring involves audio effects (FX). In ACID Pro, you can add FX to the signal path. (This is part of the DAW's DSP capabilities that I referred to earlier in this book.) For instance, you might add a reverb to your vocal track. If you do this, the ACID Pro input monitoring system enables you to hear the FX while you sing your vocals, which can help you give a more inspired performance. If you use the audio interface's input monitoring, you won't hear the FX because the audio you hear bypasses them.

On the other hand, using your DAW input monitoring tools can introduce latency in your audio. We talked about latency in Chapter 3, "Setting Up Your Computer for Music Production." You can attempt to control latency, but sometimes it's just easier to monitor through the audio interface and avoid the issue altogether.

Now you're ready to record your guitar or other instrument. If you're going to record your scratch vocal simultaneously, plug a microphone into input 2 on your sound card and repeat the procedure for checking your trim levels. Insert another new track into your project, and name it Scratch Vocals. Arm the new track, and set its record input to input 2. If you need to, turn the track's input monitoring on so you can hear it while you sing.

You now have two tracks armed and ready for recording.

Ready, Set, Record!

This is where the fun really starts! It's always exciting to get to this stage. You've set up and armed two tracks for recording. You've trimmed your input levels to ensure that you have no clipping on recording input. You're ready to record—almost.

First, although you no longer need the metronome since you have the scratch drum track to play along with, the metronome can still be helpful. You can set the metronome to give you a starting measure before ACID Pro starts recording. This enables you to get your hands from your mouse to your instrument, concentrate on the song's tempo and timing, and take a deep breath or two for relaxation before recording starts.

In the transport bar, click the Metronome Countoff button to turn the feature on. (Refer to Figure 5.1.) The button icon shows how long the countoff will be. By default, it's set to two measures. With the metronome off and the countoff on (and set to two measures), you'll hear two measures of the metronome before recording starts and no metronome while you're recording.

Now you're ready to record. Get yourself set to play and sing and then, in the Transport bar, click the Record button. The metronome starts counting off. When the count off is complete and the project starts playing/recording, start playing and singing.

When you're done with the song, click the Stop button. The Recorded Files dialog box opens, and you can decide whether you want to keep the recordings you just made. Since these are just scratch tracks, you don't have to be too picky. Even if you missed a word here and there, sang a bad note, or muffed a chord change, as long as the performance is solid enough to guide you, keep these files. Of course, if you want to try to do better, you can always record again.

Notice that ACID Pro has named the files for you with the project name appended with the track names. If you want to change the names, you can do so here. You can also delete the files right now if you're terribly disgusted with your performance! When you have a performance that you're comfortable using as scratch tracks, click Done to save the files and add them to your timeline.

After a moment, the waveforms for the files you just recorded appear in your timeline. You can see my timeline in Figure 5.7. Now would be another great time to save your project. Then click the Arm for Record button on your scratch instrument and vocal tracks to disarm them. Finally, play the project to hear the results of your recording session.

Figure 5.7

After I've completed recording my scratch tracks, I have three tracks in my project.

If you want to hear what my project sounds like at this point, open the file ImGoingHome_ScratchGuitVocals.wav from the Chapter 05 folder on the companion disc. As I said, I'm not concerned at this point about perfect recording environment or performance. If you listen closely enough to the vocal track, you might be able to hear the water heater humming and other noise. You'll also hear all my bad notes and missed chords. None of those problems matters at this point since these are just scratch tracks; it's not worth my time to go back and fix those mistakes.

Finalizing Your Song's Arrangement

One of the great things about working in a DAW on your computer is the tool set that you have available to you to work with your project. You've just recorded your guide tracks. If you're like me, when you listen to it, you're just as likely to want to change the structure of the song as not. For instance, when I listen to the tracks I just recorded, I feel like there should be a musical break somewhere—maybe a guitar or synth solo would do the trick. Of course, I didn't play that section in the song, but I can do some editing to add it now.

ACID Pro has a fantastic feature called Sections. With the Sections tool, I can define sections of my project—like verse, chorus, and so on—and then work with those sections. For instance, I might rearrange the sections or copy one section and paste the copy into another location in the song. Let's go ahead and define the sections of your song.

> **NOTE**
>
> I'm going to proceed with the discussion in this chapter (and the remainder of the book) as if you're working along with me on my project. However, you can do everything I discuss on your own song, too.

Creating Sections

Set your loop region bar to match your introduction. Choose Insert, Section. A section identifier appears above the markers, and the name is highlighted, so you can type in a more descriptive name if you choose. Type a new name and press the Enter key.

Use the same technique to create sections over the other parts of your song. You can see my section markers in Figure 5.8.

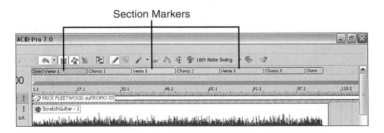

Figure 5.8
I've got all of my song's sections identified so I can easily work with them.

Rearranging Your Project

With your sections defined, you can experiment with your arrangement to see if you can come up with something you like better. For instance, I think my song could really use an instrumental break.

I'd like to have a break play over the chorus right after the current chorus 2 section. We can easily create this new section even though I didn't build an instrumental break into the song when I recorded the scratch tracks.

You can move sections to rearrange the song. For instance, let's say that for some reason I want to move the Verse 1 section so that it happens just before the Outro section. To do this, drag the Verse 1 section label toward the end of the project. As you move it, a red insertion bar appears. This indicates the target for dropping the section. Position the insertion bar between the Chorus 3 section and the Outro section and release the mouse button. This moves the Verse 1 section bar and everything in the section (the events on the timeline) so that now it occurs between the last chorus and the outro.

Play the song and you can hear exactly what it sounds like with the new arrangement. I don't like the way that sounds, so click the Undo button to undo that last move and return the song to its original arrangement.

You can also create copies of sections; this is how you'll create the new musical break section. We know we want to have the musical break play over the chorus and happen right after the Chorus 2 section. To create a copy of the section, hold the Ctrl key while you drag the Chorus 2 section to the right. When the red insertion bar appears between Chorus 2 and Verse 3, release the mouse button. This creates a copy of the section and moves everything else in the project later in the timeline to create room for the new section.

This new section will be the musical break, so right-click the Copy of Chorus 2 section label and choose Rename from the menu. Name the section Musical Break and press the Enter key.

As you can see, with sections you can experiment with all kinds of different arrangement ideas.

Editing Your Scratch Tracks

Once you've made a decision on the arrangement you want to go with, you might want to do a little cleaning up of the project. For instance, it's pretty unlikely that you used all six minutes of the scratch drum track. My drum track goes on well after I've stopped playing guitar and singing. You can edit the drum track to the length you need it so that you can keep your project tidy.

You use the same technique to shorten an event that you used to lengthen it. Just drag the right edge of the event to the left until it ends when the guitar and vocal tracks do. Remember: If you're having trouble editing to exactly the point you want, zoom in on your project.

Also, when you copied the chorus to create the break section, it copied everything in the chorus section, including the vocal. Naturally, if this is a musical break, we don't want the vocal and we can easily delete it during that section. Click the event under the Musical Break section in the Scratch Vocal track. You can see by the dark shading the event takes on that this selects the event. Press the Delete key to remove it from the timeline. Figure 5.9 shows my project after I've added the musical break section.

Figure 5.9

My project now has a musical break section.

Studio Log

In this chapter, you created a few scratch tracks that you'll use as guides when it comes time to record the real tracks. You learned some critical concepts here, including becoming familiar with the metronome, digital clipping and the problems it causes, setting up your DAW for recording, deciding how you want to handle input monitoring, and more.

You also discovered the value of identifying the different parts of your song with sections so that you can experiment with different arrangements.

As you can see, the combination of looping features and multitrack audio features can be a powerful one. With a versatile drum loop library, you can quickly add a drum guide track to your project to help you get a feel for the groove of the song while you're recording the guide instrument and vocal tracks.

From here, you'll move on to creating your final tracks. The guide tracks you created in this chapter will help you as you build the rest of your project.

6

Creating Drum Tracks

IN THIS CHAPTER

- Recording live acoustic drums
- Building drums with ACID Pro loops
- Working with oneshot files in ACID Pro

It's time to get to the serious recording. You learned some important basic recording functions in the previous chapter. But although you assembled helpful drum loops and recorded useful guide tracks in that chapter, what you record (or create) in this chapter will be useable for your final project.

You have a lot of options for creating your drum and percussion tracks, and we'll discuss most of those options here. The whole point of this chapter is to create a drum track that will inspire and drive your performance on tracks you'll lay down later and serve as a compelling final drum section for your song.

Recording Live Acoustic Drums

I absolutely love the sound of a well-recorded drum kit. The thwack of the kick as it hits you in the chest, the snap of the snare as it drives the song, the clarity of the ride cymbal as it rings rich and strong. For me, there's nothing exactly like a well-recorded live acoustic kit.

Unfortunately, there's also nothing quite like the challenge of recording a drum kit properly! Think back to our discussion of preparing your space for microphone recording. As we discussed, it's difficult enough to keep extraneous noise from bleeding into your vocal microphone. Now, multiply that one microphone by the multiple microphones it takes to record drums, and you begin to get an idea of the scope of that challenge.

Still, if you're up to the challenge and you have a space in which you can set up and wail away at the drums, the results can be quite rewarding. Let's talk about a few of the issues involved in recording drums.

How Many Microphones Will You Use?

As you're getting set to record your live acoustic drum kit, your first decision will be the number of microphones that you'll use to record your tracks.

Probably the minimum number of microphones you can use to achieve a good drum kit recording is two. Certainly that's the case if you want to achieve any sense of stereo separation on the kit. Typically you'd want these two microphones to be the same make and model. Normally these microphones would be positioned high above the kit and pointing down at it (thus the term *overheads*). You'd want one mic above the left side of the kit and the other above the right. If you don't have high enough ceilings, this can be difficult; you might have to resort instead to positioning the microphones more in front of the kit than above it.

You'll record these two mics to separate tracks in your DAW and probably pan one hard left and the other hard right. This way you can preserve the sense of stereo space that the two microphones naturally create by virtue of their different locations and proximity to various elements of the drum kit. (We'll talk more about panning in Chapter 10, "Mixing Your Song," when we turn our attention to mixing topics.)

You can actually get a pretty good sound out of this simple setup. However, certain drums can get "lost" in the overall drum mix. For example, it can be difficult to bring the kick drum out the way you'd like it in that setup.

Essentially, the only tool you have for mixing the drum kit is to adjust the placement of the two microphones. And, of course, the closer you get to any one piece of the kit, the louder that piece will sound in the overall mix. The trouble is, you can't get closer to one piece without changing the microphone's position relative to the other pieces. Thus, every move you make with the microphone affects not just the volume of your target drum but the mix of the entire kit. You might have to do a lot of experimentation to get your drum mix just right.

Once the tracks are recorded, the only mixing you can do is between the two microphones, so your mixing options become pretty limited at that point.

If you're having a lot of difficulty bringing out an individual drum, such as the kick, you can add additional microphones into your recording setup. You might position the mic right next to the front face of the kick or inside the drum through a hole cut into the drum head. With this technique—referred to as *close micing*—you end up with the kick fairly well isolated on its own separate track in your DAW. Then you can blend that track in with the mix of your overheads to add the extra punch you were looking for.

The extreme of the close micing technique involves putting an individual mic on each piece of the drum kit. The idea is to get a strong recording of each individually so that you have total control over the drum mix later.

Of course, it's impossible to get complete isolation on each microphone, and there will be bleed-through on virtually every mic in the setup. Still, if you're careful about placement and microphone selection, you can achieve a reasonably isolated recording of each piece of the kit and in that way achieve maximum control of the drum mix.

The Realities of Recording an Acoustic Kit

Obviously, there's a lot left unsaid in the brief discussion I just laid out about how many microphones you'll use to record your drum kit. The truth is, I'm not an expert at the techniques involved. However, I've done it enough to identify some of the challenges involved.

The number of microphones you own obviously affects just how you can approach this topic. If you're going to close-mic every piece of the kit, you're going to need several microphones. Add it up: the kick, snare, hi-hat, two overheads, high-tom, low-tom, floor-tom. That's a pretty basic kit, and you're already up to eight mics.

If you don't already own everything you need, you're forced to borrow, rent, or buy. If you borrow, you'll have to take what you can get. And if you rent, you're going to shell out some cash. Buying means even more cash. And don't forget to rent or buy the cables to connect all those microphones to your audio interface.

Furthermore, for each microphone you put in front of the drum kit, you're naturally going to need an input on your audio interface. It's certainly not unheard of to mic a kit with a dozen or more microphones. Anything over 10 will probably require you to have two audio devices that you can string together so you have adequate inputs. If you cringed at the cost of one high-quality audio interface, the cost of the second one isn't going to make you feel any better!

The good news? Well, if you pick your DAW right, it'll give you unlimited tracks on which to record, so at least you don't have to shell out any more money there!

As I alluded to a moment ago, there's an art to recording a drum kit. Certain microphones work better for drums than others. In fact, certain microphones work great for snare drums but not so great for kick drums. Ask the pros what they use to record drums, and you'll get a list of specialized, high-quality, and high-priced microphones that you can probably only dream about using. A great drum sound requires the right microphones.

Those of us who are pretty much amateurs at microphone technique often don't realize just how important a role the actual physical placement of the microphone can have on the quality of the recorded sound we achieve through it. (This applies to anything being recorded, not just drums.) I've heard a microphone transform from sounding okay to sounding amazing just because an audio engineer knew the right place to *put* the microphone as well as exactly what to point it at. Unfortunately, you can't just jam a cable into the mic, stick it on a stand in front of the drum, point it at the drum head, and expect to get the best sound every time. It just doesn't work that way.

If you don't have a great deal of experience with mic selection and placement, you're going to either spend a lot of time trying to find the perfect placement of every mic, or you're going to end up with inferior results.

Any time you record with a microphone, the room in which you record plays a huge role in the sound of your recordings. That's never more true than it is with drums. Different types of music use different drum sounds, as do different drummers and engineers. Some call for a *live* drum sound with lots of natural room sound (reverb), while others want a more controlled, dryer sound. In all likelihood, you're stuck with the room you have. You might be able to change the level of reflection a bit with some of the sound dampening techniques we talked about back in Chapter 2, "Setting Up Your Recording Studio Space," but for most of us, there will not be much we can do to achieve the exact sound we want.

Then there are the issues of extraneous noise coming from outside your recording space, along with the bigger problem of sound escaping from your recording space and invading the silence of those around you. Unless you have a dedicated, isolated, and fairly large space in which to record drums, (remember, you have to have space not only for all those microphones, but the drum kit itself!), you've got a real challenge on your hands.

Believe me; I have nothing against recording live drums. I wish I could always have live drums in my recordings. But for the kind of recording we're talking about in this book, it just isn't always practical or even possible. Everything I've discussed here adds up to great challenges and runs you afoul of several of the initial assumptions I laid out in the Introduction to this book. For example, you'll have to violate assumption 2, which essentially states that you won't be undertaking the extensive construction necessary to turn at least part of your studio into a highly effective drum iso booth. Otherwise, you'll be stung by assumption 4 that you are not free to make an unlimited level of noise.

If you can set up an effective system for recording live acoustic drums, that's great! I encourage the practice wholeheartedly. You can find a lot of great information on the techniques you'll need to master and the equipment you'll need to acquire to do the job right. But the realities for most of us mean we can't get the recordings we want with those traditional approaches. Combine all the challenges I've mentioned with assumptions 5, 6, and 7 (which basically state that you're open to creative solutions), and the door opens to other, far more practical—and in some ways more powerful—possibilities. These alternative methods will help you get the job done and give you great results. So let's move on to talk about some of your other options.

Recording with a Drum Machine

In the previous chapter, I gave a brief nod to recording your scratch drums with a drum machine. If you have a drum machine, you can use the techniques you learned in Chapter 4, "An Introduction to ACID Pro Fundamentals," to record the line outputs of that machine onto two tracks of your DAW.

A drum machine enables you to completely eliminate the use of microphones in creating your drum tracks. Also, you can work with headphones on or with your studio monitors at low volume while you're creating your drum tracks. Thus, a drum machine completely eliminates the limitations of your recording environment from the equation.

It sounds pretty good so far, doesn't it? Let's take a closer look at some of the issues to help you decide whether a drum machine makes sense for your recordings.

Sound Options

Drum machines offer a variety of drum sounds. However, they may work better for some types of music than others. Some musical styles call for a more electronic drum sound, and drum machines can be perfect for this type of music. In fact, some musicians seek out vintage drum machines because their less than perfectly realistic drum sounds have a character all their own and might be exactly what the musician wants for the recording.

If you're after more of a natural acoustic sound for your song, you may find it a bit of a challenge to find a sound you like from your drum machine. Still, drum machine sounds are getting better all the time, and some sound quite natural—particularly modern drum machine synthesizers or samplers.

Typically, a drum machine can mimic multiple drum "kits." For example, if you like the sound of the drums on early John Cougar Mellencamp recordings, you might choose the Kenny Aronoff kit from your drum machine. The drum machine will then do its best impersonation of the Kenny Aronoff sound.

Many drum machines also give you the power to mix and match kits. So, if you like the snare drum from the Buddy Rich kit but the kick drum from the Ginger Baker kit, you can mix and match them to build your own custom kit.

Finally, you can often alter the default sounds of a kit. For example, you might want to add a little equalization (EQ) to a kit's snare to beef it up a little bit.

Rhythm Options

Typical drum kits offer lots of different rhythm patterns—maybe even hundreds. These patterns are particularly useful as scratch drum tracks or as tracks to play along with when you're practicing or writing. They can establish a feel for you with minimum effort on your part.

However, you're probably not going to want to use those built-in rhythms just as they are for your final recordings, so typically you can modify the default rhythms and even create completely new rhythm patterns for your music. This is not always the most intuitive process on some machines, but most machines offer this capability one way or another.

Many drum machines also have some sort of finger pads that act as miniature drum heads on which you can play a rhythm of your own. These pads are often sensitive to velocity (the force with which you press the pad), so you can get a human feel into your patterns in terms of both musical timing and the volume of each hit.

You might also be able to save the rhythm you play onto your drum machine as a preset that you can call up later, or you might simply have to pass the output of the drum into your DAW and record what you play there.

Limitations

With those factors going for them, drum machines can look like an attractive alternative for laying down your drum tracks. However, unless you're specifically after the sound of a drum machine, I think there are even more attractive options out there for you.

Drum machines tend to create drum tracks that sound, well, machine like. There's no human error in them (although some drum machines may have the ability to emulate human inconsistencies in volume and timing). Although the word *error* has negative connotations, in the case of music, a certain amount of error actually enhances the finished product.

Specifically, when a human plays a drum part on a real kit, the musician's musical timing is less than perfect. Even the most solid drummer misses a beat (even if ever so slightly) here and there. Those tiny errors give the music an organic, human feel. Machines tend not to make those types of errors, and the resulting music can sound stiff, cold, and impersonal. You can build small errors into the rhythms that you create on some drum machines, but it can be a lot of work.

Another limitation is the number of rhythms the drum machine provides. Even if it has hundreds of preset rhythms, it may still not have one you feel works for your song. Remember, of all of the rhythm presets in that drum machine, only a certain subset may be useful to you for your style of music.

As I said, on most drum machines, you can modify the preset rhythms to suit your needs. However editing inside drum machines is generally not easy or intuitive.

In my opinion, there are other options for creating your drum tracks that give you every advantage of a drum machine and help you avoid many of the drawbacks.

Building Drum Tracks with Drum Loops

With the powerful editing tools inside your DAW, you have great potential for creating drum tracks that don't require microphone recording yet preserve the human feel and top-notch audio quality that you may find it difficult to achieve with a drum machine. The options it gives me for creating drum tracks is one of the reasons I really like working with ACID Pro. (We'll discuss most of those options in this section.) You should be able to translate these techniques to your DAW of choice and figure out how to accomplish the same tasks in whatever software you use.

We took a look at using loops to create drum tracks back in Chapter 5, "Creating Your Guide Tracks," when we painted in a quick scratch drum track. But in that discussion, we only scratched the surface of the technique's potential. You can do much more than simply paint a drum loop from the beginning of your project to the end and call it done. For example, you can combine different drum loops to change things up at different points during a song. Or you can cut, copy, and paste sections of the loop to modify the beat, create fills, add emphasis, and so on. Let's return to my song "I'm Goin' Home" to explore some of these ideas and build a drum track.

I'm working on the project as we left it at the end of Chapter 5, where we rearranged sections to create the final arrangement.

Play the project and listen to the drum beat. Because we added only one drum loop as the scratch drum track, it is quite monotonous throughout the song. I actually think this loop works well for the song, so even though it started out as my scratch track, I think I'll keep it and build on it for my final track.

But the drum track needs some variety. Naturally, a real drummer would play fills at strategic points in the song and maybe change up the beat a little bit at other points in the song. We can use other drum loops to do the same thing.

This loop comes from Sony Creative Software's Total Drumming loop library, which was created by Mick Fleetwood (yes, *that* Mick Fleetwood of Fleetwood Mac fame). I figure I can't go too far wrong with Mick Fleetwood drumming on my recording, so I'll stick with that library.

When Mick recorded the loops for this library, he recorded many different styles and beat patterns. All we have to do is mix and match those patterns at strategic points in the song to add interest to the drum part.

Deciding Where To Place Your Fills

There are as many ways to approach the task of building out the drum track as there are musicians who want to do it. I'll walk you through one approach that I might take, and then you can use the techniques you learn to develop your own approach.

First, I listen to the whole song again and notice places in it that feel like they'd benefit from some sort of change in the drum pattern. The change might be a simple fill or perhaps a new rhythm pattern. The point is, you'll need to decide where you want to make changes.

As you're listening, when you find a spot where you'd like to make a change, you can drop a marker there to remember it. You can either do this as the project plays or stop playback and place the marker at an exact spot where you want the edit.

For example, as I play my project, it seems to me that there should be some sort of small drum fill leading from the introduction into the first verse. I can easily see by the waveform in the vocal track that the first verse starts at the beginning of measure five. Click at measure 5.1 to place the cursor there. To drop a marker at that point, choose Insert, Marker. An orange marker now appears at the cursor location. You can give the marker a descriptive name that will help you remember what it's there for. Just right-click the marker and choose Rename from the pop-up menu. In the text box that appears, type a name for the marker. Because we want a small fill to lead into the verse, type Fill in the box, and press the Enter key.

Figure 6.1 shows my project now that I've added the new marker.

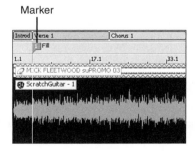

Figure 6.1

The marker at the beginning of measure 5 makes it easy to remember that I intend to create a drum fill at this location.

Go through the rest of your project, and mark the points where you want something different to happen with the drums.

MARKERS AREN'T YOUR ONLY OPTION

Using markers to remember important points in your project is one approach. In reality, though, I tend to take care of the change as soon as I decide I need it. In other words, I typically don't really set markers throughout my entire project. Instead, if I find a spot in which I'd like a fill, I stop playing the project and create that fill before I move on to listening to the rest of the project.

This is especially true for a project which I've divided into sections like we have here. Those section labels can help determine where to make changes in the drum pattern because the transitions between sections are logical places to create drum transitions.

However, that doesn't diminish the usefulness of the marker techniques we just discussed. Markers are incredibly valuable tools that you'll use for a variety of reasons. Any time you have an important location in your project that you need to remember for later, drop a marker at that location. You can have as many markers in your project as you need.

Creating Fills with Different Loop Files

Let's create the fill for the marker we just placed before we move on to the rest of the song. First, drag the bottom of the drum track header down to make the track taller so you can more effectively see what you're working with. I've made mine tall enough so that I can see the waveform but left it short enough that I can still at least partially see the other two tracks.

Now, if your cursor is not still at the same location as the marker, click the marker. When you do, the cursor instantly jumps to the marker location. That's a valuable thing to know. Markers make it easy not only to remember important locations in your project, but also to return the cursor to those locations precisely and instantly.

I feel like a two-beat drum fill would work nicely here, so we'll need to create space for it in the track. In the toolbar, click the Erase tool to select it. Then use your mouse wheel or your up-arrow key to zoom into your project. Keep zooming until you can clearly identify the beats of the measures around the cursor, as shown in Figure 6.2.

Now that you can easily identify the individual beats of the measure you're working with and you have the Erase tool, click the drum waveform between beats 4.3 and 5.1. This erases that portion of the drum event and leaves a hole in your track like the one shown in Figure 6.3.

Figure 6.2
I've zoomed in far enough that my ruler marks and beat ruler make it easy to identify the individual beats of the measures around my cursor.

Now that you have the hole in your track, you just need to find another drum loop to fill it. First, click the Draw Tool button in the button bar to change back to ACID Pro's main editing tool. In the ACID Pro Explorer window, navigate to the drum loops on your loop collection and start previewing loops that might work. Because the drum beat I'm using in my project comes from the Mick Fleetwood library, it makes sense to return to that library to preview other loops there to see if I can find something I like.

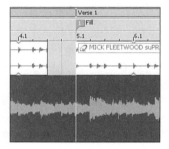

Figure 6.3
I've erased a two-beat portion of my drum track to make room for the drum fill I want to add.

TIP

When you're previewing loop files, look at the bottom of the Explorer window for information about the loop, including how long (in beats) the loop lasts. Because you're trying to fill a two-beat hole in your drum track, you'll want to find and test loops that last for two beats.

When you find a drum fill that you like, drag it into the hole that you created in the drum track a moment ago. Then snap it to the ruler mark at beat 4.3 and release the mouse button. This fills the hole with a new event that holds the drum fill. Play the project from just before the fill to see if you like it.

Trimming a Loop to Just the Portion You Need

Sometimes you need a fill of a certain length, but the loop file that you find doesn't fit the length you need. For example, I feel that another two-beat drum fill would work well in the transition between verse 1 and chorus 1. But let's say that none of the two-beat drum fills in my loop collection quite gives me what I want. On the other hand, I've found a four-beat drum fill that I like. I could expand the hole that I built into my drum track to hold the fill from two to four beats. But if I really want a two-beat fill, instead of making the hole for the file longer, I could simply use just two beats of the four-beat fill file I found. Let's work through that scenario.

First, create a four-beat hole in your project leading from the first verse into the first chorus. In my project, I create a hole from beat 20.1 up to beat 21.1. I know I only want a two-beat fill, but because the fill I want to use lasts for four beats, I want to create a four-beat hole temporarily. Now drag the four-beat fill into the hole in your drum track.

Because you want only two beats of the fill, you'll have to trim the fill down. In my case, I want the last two beats of the drum fill, so I'll need to trim off the first two beats. To trim an event, point to the edge that you want to trim off. The mouse icon changes to a box with a right-/left-pointing arrow. When you see this icon, you know you're ready to trim the edge of the event. If, like me, you want to trim off the first two beats of the event, drag the left edge of the event to the right until it snaps to the ruler mark at beat 20.3.

Now your fill is the right length, but you have a two-beat hole in your track preceding it. Not only can you trim events to make them shorter as you just did, but you can make them longer. So trim the right edge of the main drum event to the right until it snaps to the left edge of the fill event (which you trimmed to beat 21.3 a moment ago).

Now your hole is filled, and you have a two-beat drum fill that you created from a drum-fill loop that is actually twice as long as you needed. This kind of trimming of events, although a deceptively simple task, is an extremely powerful technique because, as you did here, you can trim events down to just segments of loop files to customize your project.

Figure 6.4 shows a portion of my project after I've gone through it and customized my drum track with different drum loops and fills. Notice that now instead of just one steady event on the drum track, I've got multiple events of different lengths. I've used these to add variety to the drum track. If you want to hear what my project sounds like with this new drum treatment, play the file ImGoinHome_DrumFills.wav from the Chapter 06 folder on the companion disc.

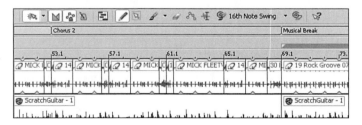

Figure 6.4

My drum track now contains multiple events on the drum track to add variety to the song's beat.

TIP

If you open an existing project, you can do some experimenting to learn more about just how it was assembled. Trim events to make them longer or shorter to see whether you can find places where just a portion of a loop file was used to create a fill. Move things around and see if you can make a drum arrangement that you like better than the existing one. The point is, you can learn an awful lot by deconstructing someone else's project. So go ahead and experiment if you can find a project someone's willing to let you use. You can always use the startup project if you want to. See what techniques have been used that you might be able to utilize in your own project.

Building Drum Tracks with Oneshot Files

As you learned in the previous section, you can use drum loop files to create a nice drum track for your project. However, the loop approach has its limitations. Obviously, you're limited to the loop files you actually have in your collection, and you might not have a loop that gives you exactly the feel you want. Besides that, you're limited to the fills that the loop developer decided to record. Also, you have no control over the mix of your drums; you're stuck with the mix that the loop developer gave you, so if you would like the kick to be louder or you want to put an effect on the snare, you're out of luck because you can't do something to one piece of the kit without affecting everything else.

I find these limitations unacceptable most of the time, but I wanted to take you through that discussion for the valuable techniques you learned during it. You'll use many of those techniques as we build a new drum part in this section.

Introducing Oneshot Files

Here we'll learn another, more versatile approach to building drum tracks. This approach involves using another type of recorded file called a *oneshot* file. With this technique, you can custom make a drum part exactly as you want it. It can be a time-consuming process, but when done correctly, the results are exceptionally rewarding. With this technique, you'll create drum tracks that are virtually indistinguishable from a track that was played live. In fact, I've used this method to create drums that have fooled not only my fans, but other musicians and recording-savvy colleagues into thinking that my recordings were done with a live drummer in the studio. The results can be that convincing!

So what exactly is a oneshot? Recall in Chapter 4 that you added loops to your project. When you dragged those loop events through your project, they just kept drawing over and over until you stopped, thus creating an event that was as long as you wanted it to be and was entirely filled by the looping file. You used the same technique to create your drum track earlier in this chapter.

Unlike a loop file that has been created such that it can repeat endlessly and fill whatever length of event that you want it to, a oneshot file does not repeat. When you draw it into your project, it draws in just once—thus the term *oneshot*.

Oneshot files typically hold things that you wouldn't want to repeat endlessly, or for that matter, even more than once. For example, the drum loops you've been using contain a recording of the whole drum kit playing a rhythm. Because it's the whole kit, it makes sense when you repeat it over and over because it creates a nice drum track.

On the other hand, think of a cymbal crash recorded alone. Or a snare hit. If you repeated those over and over, it'd be nothing but annoying! So the loop developers put these types of sounds into oneshot files. You can think of oneshots as building blocks. If you put enough of them together in a logical arrangement, you can create something useful. That's what we're going to do here as we build a new drum track from scratch with oneshots.

Arranging Your Oneshot Files on the Timeline

Unlike building your drums with loops on a single track, we're going to use several tracks to build the drums with oneshots. In fact, we'll use a new track for every piece of our virtual drum kit. In other words, we'll use one track for the kick drum, one for the snare, and so on.

In the Explorer window, navigate to the folder that holds your oneshot files. Typically, the loop developer puts the oneshots in a readily identifiable location on the loop library disc, such as in a folder called Oneshots. If you don't have any of your own, you can find a collection of oneshots in the Sony Sound Series Sampler folder on the companion disc. (I'll proceed as if you're using these.) These oneshots again come from our old friend Mick Fleetwood.

You'll develop your own system after you get more experience, but it makes sense to start with the kick drum because that (along with the snare) typically forms the basic beat of a drum pattern. So drop the kick drum file onto a blank area in the timeline to create a new track for it. Position the new event at the beginning of the project so that it sits at beat 1.1 of the song.

Trim the right edge of the new kick drum event to the right. As you do, notice that, unlike the loop files you used earlier, this file fills only a portion of the event after you surpass the file's natural length. That's one fundamental difference between a loop file and a oneshot. Figure 6.5 shows my event after I've trimmed it to be longer. You can see that most of it is empty.

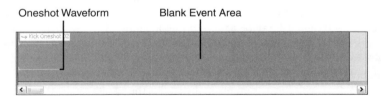

Oneshot Waveform   Blank Event Area

Figure 6.5
Even though the event in this figure extends to the beginning of measure 6, the oneshot's waveform doesn't even last up to measure 2.

TIP

Another important difference between a oneshot and a normal loop file is that a oneshot file does not contain tempo information the way a loop file does; thus, a oneshot plays at the same tempo regardless of your project's master tempo setting. In Chapter 12, "Delivering Your Music," you'll see an example of why it's important to remember this critical difference between the two file types.

CAUTION

In general, always make sure to make an event that holds a oneshot as long as it needs to be to hold the file's entire waveform (even if the waveform looks flat to you). If you make the event so short that it cannot hold the entire waveform, you'll be cutting off part of the file's sound. This causes the audio to cut off abruptly instead of decaying to silence naturally and can thus make your project sound unnatural. There are, of course, exceptions to the rule, as you'll see a bit later, but don't cut the event short unless cutting off the sound is what you really intend to do.

As I stated, you can think of oneshots as building blocks. So now you just need to use the kick one-shot to build your kick drum pattern. In my song, I thought the introduction would be nice with a bit of a sparse drum pattern, so I decided to place a lone kick drum hit at the first beat of each measure of the introduction. Once the track holds the file, you can use the ACID Draw tool (the default tool that's shaped like a pencil) to draw in additional events.

First, you'll probably need to zoom in to the beginning of your project until you can see the first beat of every measure on the beat ruler. Then point to beat 2.1, hold the mouse button down, and drag to the right. This draws another event into the track at that point. Notice that with a oneshot, the event stops drawing when it reaches the file's natural end, so it doesn't matter if you draw too far. Place two more kick drum events at 3.1 and 4.1.

After listening to the introduction with the new kick drum events in it, I decided that a double kick hit would sound nice at beats 2.1 and 4.1. I want the first hit to happen on the eighth note preceding the first beat in the measure and the second to land on the first beat.

Click at beat 2.1 to place your curser there, and zoom in until you can identify each beat of the measure in the beat ruler. Notice that as you zoom in, the resolution of the beat ruler gets finer and finer, so you can identify eighth notes, sixteenth notes, and even finer note increments as you zoom farther and farther into your project. Stop zooming once you see that you have a ruler mark on eighth notes.

Draw a new kick event starting at the eighth note after beat 1.4 (position 1.4.384), and stop drawing when the new event meets the existing event at beat 2.1. This is an instance when it's acceptable to cut a one-shot short. Add another event starting at beat 3.4.384 and extending to beat 4.1. Now play the project and listen to your new kick pattern.

Adjusting the Volumes of Individual Oneshot Events

Now you've got the timing right, but you have to do a bit more work if you want to be totally convincing. Because you've used the same oneshot for each of these kick events, they have identical volumes. That's not natural, because a drummer would never be able to kick the drum head with exactly the same force every time. Nor would she want to. Varying the volume of drum hits is one of the things that makes a live drummer sound organic and natural as opposed to the constant repetition of a machine.

So, if you're going for a live-drummer feel and you want your drums to be totally convincing, you're going to have to get in there and give these drum hits different volumes. For these double hits, I want the first hit of the pair to be weaker than the second. You can change the volume of any event on your timeline independently of every other event.

To change the volume of the first kick in the pair around 2.1, drag the top edge of the first of the two events down. As you do, you see a blue line that indicates the current volume level, and a ToolTip shows you a gain value that gets increasingly more negative as you drag down. The farther you drag the line down, the quieter you make the event. You'll have to decide by trial and error just how quiet to make the event, but you'll find a good level soon enough. I settled at around –6 decibels (dB). Reduce the gain of the first event in the kick pair around beat 4.1 in the same way.

WORTH EVERY SECOND

This process of adjusting the volume of individual events is part of what makes this method of creating drum tracks so time consuming. But it's also critical to creating drums that sound like they were played by a human and not a machine. (Of course, if your music calls for the machine sound, you have far less work to do!) The temptation will almost certainly arise to skip this detail—especially when you have to start adjusting the volume of every hi-hat event that you've spread across your project on eighth notes (which you'll do later)! But don't give in to that temptation. You won't regret the time it takes to do this. Think of it this way: If you were to go into the studio to record drums, it'd probably take you much longer than it'll take to do this. And it'd cost you a whole lot more money!

Also, you'll find that you don't have to be very exact about it. After all, a live drummer doesn't hit the drums with exact knowledge of how loud the hits are.

One trick I use all the time is to paint in all my events and then quickly go through the project making random adjustments in a given range. For example, I'll decide that I want to adjust all my hi-hat event volumes to somewhere between 0.0dB (the event's natural volume) and –4dB. Exactly where each one lands isn't that important. You can further affect the feel of your tracks if you decide that, for example, every hi-hat event that falls on the first beat of a measure will be louder than all other hits in the measure. You'll soon get a feel for creating dynamics with this method, and you'll find that it doesn't take nearly as long as it sounds like it would right now.

Finally, remember that nothing you do has to be final. If, after you randomly set these volumes, you decide that something isn't quite right, you can always go back in and make further adjustments.

Figure 6.6 shows the kick pattern I've created over the introduction.

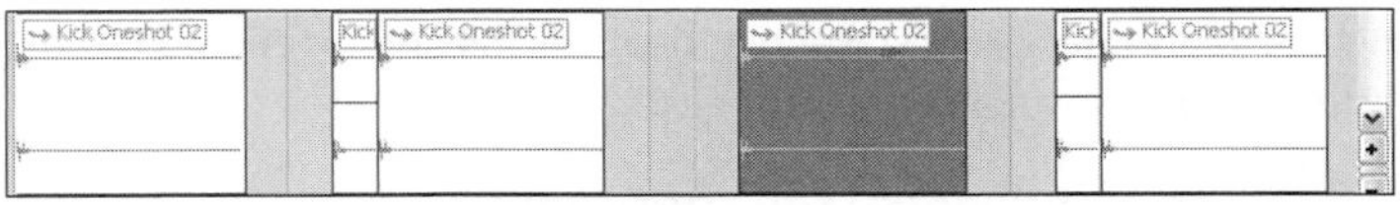

Figure 6.6
Using a series of events on the kick drum track, I've created a kick drum pattern for my introduction.

Copying and Pasting Events

Different sections of your song may well have different drum patterns. For example, in my song I'm going to want a kick drum pattern that's less relaxed than the one I've created for the intro that centers around the first beat of the measure. Because in many types of pop music the kick drum hits on the first and third beat of the measure, that's what I want to create for my song.

I've decided on a pattern similar to what I created for the intro, where the first beat of the measure gets a single kick and the third beat gets a double kick. However, it feels right to me to have the first hit right on beat 3 and the second hit of the pair on the eighth note following beat 3. It also feels better to me if the first hit of the pair is louder than the second hit.

Use the same methods you used for the intro section to create one measure of kick drum over measure 5 of the song that follows the pattern I've described. Remember to cut an event short at the point where it meets the next event, including the last event in the measure, which will end right at the first beat of measure 6 (because a new event will start at beat 6.1). Figure 6.7 shows measure 5 of my project with my new kick drum pattern in it.

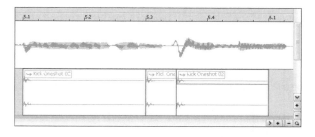

Figure 6.7

Measure 5 has a slightly different pattern than the intro section. This pattern will become the basis for the remainder of my song.

Okay, so I've got 5 measures of kick drum completed. That only leaves about 120 measures more before I can move onto the snare drum! Well, it's not quite as bad as it sounds. We can use the copy and paste features of the DAW to make quick work of filling in events for the rest of the kick drum track.

Because we're using measure 5 as the model for the rest of the song, we'll copy the events in that measure. Click the event that starts at beat 5.1 to select it. Then hold the Shift key and click the end of the last event in the measure. (That is, click at beat 6.1.) This selects all the events in the track between the first one you clicked and the second one. In other words, this selects all the events in measure 5 of the kick drum track.

Now right-click one of the selected events and choose Copy from the pop-up menu. If it's not already there, click at beat 6.1 to place the project cursor at that location. Then choose Edit, Paste Repeat. In the Paste Repeat dialog, you can specify the number of times you want to paste the contents of the Clipboard (where you copied the events on measure 5 a moment ago) into the project. You can paste a maximum of 100 times, so enter 100 into the Number of Times to Paste field. You want the events to be pasted end to end, so select the End to End radio button. Click OK.

Instantly, your kick drum track is filled up to measure 106 with copies of the pattern you created for measure 5. Choose Edit, Paste Repeat again, enter 16 into the Number of Times to Paste field, and click OK. Now you've got kick drum all the way up to the last beat of your project. Draw in one more event at beat 122.1, and your kick drum track is completely populated.

Now go through the track and do a little volume randomization, as I discussed a bit earlier, to give more of a human feel.

To hear how my project sounds with my kick drum track complete, play the file ImGoinHome_KickDrum.wav from the Chapter 06 folder on the companion disc.

Working with Multiple Files on a Track

When my kick drum is mostly in place (I say "mostly" because I'm almost certainly going to want to change the pattern at various times in my song), I turn my attention to the snare drum. Find a snare oneshot that you like, and add it to a new track in your project.

I've chosen a snare sidestick hit for my intro and placed it on every second and fourth beat of the intro measures. I've chosen a full snare hit for the rest of the song. I know that I want the snare to hit (generally speaking) on the second and fourth beat of every measure as is typical in rock, country, and other pop-based styles of music.

The first snare hit will be at beat 5.2, so zoom far enough in that you can identify quarter beats and drag the snare oneshot that you want from the Explorer window onto the same track that holds the sidestick oneshot events. Drop it at the ruler mark for beat 5.2. You know that the next snare hit will be at 5.4, and you can see that the event at 5.2 stretches past 5.4. So trim the event at 5.2 so that its right edge stops at 5.4 (where the next event will start).

This track now holds events made up of two different files: the sidestick file and the full snare hit file. Notice that the track header (make the track header taller if you need to) lists the active file for the track. Click the name of the active file, and you can see all the files that the track uses. You can choose the file you want to draw onto your track from this list. Make sure you choose the full snare file. Figure 6.8 shows the file drop-down list from my project.

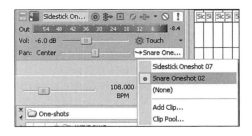

Figure 6.8
Each track can use any number of files, so make sure to choose the file you want to paint onto the track.

Now use the copy and paste repeat method to fill the rest of your track in with snare hits. You'll have to paste repeat a few times. If you paste too many events in, just delete the ones that extend beyond the end of the song.

To listen to my project with the snare track added to it, play the file ImGoinHome_KickSnare.wav from the Chapter 06 folder on the companion disc.

Using the Paint Tool and Alternate Grid Spacing

Now that you have the kick and snare, let's add the last of the basic drum tracks: the hi-hat. For this song, let's put a hi-hat event at every eighth note (another common beat for pop music). Although we could use paste repeat again to accomplish this, another method will be quicker in this instance because there will be so many events on this track.

Click the Paint Tool button in the button bar to select the Paint tool. This tool enables you to paint events freeform across your project. In this case, we're going to paint the hi-hat event across the entire length of a new track. But the events will (as usual) snap to the ruler marks, which we can use to our advantage here. First, let's change the ruler mark spacing to eighth notes. Choose Options, Grid Spacing, 8th Notes. This changes the ruler marks to one at every eighth note regardless of the project zoom level.

Now zoom out of the project far enough that you can see the entire song. Drag a hi-hat oneshot file from the Explorer window onto the timeline to create a new track. (For my song, I chose a closed hi-hat sound.) Then drag across the entire hi-hat track. As you do, you paint in hi-hat events at every eighth note. Be careful not to drag into one of the other existing tracks, or you'll replace what's already on that track with new events. If that happens, stop painting and click the Undo button; then start painting again.

After the hi-hat events are painted across the project, you can delete them where you don't want them. For example, if you don't want them during the intro section, switch back to the Draw tool, select the hi-hat events that you don't want, and delete them. I've deleted mine so that the first one now starts at beat 5.1 instead of at the beginning of my project.

Once again, all these hi-hat events have been painted in at the same volume. To make the sound convincing, go through the project and randomize their volumes. I think a real drummer has a tendency to hit the hi-hat a little harder every time he hits the snare, so I tend to keep my hat hits at beats 2 and 4 of each measure a little louder than the others.

To listen to my project with the new hi-hat track in it, play the file ImGoinHome_KickSnareHats.wav from the Chapter 06 folder on the companion disc.

Duplicating a Track and Swapping Files

Now that I've got all those hi-hat events in my project, I realize that maybe instead of the hi-hats during the choruses, I'd rather have a ride cymbal. At first, it might seem like you just did a lot of work adjusting those hi-hat volumes during the chorus, and now that work's wasted. Thankfully, that doesn't have to be the case.

You've got all the hi-hat events in the right places during the chorus; it's just that they're currently playing the wrong loop. Here's how to fix that problem. First right-click the track icon (the color square with the track number in it) for the hi-hat track and choose Duplicate track from the list.

Now you have two identical tracks full of hi-hat events. On the original hi-hat track, select all the events under all three choruses, the musical break, and the outro and press the Delete key on your computer keyboard. On the new track (the one that will become the ride cymbal track), select the events under the three verses and delete those. Figure 6.9 shows a portion of my project after I've deleted the appropriate events from both tracks.

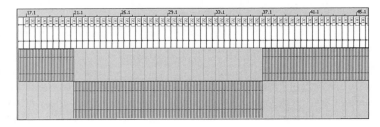

Figure 6.9
The two hi-hat tracks now have an alternating pattern between them.

TIP

Earlier you selected an event and then held down the Shift key while clicking another event, which selected all the events that fell between the two events you clicked on. Another helpful technique is to hold down the Ctrl key while you click events. This adds the clicked event to the current selection if it's not already selected and removes it from the selection if it is already selected.

Now, from the Explorer window, drag a ride cymbal oneshot to the scribble strip of the track that you want to hold the ride cymbal. (Remember, the scribble strip is the area in the track header where you name the track.) When you do this, a dark highlight surrounds the scribble strip. Release the mouse button to swap the hi-hat file with the ride cymbal file. Now all the events on this track use the ride cymbal instead of the hi-hat. Play the project and listen to the difference it makes.

To hear my project with the new ride cymbal track, play the file ImGoinHome_Ride.wav from the Chapter 06 folder on the companion disc.

Trimming Your Oneshot Events to Ensure Natural Decay

Paying close attention to the details will help you create a convincing drum sound. Remember, you want to make sure that every sound is allowed to decay naturally unless it runs into the beginning of the same sound on the same track. So you need to check every place in your project where the right edge of an event does not touch the left edge of another event that occurs after it in the track.

For example, each event in the snare track touches the one that follows it except for the last event in the project. Therefore, we don't need to worry about natural decay of any snare hit except the last one, which we need to check. Click to place your cursor at the end of the last event in the snare track, and zoom in so you can see the waveform in detail.

The only way to see whether this event is long enough to allow the last snare hit to decay fully is to trim the edge. So trim the right edge of the last snare event until you see the waveform in the event stop. It's okay to leave the event a little longer than it needs to be. In fact, that can be helpful because it gives you a clear visual that the sound in the event has died completely away before the event ends.

Then, in the same way, check any event in the hi-hat and cymbal tracks that don't touch the next event in the track. You'll find that all of them need to be extended considerably to allow the sound in the file to decay completely. Make all the adjustments necessary. Figure 6.10 shows a portion of my project after I've extended my events to ensure that my cymbals are decaying naturally.

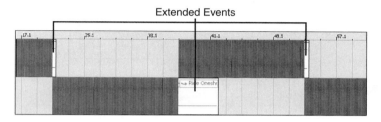

Figure 6.10

If an event does not touch the next event in the same track, extend that event as long as necessary to ensure that the sound dies away naturally.

Building Drum Fills with Oneshots

Next, it's time to build a few custom drum fills to add even more interest to the drum parts. This is where you can really get creative. You get to decide where to put the fills, how complex to make them, what drums to use in them, what dynamics to use for the fills, and everything else related to it.

TIP

When I build my drum fills, I try hard to create only fills that it would be theoretically possible for a real drummer to play. For example, a real drummer has only two arms and thus could not possibly hit the high hat, a cymbal, and a snare drum simultaneously.

Of course, you can do whatever you want to with your fills, but because I'm aiming for maximum realism, I try not to create a fill that would be impossible for a drummer to play.

Let's create a simple fill that transitions from the intro drum beat to the beat during the verse 1 section.

The first step is to imagine the fill. Play your project and let your imagination play drums along with it. Try to conjure up a fill that would work for this section. Once you have that fill in your mind, you can build it.

Recall that earlier you added a marker to your project to help you remember an important point. We'll use markers again to help build this fill. When you added the marker earlier, you did so by placing the cursor at a specific location and then choosing Insert, Marker. However, you can also insert a marker with a shortcut—pressing M on your keyboard. The powerful thing about this shortcut is that it works even when the project is playing. You can use that shortcut then to tap out the rhythm of the fill you imagine as you play your project.

Try it. Play the project, and when it reaches the point where you want to add your fill, tap out the rhythm of the fill on the M key. Each time you hit the key, you drop a marker in your project, as you can see I have in Figure 6.11.

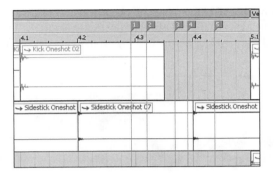

Figure 6.11

I've tapped out the rhythm of my imagined drum fill on the M key, which has added several markers to my project.

Now you just need to decide what drums you want to use for the fill and line them up with the markers. Keep in mind that you may have to delete part or all of some existing events to make room for the new events you're about to add. I'm going to use my snare, a high-rack tom, and a low-rack tom. Because I don't have the two toms in my project yet, I'll have to add them. I'll end the fill with a crash cymbal on the first beat of the verse, so I'll have to add that, too. Finally, because a drummer wouldn't normally hit a crash cymbal and the hi-hat at the same time, I'll have to delete the hi-hat event at the first beat of the verse. Figure 6.12 shows my project after I've built this drum fill.

TIP

You'll undoubtedly find that your markers do not line up perfectly with the ruler marks in your project no matter how far in you zoom. After all, you're not a machine! I sometimes leave these timing errors in my projects (unless they're so far off that they sound bad) because they add a little of the human touch to my tracks.

However, you'll find that when you try to line your events up to the markers, the events want to snap to the ruler marks and not your markers. That snapping feature is a great help most of the time, but not in this instance. To override this snapping behavior so you can line up your events with the markers exactly, hold the Shift key as you drag the event.

As a final step to building my drums (actually, I usually do this as I go along), I like to organize my drum tracks in a specific order. You can easily change the track order in ACID Pro to suit you. For example, I like my toms to be right below my snare track. To reorder your tracks, just drag the track header for the track you want to move to a new position in the list. Also check the scribble strips for each track and make sure they're each named something useful to you.

To listen to my song after I've added all my drum fills, play the file ImGoinHome_OneshotDrums.wav from the Chapter 06 folder on the companion disc.

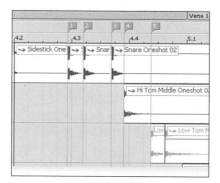

Figure 6.12
I've added drum events (including some on new tracks) and lined them up with the markers to create my drum fill.

Creating MIDI Drum Tracks

If you want to get the best of the control over your drums that building with oneshot files gives you along with the totally human feel of a live drummer, you'll want to give serious consideration to using MIDI to create your drum tracks. I'm going to save a thorough discussion of this topic for Chapter 7, "Utilizing MIDI in Your Projects." In that chapter, we'll explore using an electronic drum kit that outputs MIDI along with a drum synth to create totally convincing drum tracks. If you have access to such a drum set and a good drummer to play them, make sure you read Chapter 7!

Studio Log

ACID Pro (and perhaps your DAW) gives you some powerful techniques to create drum tracks without going through the nightmare of trying to record live drums. It takes real expertise to record live drums properly, not to mention a lot of expensive microphones, a nice live-sounding room, and tolerant neighbors. Therefore, it's great to use drum loops and oneshots that have already been professionally recorded for you by top-notch players in the best pro studios by engineers and producers who have the expertise and gear to do it properly.

If you want to create your drum tracks relatively quickly and you have a good library of drum loops, you can use looping techniques to get the job done. However, if you can't accept the limitations of using someone else's beats and fills, you can break out your oneshot building blocks and construct your drum patterns completely from the ground up. Of course, that ultimate control comes at the price of time, because it takes a bit of work to do it right. But in the end, you'll probably find the results of that extra work very satisfying.

By the way, you can always combine the two methods to create your tracks. Start with a drum loop and spice it up with oneshots. That works, too. Still, if I can't use a live drummer, the oneshot approach is the way I go nearly every time.

Utilizing MIDI in Your Projects

Many of us have held, or still hold, the conception that MIDI is the exclusive domain of keyboard players. After all, those guys and their crazy synths started the whole MIDI thing in the first place. So if you don't play the keyboards, you can skip this chapter, right?

Nothing could be further from the truth. In this chapter, you'll learn why every person reading this book—every musician who wants to record when making noise is not a viable option—needs to understand MIDI. You'll learn how powerful the technology is and how to use it in your projects whether you play keyboards or not.

You'll not only learn how to "program" your music with MIDI by drawing notes into the timeline, you'll learn how you can use MIDI to record live performances. For example, we'll talk about recording a live drummer playing on a drum-pad MIDI controller through an incredibly realistic-sounding synth to achieve a fantastic, natural drum sound. And what you learn there you'll be able to apply to any MIDI controller and any synth sound you need.

We talked a bit about MIDI back in Chapter 4, "An Introduction to ACID Pro Fundamentals," but that discussion was really just an introduction to the technology. As I mentioned back in that initial discussion, MIDI has developed a bad reputation among many musicians and listeners. We'll talk a little bit more about how that reputation developed, and we'll prove the reputation is undeserved.

I'll warn you, though; I have to lay out several concepts in a logical sequence, so you won't begin to hear those "natural-sounding" results until around midway through the chapter. So I ask you to stick with it and excuse what might sound like cheesy MIDI sounds until you've learned enough that I can introduce the technologies that make it all worthwhile.

We'll start where we left off in Chapter 6, "Creating Drum Tracks," and use MIDI to put our drum tracks together. Then we'll talk about recording other instrument tracks with MIDI, collaborating long distance, and editing your MIDI once it's in your project. In the process, you'll learn how to work with external MIDI controllers and internal soft synths that will give you the flexibility and power you need, along with the natural, organic results you demand.

Manually Assembling a MIDI Drum Track

In Chapter 6, you learned to use oneshot files as building blocks to create authentic-sounding drum tracks. You can do the same thing using MIDI and that's a good place for us to start so that you can get a handle on how MIDI works in your timeline.

Because I'm using ACID Pro, I can do all my MIDI work without leaving the project I've already started. That's because ACID Pro features a powerful MIDI sequencing component. If your DAW doesn't possess MIDI sequencing functionality, you'll have to use a standalone application to work with MIDI, commonly referred to as a *MIDI Sequencer*.

For this discussion, I'm going to go back to the project I've been working on. I'll start with a version of the project that existed way back before we started creating drums in the previous chapter.

Setting Up a MIDI Track

If you're going to utilize MIDI in your project, you'll start by adding a MIDI track. Unlike the audio tracks you've seen throughout the past few chapters, MIDI tracks don't create noise; as we discussed, MIDI is just information that your sequencer feeds to a synth. It's the synth that creates the audio you hear when you play the track. We'll talk more about this later, but it's a key concept because it gets right to the core of why MIDI has often been so unfairly judged.

To insert a MIDI track into your ACID Pro project, choose Insert, MIDI Track. This adds a MIDI track below the existing tracks in the project. Because we'll be concentrating on this MIDI track, let's make it the first track in the project. To do that, you might need to scroll down in the timeline to see the new track. You can use the scrollbar at the right edge of the timeline to do that. Once you can see the new MIDI track, drag its track header up. As you do, you'll see a dark insertion line showing you where the track will be dropped if you release the mouse button. Position the insertion bar so that it sits above the first track, and release the mouse button. Your MIDI track now occupies the first position in the track list. Drag the bottom of the track header down to make the track taller so that you can see all its controls.

TIP

Remember, whenever you want to select a track header or drag it to a new location, aim for the track icon when you click. There are a lot of controls and buttons in the track header, and if you inadvertently click one of them, you may get a result you don't want. The Track icon is a "safe-click" zone. The only thing that happens when you click there is that you select the track header. So, if you always aim for the track icon, you'll never accidentally click any other button or control. If you happen to click a control and it performs an operation you didn't want, click the Undo button in the main toolbar to undo the edit.

Figure 7.1 shows my project now that I've added my MIDI track and reordered the track list to put the new track first.

Figure 7.1
My new MIDI track sits at the top of my track list.

You can see that the track header for a MIDI track holds more controls than the headers for audio tracks. MIDI has many capabilities that we won't touch on in this book. (MIDI is another of those topics that warrants a book of its own for a full discussion.) You can use the controls in the track header to adjust many of them.

In the timeline, the MIDI track contains nothing. You can drag an existing MIDI file from the Explorer window to the track (we'll do that later), you can use a MIDI controller to record information onto the track (we'll do that later too!), and you can draw in new MIDI notes by hand. That's what we're going to do now.

Before you can draw MIDI notes into the timeline, you'll have to create a MIDI *event* to hold those notes. Point the mouse to the timeline for the MIDI track. The mouse icon changes to a pencil shape. Just like you drew oneshot events when you created drums in Chapter 6, you paint your MIDI event here.

Let's start with a one-measure event. Zoom into the project until you can clearly identify where the first measure of the song starts and ends. Click at the beginning of the track and drag to beat 2.1. This draws an event into the MIDI track that spans the first measure. As you can see in Figure 7.2, the event is blank.

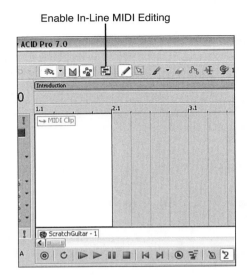

Enable In-Line MIDI Editing

Figure 7.2

The project now contains a one-measure-long blank MIDI event.

Adding MIDI Notes

Now we just need to populate the blank MIDI event with the MIDI information that directs the software to create the sounds we want. To do this, click the Enable In-Line MIDI Editing button.

As Figure 7.3 shows, the timeline now contains a piano-style keyboard section and shading that runs through the length of the track. The keyboard acts as a software MIDI controller (which will come in handy if you haven't yet connected a hardware controller). The track shading helps you identify the note that corresponds to the keyboard when you're working far away from the keyboard in the timeline. Specifically, the darker shaded lines—which I'll call *note lanes*—correspond to the black keys on the keyboard.

Click a key on the track's keyboard. You hear a piano sound that corresponds to the note on the keyboard that you click. Click other keys. Notice that the farther toward the right end of the key you click, the louder the note sounds. In other words, these keys emit a different MIDI note velocity depending on where you click them.

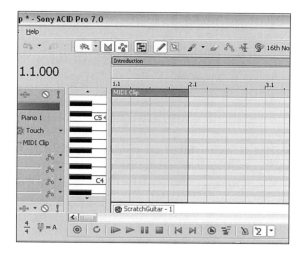

Figure 7.3

Once you've entered In-Line MIDI Editing mode, the MIDI track contains a software keyboard-style controller and shaded note lanes.

VELOCITY TRANSLATES TO VOLUME

In MIDI, *note velocity* translates to volume of the note played through the synth. So to control volume, you assign a velocity value to the note. That velocity value is passed on to the synth and defines the note's volume.

MIDI can define any of its parameters with one of 128 possible values. Those values (ranging from 0 to 127) define the parameter. If a MIDI note has a velocity value of 0, you can't hear it because it is the lowest possible velocity (and thus the lowest possible volume from the synth). A note with a velocity of 127 is the loudest possible MIDI note.

Most hardware controllers can sense how hard you push a key (or other control) on the controller. The force you use to press the key dictates the MIDI note velocity of the resultant note. Because a mouse click is the same no matter how hard you press the mouse button, the track's MIDI controller keyboard needed a different way to define velocity. Thus, the position of your click on the key defines note velocity for the MIDI note.

Click somewhere inside the MIDI event you created and drag the mouse to the right. As you do, you draw a MIDI note into the event, and you hear the note that you're creating. Draw one note at each beat of the measure. Play the project, and you can hear the tune you just created.

NOTE

Notice that where you draw on a MIDI track determines what function you'll perform. If you drag outside an existing MIDI event, you'll draw a new empty event into the track. If you draw inside an existing MIDI event, you'll draw MIDI notes into that event.

SOLOING A TRACK

When you play your project at this point, it very possibly sounds like your piano player has returned to his heavy drinking days! That's because you probably didn't think about how the notes you were drawing would work with your scratch guitar and vocal tracks. (Remember them?)

While you're experimenting, you can solo the MIDI track. Soloing a track temporarily takes all other tracks out of the mix so that you hear just the one you soloed. That can be helpful in many cases, like this one and like others that we'll see when we discuss mixing your project in Chapter 10, "Mixing Your Song."

To solo your MIDI track so you can hear the results of your work without the guitar and vocal in the mix, click the Solo button in the MIDI track's track header (the button with the exclamation point icon). When you're done listening, click the Solo button again to unsolo the track and bring the other tracks back into the mix. Every audio and MIDI track has its own Solo button.

Choosing Your Synth Sound

While it's pretty cool that you can create a piano part for your song, we didn't really want that at this point. Instead, we were trying to create drums. This is one of the powerful features of MIDI. Once again, I'll repeat that MIDI doesn't create sound; it merely creates instructions that the synth follows to make the sound. So the MIDI doesn't depend in any way on what sound you want it to make. In other words, after this MIDI is on the timeline, you can assign any sound from your synth to it and produce that sound.

Depending on how you set the controls of a synth, it can create many different sounds. Many synths have preset sounds, often referred to as *programs* or *patches* that you can choose to quickly change the sound produced by the synth as it follows the MIDI instructions. The MIDI track header contains a Program button that enables you to choose different MIDI patches. Click the Program button and choose a different sound from the drop-down list. The synth gives you lots of different Program options, as you can see in my Program drop-down list shown in Figure 7.4.

Because we want to create drums, click the Program button again and choose Drum Kits from the pop-up menu. Then choose Standard from the cascading menu.

Notice that the piano-style keys change to names of various drums and percussion instruments. You might also notice that the notes you drew into the timeline have disappeared from sight. Don't worry; they're still in your project. It's just that they're associated with sounds that don't currently appear in the list. Click the arrows at the top and bottom of the list of drum sounds to scroll through them until you can see your notes on the timeline again. Figure 7.5 shows my project, and you can see that the notes I drew in earlier are associated with the splash cymbal, tambourine, ride bell, and Chinese cymbal sounds. Play your project to hear the sounds generated by the MIDI notes you added.

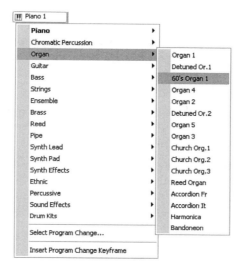

Figure 7.4

The synth's Program list shows that it can create a variety of sounds.

Figure 7.5

My MIDI notes are now associated with the drum sounds instead of the piano program.

NOTE

Don't worry if you don't like these drum sounds. We'll discuss options for much higher-quality sounds later in the chapter. For now, we'll stick with these sounds while we discuss these basic MIDI principles and techniques.

Arranging the MIDI Notes

Now that we've got the sound we want, we can turn our attention to creating the drum beat that we want for the song. This process is similar to the one you went through to create drum beats with oneshots back in Chapter 6. This time, however, you'll adjust the position of your MIDI notes instead of audio oneshots to create the patterns you want.

You already have four notes in your project, but of course you're not committed to where you placed them. In fact, you're not committed to any aspect of those notes because you can change any of those aspects.

It might help to zoom into your project even further to see each quarter note of the measure in the beat ruler. Now scroll through the list of drum names until you find Bass Drum 1 and Acoustic Snare in the list. When you know where they are, scroll back if you need to so you can see the notes you've already drawn into the event.

When you find them, click the first note to select it, hold the Shift key, and click the last of the four notes. This selects all of them. Drag the selected notes in whatever direction (up or down) you need to to drag them to the Bass Drum 1 and Acoustic Snare tracks. As you drag to the bottom of the event, the list of drum sounds begins to scroll so you can find the sounds you're after. You can hear the sounds play as the notes pass over them.

When you get in the right neighborhood, drag the notes individually to position them so that two notes sit on the Bass Drum 1 note lane (at beats 1 and 3) and two sit on the Acoustic Snare lane (at beats 2 and 4). Play the project to hear what you've created. Suddenly you've got a drum track to go along with the other tracks at the first measure!

Of course, you're far from done. You might want to create the same double-kick drum pattern that we used when we used oneshots to create the drums back in Chapter 6. Draw another note into the Bass Drum 1 lane at the eighth note between beats 3 and 4.

Next, draw a note in at every eighth note on the Closed Hi-Hat track. You now have your basic beat in place. Figure 7.6 shows the first measure of my song with the basic beat in place.

Depending on your style of music, you might want to create the same kind of dynamics that you created when you were working with oneshots to achieve a more human feel. We will use the MIDI note velocity setting we already discussed to create dynamics in the volume of individual notes.

When you use the Draw tool to add notes to your timeline like you did here, those notes come in with a velocity of 64 (essentially halfway between the extreme MIDI values of 0 and 127). Typically, I like to have my velocities as high as possible and then back off of some of them to create dynamics. You'll probably develop your own technique, but that's what I like, so I'm going to set all these notes' velocities to 127.

Right-click any note in the event and choose Select All in Event from the pop-up menu. This selects all the notes in the event. Right-click any of the selected events and choose Velocity from the pop-up menu. Notice that you have several options here, as you can see in Figure 7.7, including Set To, which enables you to set any MIDI value for the velocity of the selected notes. For now, select Set to Maximum from the cascading menu to set the velocity for each selected note to the maximum possible value of 127.

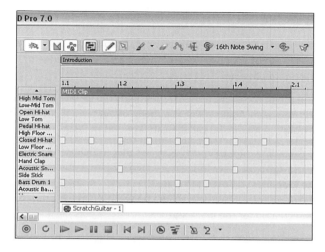

Figure 7.6

I've created my kick, snare, and hi-hat basic beat for the first measure of my song.

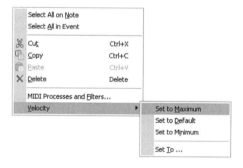

Figure 7.7

You have several options for setting the velocity of the selected note or notes.

Now that you've set all the note velocities to the maximum, you can back off of certain ones to create dynamics. For example, let's set the second of the two bass drum notes at beat 3 to a lower volume. First, click in a blank spot on the track to deselect all the selected MIDI notes. Then right-click the drum note and choose Velocity, Set To. A text field appears above the note. Type a value into that field (I used 110) and press Enter. In the same way, change the velocity values of your hi-hat notes to create dynamics there as well.

TIP

For a handy shortcut to change a MIDI note's velocity, double-click the MIDI note. This brings up the same text field that you saw when you navigated through the pop-up and cascading menus.

Creating Drum Fills

Now that you've got the basic beat in place, you can apply it across the rest of the project and add in drum fills. Zoom all the way out of your project, and then drag the right edge of the MIDI event to the right until it lasts for the entire project.

Right-click the bar at the top of the event (the one that holds the event name) and choose Event Clip (MIDI Clip) from the pop-up menu. Again, a cascade menu offers several options. For example, you could choose Rename from the menu and call the clip Basic Drum Beat.

Choose Loop from the cascading menu. Figure 7.8 shows that this causes whatever you've drawn into the event (in this case, just what you have in measure 1) to loop repeatedly until it fills the entire event. It's not unlike the loop files you used to create the first drum track back in Chapter 6. Play the project and listen to the drum track. Of course, there's no variation in the drum pattern because you're simply looping what you created for the first measure.

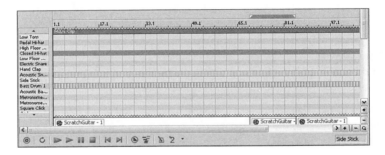

Figure 7.8

The MIDI information now loops to fill the entire event.

Now, let's say you want a fill leading from the introduction into the first verse. The first verse starts at measure 5, so place your cursor at beat 5.1 and zoom into the project so that you can see the quarter notes around measure 5.

TIP

Remember that you can double-click the Measures and Beats value in the Time Display area, type the location you want to go to, and press the Enter key to jump instantly to that location.

You can use the same method of tapping out the rhythm of the drum fill with the M key to drop markers that you learned in Chapter 6. Or you can just add MIDI notes and adjust them as you see fit to create the fill you want.

However, you have something to keep in mind. Because this event contains one measure of MIDI information that loops to the end of the song, any change you make to the event at any measure in the song is going to affect every other measure of the song. In other words, if you create a fill at the end of measure 4, that same fill will exist at the end of every other measure (because every measure is just a repeat of the original measure).

In some ways, this is good. For example, if you decided to create a double-kick drum around the first beat of every measure as well as the third, you'd only have to add it once, and it would apply across every measure in your project.

However, in the case of creating the occasional drum fill, this is not a good situation because you don't typically want the same fill in every measure. So how do you get around the problem?

Again, you could go about it in a couple of different ways. Here's one that works for me. The drum fill I want to create starts at beat 4.3 and goes to beat 5.1. I can create a hole in my track over that time period and fill it with a new MIDI event. That new event will hold my drum fill.

First, click the bar above the MIDI event right at beat 5.1. This places the cursor at that location and selects the MIDI event. Then choose Edit, Split At Cursor. This cuts the MIDI event into two separate events, one on each side of the cursor, which defined the split point.

Edge trim the right edge of the first event (the one that now stops at beat 5.1) to the left so that it stops at beat 4.3 instead. Then click the Paint Clip Selector button in the track header. From the drop-down menu, choose Create Empty MIDI Clip. This places an empty MIDI clip in the Paint Clip Selector list and makes it the active event (that is, the one that will be drawn into the project when you drag with the Draw tool).

Draw in a new event between beats 4.3 and 5.1. The event is empty. Now just draw the notes that make up your drum fill into the new empty event. In Figure 7.9, you can see my new event (called MIDI clip – 1) with the drum fill, including a couple of extra snare hits along with a couple of tom hits leading into measure 5. Adjust your MIDI note velocities to create the desired dynamics, and your fill is complete.

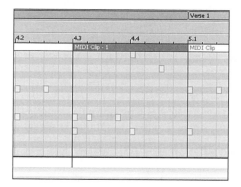

Figure 7.9

I've created a new event between beats 4.3 and 5.1 and drawn a drum fill into it.

Now you can move on to creating other fills in your project. You can use the one you just created somewhere else in the project if you don't mind using the same fill more than once. Just make a hole for it in the track, select it from the Paint Clip Selector list, and draw it in wherever you want it.

There's a lot more you can learn about editing MIDI note in your sequencer. But the basic techniques we've talked about here can give you a great start on building drum tracks that work for your song.

But what about the drum sounds? Are you stuck with these somewhat cheesy-sounding drums? Naturally not! Let's talk a little bit more about the sounds your DAW and MIDI sequencer can make from the instructions you feed it via MIDI.

Routing Your MIDI Through a Soft Synth

All along I've been saying that MIDI doesn't make any sound on its own. It needs a synth to create the audio. So how then did we hear the piano and drums that we were working with in the previous discussion?

The answer to that question, interestingly enough, sheds some light on how MIDI came to develop such a bad reputation among those who don't understand the technology.

Downloadable Sound Soft Synths

MIDI does indeed need to be fed to a synth (and remember, I'm using the term *synth* to refer generically to both synthesizers and samplers) to create audio. It didn't take musicians long to realize that if they wanted anyone to hear their music, the listener needed to have a synth to play it through. But the vast majority of computer users weren't about to go out and buy a synth just so they could hear the MIDI on some web page (for that matter, they weren't even aware that they had to).

So to make MIDI "just work," soft synths were added to computer operating systems. This way, if a MIDI file was encountered, at least there would be something to create audio according to the instructions.

On the Windows operating system, the soft synth comes in the form of a file called a downloadable sound (DLS). This file contains various synthesized sounds that are used to play back any MIDI files that the operating system encounters.

Although it's nice to know that any MIDI file will play on your computer, the sounds in the DLS do not necessarily produce an accurate rendition of the sounds they're meant to mimic.

Furthermore, the way those sounds are mapped out in the DLS may be substantially different from the way they were mapped out in whatever synth the musician was listening to while creating the music. So what might have sounded like a lush, rich string section to the composer may end up sounding like a glockenspiel and a gong to the listener who's hearing the audio created by the DLS or some synth other than the composer's.

These are the very reasons why so much of the music generated by MIDI sounds, well, horrible. And that's partially where MIDI got its bad reputation.

But now that you know that, let me assure you that music created with the help of MIDI technology doesn't *have* to sound bad. It's still true that if you deliver a MIDI file to your listeners, you are totally dependent on the quality of the synth they're using to give them the intended experience.

But if you turn that MIDI into audio and *then* deliver the file, your fans will hear exactly what you wanted them to. And they'll probably never know that you used MIDI to create it. In fact, most people would be amazed at just exactly how much MIDI-generated music they've heard—and thoroughly enjoyed—on the radio, at the dance club, and so on. That's what your DAW or MIDI sequencer and a good synth will do for you: Turn those MIDI instructions into great-sounding audio that you can weave into your project and deliver to your fans.

ACID Pro and DLS

When the developers of ACID Pro decided to include MIDI capabilities in the application, they, too, realized that they needed to provide a way for the user to hear audio generated from any MIDI file they added to or created on the timeline. So they turned to the operating system's DLS file because it was assured to be on everyone's operating system. That's why when you created the MIDI drum notes earlier, you heard drums immediately. But it's also why the drums don't sound great.

The developers of the software decided that hearing low-quality synth sounds was better than hearing nothing, so by default when you listen to the audio generated by MIDI instructions, you hear it through the operating system's DLS soft synth. Other DAWs and sequencers may utilize the DLS in a similar fashion.

To hear the introduction to my project with drum sounds created by the default DLS, play the file ImGoinHomeIntro_DLSDrums.wav from the Chapter 07 folder on the companion disc.

But naturally, ACID Pro gives you a way to take things to a different level if you want to. The operating system's DLS isn't the only game in town. Many other DLS files of much higher quality are also available. (I've included some DLS files from Sony Creative Software in the DLS Instruments folder on the companion disc.)

Virtual Studio Technology Instruments

As I mentioned, DLS files are not the only option available. Many extremely high-quality soft synths are created as Virtual Studio Technology instruments (VSTi). A good VSTi works with any DAW or sequencer that supports the technology and can produce really astounding audio. VSTi technology plays a huge role in enabling you to create fantastic-sounding music when you don't have a professional-quality space to make it in. I can't say enough about how much I appreciate VSTi for my recording projects!

Choosing a Different DLS Soft Synth

Now that we know such high-quality synth options exist, let's use them for our drum tracks. I mentioned that I've included several DLS files on the companion disc, so let's start by swapping out the default DLS with one of these higher-quality ones.

I didn't mention this at the time, but when you inserted a MIDI track to your project, ACID Pro loaded the default DLS soft synth for you. To see this, we'll have to talk a little bit about the ACID Pro mixing console. We'll use this tool much more extensively in Chapter 10, when we turn our attention to creating a great mix, but we need to touch on it here, too.

Figure 7.10 shows that, by default, the Mixing Console window appears docked at the right side of the window docking area.

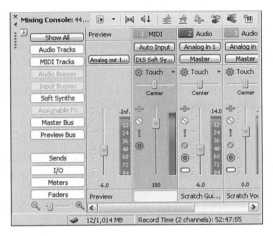

Figure 7.10

The window docking area holds the mixing console.

Think of the mixing console as a software version of a hardware mixer. It gives you controls that you can use to adjust various parameters and characteristics of your project's tracks, such as track volume and panning. It also gives you control over track signal routing so you can specify where you want the audio from each track to go (the master bus, effects, and so on).

However, the mixer also contains controls for other things in your project. For example, when we talked about some basic routing topics back in Chapter 4, we discussed how the audio from each track in your project routes to the Master bus and from there to the outputs of your audio device and on to your studio monitors. The mixing console contains controls for the Master bus as well as for the tracks in your project.

But the Master bus is not the only type of bus your project can have. In Chapter 10, we'll add different types of busses that will give us powerful options for controlling the audio. When you inserted the MIDI track earlier in this chapter, ACID Pro created one of those other bus types for you, called a Soft Synth bus.

The Soft Synth bus contains tools for controlling the properties of the soft synth. As we've discussed, the soft synth creates the audio described by the instructions from your MIDI track. We also discussed how, by default, ACID Pro uses the operating system's DLS file to create that audio.

To see the Soft Synth bus in the mixing console, you'll probably have to use the scrollbar at the bottom of the console window to scroll past the track controls until you can see the bus controls. Figure 7.11 shows that my mixing console window holds two busses: the Master bus and a Synth bus. Notice that at the bottom of the Synth bus, a scribble strip (similar to those you've used on tracks) identifies the synth that the bus uses.

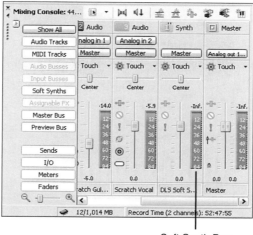

Soft Synth Bus

Figure 7.11

The Mixing Console window contains a Synth bus, which gives you control over the soft synth that creates audio for your MIDI track.

NOTE

There is a group of controls in the mixing console for each track and bus in your project. These groups of controls are called *channels*.

MIDI TRANSFORMED TO AUDIO

Play your project. As it plays, look at the output meter for your MIDI track. You'll notice that the meter has a distinct feel to it. By this, I mean that meter transitions distinctly from one level to another. That's because the MIDI track meter shows the level of MIDI note velocity and jumps instantly from one velocity to the next as the cursor moves through the song.

Now look at the meter for the synth channel. You'll notice that this meter has a more organic, less distinct feel. Instead of jumping instantly from one level to the next, the meter sort of eases between levels. That's because this meter represents the volume of the audio that has been created by the synth. In other words, what went into the synth as MIDI information has been transformed to audio that comes out of the Soft Synth bus and routes to the master mix so you hear it along with the audio from other tracks in your project. The Soft Synth bus meter reacts to the natural decay that exists in audio but does not exist in MIDI information.

To change the synth that you're routing the MIDI track information through, double-click the number label at the top of the Soft Synth bus channel. This opens the Soft Synth Properties window that you can see in Figure 7.12.

Figure 7.12
The Soft Synth Properties window shows the controls that you can use to manage the DLS soft synth.

The Voice Set drop-down list shows that this soft synth is set to use the GS sound set, which is the operating system's DLS. The Available voices list shows all the different sound groups, or voices, the DLS contains. If you scroll down far enough in the list, you'll see that the Standard patch of the drum kit voice type is selected. That is, of course, the patch you selected earlier.

The Soft Synth Properties window contains another software controller. Click any of the keys on the controller to hear the sound associated with it.

Now let's change to a different DLS. Click the Open DLS Voice Set button. In the Open DLS Voice Set dialog box, navigate to the *DLS* Instruments folder on the companion disc. Scroll through the list, and you'll see several drum sound DLS files. Select one of those files from the list and click the Open button.

ANOTHER FAMOUS DRUMMER AT YOUR DISPOSAL

The DLS Instruments folder contains three DLS files called Vitale Kit 01, 02, and 03. These sets of sounds were recorded by Joe Vitale and his son Joe, Jr. These guys know drums, and they know how to record them! Joe Sr. played drums with all kinds of famous acts, including Joe Walsh; Crosby, Stills, and Nash; and more. Both Sr. and Jr. are involved in many high-profile projects, but they still find time to create great-sounding loop libraries and DLS files for Sony Creative Software.

So if you want the sound of another famous drummer on your recordings, you can use one of the Vitale DLS files.

The Soft Synth Properties window now lists the Vitale kit that you just added. Select it from the Available Voices list, and click the controller keys to hear the sounds.

Back in your timeline, notice that the drum names have disappeared from the list and have been replaced with numbers. This DLS doesn't have the drum names built into it, but it follows a fairly standard organization scheme, so you can load the names manually if you want them.

To do so, click the Program button in the track header, choose DrumMaps from the pop-up menu and then choose Select Drum Map from the cascading menu, as shown in Figure 7.13.

Figure 7.13
You can load a drum map for any DLS or synth that doesn't have its own.

The Track Properties window opens with the Output Settings tab active and set to show ACID Pro's available drum maps. Select the check box for the Standard Set drum set and click the window's Close button. The drum map is now loaded, and drum names appear in the list on the MIDI track.

If you need to, scroll through the list until you can see the MIDI notes that you added to the track earlier. Play the track, and listen to the new drum sounds. If you want to hear the introduction of my song with drum sounds from the Vitale Kit 02, play the file ImGoinHomeIntro_VitaleDLSDrums.wav.

CAUTION

Although DLS files can sound great, ACID Pro plays them through the same synthesis engine that the operating system supplies for the default DLS file. That synth engine is not the greatest quality synth available. Therefore, you may hear noise artifacts when you play the DLS sounds. Those same artifacts will become part of your song. Some VSTi synths (which we'll talk about shortly) enable you to load DLS sounds into them. Your DLS files will probably sound better when played through a high-quality synth engine from a VSTi synth than they do when played through the operating system's engine.

Try some of the other DLS drum sounds to see how they affect the sound of your project.

Routing Your MIDI Through a VSTi

I mentioned VSTi technology a bit earlier in this chapter. You can find many VSTi packages that synthesize drum sounds. There are several freeware packages available online (though I can't recommend any because I've never used them). Packages that you pay for range in price from about $50 and up.

The ACID Pro 7 package includes a VSTi soft synth made by Submersible called KitCore. I'm going to load KitCore and use its sounds for the drums that I've built for my project.

Unlike DLS files, a VSTi acts as a plug-in to your DAW software and requires installation on your computer. I talked about the concept of plug-ins way back in Chapter 1, "Laying the Groundwork for Recording." The plug-in comes with its own executable installation file. You install it just like you install other applications on your computer.

> **TIP**
>
> During the installation process, your VSTi's installer will ask where you want to install the application. You can generally stick with the default for this folder. Then the installer might ask you where you want the reference for the plug-in to reside. You should give thought to this question.
>
> When ACID Pro starts, it scans a folder located at C:\Program Files\Vstplugins and then loads any plug-ins it finds there so that they are available for you to use. Often, plug-in installers do not choose the Vstplugins folder as their default location. If your VSTi chooses a different location, ACID Pro won't find your plug-in at startup. I'll show you how to find and load the plug-in regardless of which folder the reference resides in, but it's a more automatic process if you change the location to the Vstplugins folder during installation.

After you've installed the plug-in, start ACID Pro again (I'm assuming you closed it as a matter of good software installation policy during the installation of your plug-in) and open the project you've been working on.

In the mixing console, double-click the number label at the top of the Soft Synth bus to open the Soft Synth Properties window again. If you've been following along, your Soft Synth bus is still set to one of the Vitale Kit DLS files.

Instead of choosing a new DLS file like you did earlier, you're going to load an entirely different soft synth, so click the Edit Soft Synth button. This opens the Soft Synth Chooser. Figure 7.14 shows my Soft Synth Chooser. You can look down the list to see all the VSTi soft synths that ACID Pro has detected on my system.

Figure 7.14

The Soft Synth Chooser lists all the soft synths that ACID detects on your system.

If you know that you've installed a soft synth and you don't see it in the list of available synths, you'll have to help ACID Pro find the location where you installed the plug-in and you'll use the Plug-In Manager to do that. Click the Cancel button to close the Soft Synth Chooser window. Choose View, Plug-In Manager.

In the Plug-In Manager, shown in Figure 7.15, click the Configure VST button. In the VST Configuration dialog box, click the Add button.

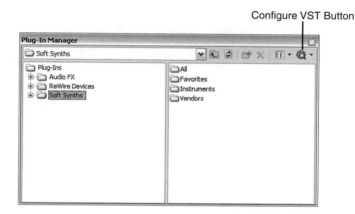

Figure 7.15

The Plug-In Manager gives you control over the effect plug-ins and VSTi plug-ins that you've installed on your system.

Then browse to the location on your computer drives where you installed the reference to the plug-in you want to use. When you've specified that folder, click OK. Click the Scan button. When the scanning process finishes, click OK to close the VST Configuration dialog box. Check the appropriate folder in the Plug-In Manager to confirm that your VSTi is listed.

Now, close the Plug-In Manager window and click the Edit Soft Synth button in the Soft Synth Properties dialog box again. This takes you back to the open Soft Synth Chooser dialog box. Your VSTi now appears in the list. Select the soft synth that you want to use from the list (I chose KitCore), and click OK.

The soft synth's interface now appears in the Soft Synth Properties window. Figure 7.16 shows the interface for KitCore after I've loaded it into my project.

You can click the various buttons in the KitCore interface to hear the sound associated with it. You can also choose from several drum kit sounds. Click the Presets drop-down arrow to see all the choices, and select one from the list. Play your project to see if you like the drum sound for your project. If you don't, try a different one.

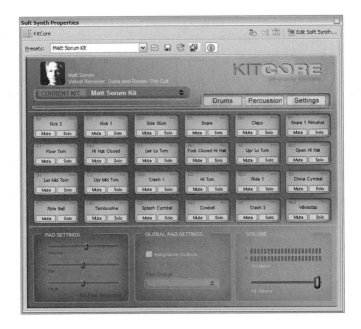

Figure 7.16

The KitCore interface as it appears in the Soft Synth Properties window.

If you want to hear my song's introduction with two different kit sounds from KitCore, play the files ImGoinHomeIntro_KC_BenSmithModslam.wav and ImGoinHomeIntro_KC_MattSorumKit.wav from the Chapter 07 folder on the companion disc. Notice how different the two drum kits sound. Even more than that, notice how good they sound!

Using a MIDI Controller and a Live Drummer to Record MIDI

For the ultimate in achieving a live feel, the only thing missing from our setup is the live drummer. We discussed the concept of MIDI controllers back in Chapter 4. Recall that MIDI controllers come in a variety of different forms. One of those is a set of pads arranged like a traditional drum kit that a live drummer can play to trigger MIDI messages. We can then record these MIDI messages into the ACID Pro timeline as MIDI notes.

Let's say we want to use such a controller to record MIDI into the timeline instead of drawing the notes by hand as we have been up to now.

TIP

There's no rule against using a combination of techniques to get MIDI notes onto the timeline. For example, you can record MIDI notes from your MIDI controller to the ACID Pro timeline and then manually add notes that the drummer didn't play. Maybe you wish the drummer had played a fill in a certain spot that currently lacks one. You can draw the fill manually.

I want to record my drummer friend M. Scott Young (who you met back in Chapter 1). Although assembling the drum tracks myself with the techniques we've discussed so far gives me the ultimate decision-making control, I like to collaborate with a drummer who can offer valuable ideas on beats and rhythms.

Scott and I, having settled on a beat and tempo for our version of the song, will record his drums (via MIDI) while simultaneously recording my scratch guitar and vocal tracks. This way we can play live together and establish a live feel for the song.

So we have some setup to do. Start a new project and insert two audio tracks along with one MIDI track. Route your guitar and vocal tracks so that they're listening to the inputs on your audio device that you've plugged each into; then set up the tracks to record. If you need a refresher on how to set up your project to record audio into these tracks, refer to Chapter 5, "Creating Your Guide Tracks."

Now let's set up the MIDI track to record MIDI data from your controller. First you need to connect the MIDI controller to your computer. If your audio device has MIDI jacks, you can use those. If your audio device doesn't have MIDI jacks, you may need to purchase a standalone MIDI interface unit. Such units can interface with your computer via a USB connection. In fact, some MIDI controllers send MIDI out a built-in USB jack in addition to their traditional MIDI jacks. If your controller does this, you won't need a MIDI interface device because your computer already has USB ports that you can use. Keep in mind that you might have to install some sort of software driver to enable your controller to communicate as a USB device with your computer. (Such a driver should ship with your controller if the controller requires one.)

In my setup, my AudioFire 8 audio device has a MIDI In jack and a MIDI Out jack. This enables my computer to send and receive MIDI data. In this case, I want to receive MIDI from the MIDI controller, so I plug a MIDI cable into the MIDI Out jack on the controller and then to the MIDI In jack on my audio device.

MAKING YOUR CONTROLLER TALK TO YOUR SOFT SYNTH

Remember that MIDI information can have one of 128 values. Each pad on your MIDI drum controller has a distinct value. Likewise, each drum sound in your drum synth has a distinct value. You may need to verify that your MIDI drum pads correspond to the sounds in the VSTi drum synth you're using.

For example, if you find that when you hit the snare pad, you hear a sound other than a snare sound (or perhaps no sound at all), you don't have agreement between your controller and your synth on what value the snare sound should be.

You might be able to change the value assigned to the snare at the controller, the synth, or both. But wherever you make the change, it's critical to get the controller and the synth to use the same values for each specific sound.

Now that my hardware connections are made, I need to open the lines of communication between my audio device's MIDI ports and my DAW. In ACID Pro, choose Options, Preferences and click the MIDI tab. Figure 7.17 shows my MIDI preferences. Because you want to record MIDI coming into ACID

Pro, select the check box for your MIDI input connection from the Make These Devices Available for MIDI Input section. Click OK to close the Preferences dialog box.

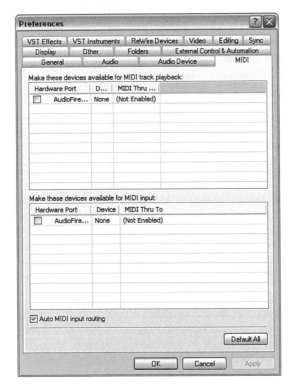

Figure 7.17
Establish communication between your controller and ACID Pro on the MIDI tab of the Preferences dialog.

Now make sure your controller is properly set to generate MIDI, and start beating the drum pads. You hear the sounds that the soft synth creates according to the MIDI you're sending it by hitting the drum pads. Remember, initially you'll hear the default DLS sounds, but if you route the Soft Synth bus to a drum VSTi plug-in, you'll hear the sounds from that instead. Click the Arm for Record button in the MIDI track header.

When you're satisfied with the record input levels you're getting in your audio tracks (make sure you're not clipping!), you can start recording. Remember that you might want to use the metronome to keep everyone at the right speed. When I'm recording with a drummer, we often don't use the metronome, but we usually want the metronome count-in to be active.

When you're ready, click the Record button in the Transport toolbar and begin playing. ACID Pro simultaneously records the two tracks of audio and the MIDI information coming from the controller to the MIDI track. When you're done with the song, click the Stop button.

After you save your recorded files, you have your audio and MIDI drum tracks in your project. Unarm all the tracks and play your project to hear the results. Figure 7.18 shows my project after the recording.

Figure 7.18

The project now has two tracks of audio and a track of MIDI—all recorded simultaneously.

> **NOTE**
>
> Notice the line running through the drum track in Figure 7.18. That line, called an *envelope*, represents the recording of the state of a foot switch that is part of the drum controller. It emulates the hi-hat pedal. As I've mentioned, MIDI can convey many types of information, and ACID Pro can record that information. Every time Scott pressed the hi-hat foot pedal or released it, the movement was recorded by the envelope. This adds even more realism to the drum sound.

If you want to hear what Scott and I came up with for my song, open the file ImGoinHome_ LiveDrummer.wav from the Chapter 07 folder on the companion disc and listen to the MIDI- generated drums along with my scratch guitar and vocal tracks.

> **NOTE**
>
> Remember, although I used a drummer and a drum-style MIDI controller to record a live drum performance, you can use a MIDI controller of any form to do the same thing. All you have to do is connect your favorite MIDI controller, route the MIDI to the synth that has your desired sound, and you can play and record your live performance.

Working with Soft Synths for Keyboard Sounds

As you've seen here, there are a lot of options for creating the drum sounds you want your MIDI files to generate. Hopefully you're starting to get a handle on the power that MIDI technology brings to your projects, especially when you combine it with high-quality DLS files or VSTi plug-ins.

The really cool thing is that you don't have to mess with the MIDI to try these different synths. After you've arranged your MIDI notes (referred to as *sequencing* your MIDI track or tracks), you can just swap out different soft synth sounds until you find the one you like for your tune. You can work with any sounds, not just drums sounds like we have here. For example, you can record or assemble a melody in a new MIDI track and assign a piano sound to it. Then you can try a violin sound. And then maybe a horn, and so on until you find the sound you like.

As you'll see later when we turn our attention to mixing in Chapter 10, you don't have to settle with exactly the sound you get out of your soft synth. Your DAW or sequencer most likely features several ways to add additional effects to the sounds your soft synths create.

I'll create a simple organ line for my song to demonstrate how all this works.

Now, I can sort of fumble my way across a piano keyboard and play a couple of things, but I'm no keyboardist by any stretch of my active imagination. So I can either construct my keyboard parts in the same way I constructed the drum part earlier—drawing the melody in note by note—or I can attempt to play the part and go back to edit out the mistakes later.

First, close the Soft Synth Properties dialog. Then choose Insert, MIDI Track to insert a new MIDI track to your timeline. Rearrange the tracks as I showed you earlier so that the new MIDI track sits just below the drum track.

In the Mixing Console window, scroll until you can see the Soft Synth bus. Notice that after your project contains a Soft Synth bus, adding new MIDI tracks does not insert new busses. The new MIDI track simply routes to the existing Soft Synth bus.

In this case that won't work, because the existing Soft Synth bus is set to play drum sounds, and we want an organ sound. Because ACID Pro enables you to add more than one Soft Synth bus, we can easily get around the problem, so that's what we'll do.

In the mixing console, click the Insert Soft Synth button. The Soft Synth Chooser opens and shows all the available soft synths. If you don't have a VSTi plug-in that can give you an organ sound, choose the DLS soft synth from the list.

TIP

Check the DLS files available in the DLSInstruments folder on the companion disc to see if there is one that gives you the sound you're looking for.

I've loaded a VSTi plug-in called B4 Xpress made by Native Instruments onto my system. This plug-in mimics the famous Hammond B-3 organ, which is perfect for what I want, so I choose that from the list and click OK. The B4 Xpress interface opens in the Soft Synth Properties window, as you can see in Figure 7.19. Click the keys in the software MIDI controller to hear what this synth sounds like.

Click the MIDI Output button in the track header for the new MIDI track and choose Soft Synth 2 (B4 Xpress) from the menu. This routes the MIDI from this track to the organ synth instead of the drum synth.

Figure 7.19

The B4 Xpress interface in the Soft Synth Properties window.

Now draw or record the MIDI for your organ track. Figure 7.20 shows my introduction with the new MIDI organ track.

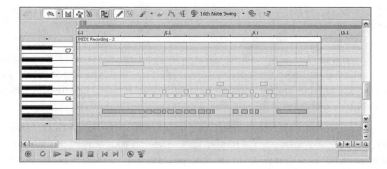

Figure 7.20

My second MIDI track feeds information to my B4 Xpress soft synth to create an organ part for my song.

Long-Distance Collaboration

One of the real benefits of the techniques we've been using is the potential for collaborating with colleagues even though there may be miles between your studios. You can send files back and forth across borders and oceans via the Internet so that other musicians can work on your song with you.

For example, I'm not happy with the organ part I just created in my song. (I'm so unhappy with it, in fact, that I didn't create a file for you to hear, although any of you savvy MIDI users can look at Figure 7.20 and re-create it in your own sequencer if you really must hear it!) Luckily, my good friend Brian Orr, who you can see in Figure 7.21, is a monster keyboard player. However, Brian lives miles away across the border in Canada, and we just can't get together as often as we'd like to.

Figure 17.21

Keyboardist, composer, and good friend Brian Orr contributed an organ track for my song.

But the miles between us don't stop us from collaborating on music. I sent Brian an email message asking for help with the keyboard track on my song. I left it up to him to decide what to play and even what sound to use. Now that he's agreed to record a part for me, I just need to get him a recording of the song to play along with.

We'll talk in much more detail about creating files that you can let people listen to even if they don't have a version of your DAW software in Chapter 12, "Delivering Your Music." But for now I'll show you how to make a quick MP3 file that you can email to your partner so that he or she has a reference to record along with.

To create an MP3 file (and any other mixed file that listeners can play on their computer or personal player), choose File, Render As. In the Render As dialog box, navigate to the location on your computer where you want to save the file and give the file a name. Note that the File Name field is automatically filled in with the name of your project, but you can change it if you want to.

Choose MP3 audio from the Save As Type drop-down list. Use the Template drop-down list to choose the bit rate you want to use for the file, as shown in Figure 17.22. Remember, the higher the bit rate, the better the audio quality of the resulting file, but the larger the file size. If you intend to email this file, you may need to choose a lower bit rate to keep the file size down even if it means less than optimal quality.

After you've made your choices, click the Save button. After a few moments, you have an MP3 version of your song in the specified location on your computer drive.

Figure 7.22

Choose a template for your file.

Now email that MP3 file to your partner. In my case, I sent the file to Brian, who loaded it into his DAW or sequencer and listened to it while he recorded a keyboard part to it. Brian recorded the part as MIDI and sent that MIDI file back to me.

After you receive the MIDI file from you partner and copy it to your computer drive, use the ACID Explorer window to navigate to it and drag it into your project. Then route the track that holds it to a soft synth. Now your partner's file is part of your project!

AVOID THE "GOTCHA" IN SHARING MIDI FILES

Remember the earlier discussion of MIDI-generated music not sounding to the listener the way it did to the composer? When you're collaborating long-distance as described here, you really have to be clear with one another about exactly how the file is supposed to sound.

For example, Brian and I decided that because we both have the B4 Xpress VSTi that I used earlier, he'd use that to create the sounds he wants. That makes it easy for me to get exactly what he intended into my project. I simply drop his MIDI file into my timeline from the Explorer window and route it to the B4 Xpress using the patch he specified.

Still, as a precaution, Brian rendered out an MP3 file of his performance and sent that along, too, so that I could hear exactly what he wanted the file to sound like. In fact, if I want to, I can just use the audio file (I'd have him send a full-quality, uncompressed file format rather than an MP3 file) in my project, and then I don't have to worry about getting the synth sound right. Why? Because when Brian created the mixed audio file, the synth sound became "baked" into the audio file, just as if he'd recorded the audio outputs of his keyboard instead of sending me a MIDI file.

An advantage to sending an audio file is that Brian knows that it'll sound exactly like he wants it to when I add it to my project. A disadvantage is that I won't be able to change it in any way (change the melody, change note volumes, or try different sounds). A MIDI file's extremely small file size makes it easy to send via email instead of something like FTP. It's also a flexible, totally editable file that I can change as I see fit—which, though I may see as an advantage, Brian may see as a disadvantage!

If you'd like to learn more about Brian and his music, visit his website at www.brianorr.com.

To listen to my song with Brian's keyboard part in it, open the file ImGoinHome_keys.wav from the Chapter 07 folder on the companion disc.

Studio Log

This chapter covered a lot of ground. You learned that you can use MIDI to assemble drum parts in much the same way as you did in Chapter 6 with oneshots. Your DAW probably provides a way for you to hear the MIDI you create without extra routing work. ACID Pro defaults to the relatively low-quality DLS soft synth built into the operating system. But there are many different options for creating higher-quality sound. Other DLS files and especially VSTi plug-ins enable you to create realistic-sounding drums.

You can also use a MIDI controller to record a performance (as MIDI information that gets sent to a soft synth). This gives your project an even more realistic, human feel.

Naturally, when you know the techniques for creating and routing MIDI for drums, you can apply that knowledge to any type of instrument that your synth can mimic.

All this makes long-distance collaboration a reality because the MIDI created on one sequencer will work in any other sequencer and in your DAW (if your DAW supports MIDI tracks as ACID Pro does).

This chapter shows just how powerful a tool MIDI is and hopefully dispels any doubt that you may have had about MIDI being a useful and legitimate tool for your recording work.

Recording Electric Keyboards, Guitars, and Basses

One of the technologies that, along with MIDI, has really blasted the home recording market wide open involves amplifier emulation (amp emulation). The bulk of this chapter focuses on this powerful technology. As a guitar player, this for me personally is one of the most exciting areas of home recording.

Now that you've got your drums in place using the techniques you learned in Chapters 6, "Creating Drum Tracks," and 7, "Utilizing MIDI in Your Projects," you've got a solid base on which to build the rest of your song.

In this chapter, we'll concentrate on electric and electronic instruments. Specifically, you'll learn some great techniques for recording keyboard audio (as opposed to keyboard-generated MIDI as described in Chapter 7) and electric guitars and basses.

During the course of this chapter, you'll review the techniques involved in recording an audio track, including input routing and input monitoring. You'll also exploit the power of amp emulation technologies and learn to add audio effects to your tracks in the process.

In most of the discussion in this chapter, I'll refer to recording an electric guitar, mainly so I don't have to keep writing "electronic keyboard and electric guitar or bass." However, keep in mind that most of the techniques I discuss here are equally applicable to—or at least quite similar to—an electric bass and the audio outputs of an electronic keyboard.

Essentially, we're talking about recording the audio output of an electric instrument. Though the details may vary for different instruments, the basics of how you approach the task are pretty much the same no matter what electric instrument you're recording.

Recording an Amplifier with a Microphone

Assumption 4 from the Introduction to this book states that you aren't free to make unlimited amounts of noise during the recording process. But if that assumption doesn't apply to your situation, you may want to record your instrument with a microphone in front of the amplifier you play through.

Few would dispute the assertion that micing your amplifier gives the best, most natural recording results—*if* you have the right microphone and the skills to use it correctly. Still, if the lack of proper equipment or inexperience with technique prevents you from achieving an optimal microphone recording, you may actually get better results by eliminating the microphone and using one of the techniques we'll discuss later in the chapter to record your instrument. There are several issues (besides the neighbors, your sleeping family members, and the dog howling at the moon) to consider when recording your instrument's amplifier with a microphone.

> **NOTE**
>
> Of course, if you have the facilities to record through a microphone but lack the experience, making a few mistakes is not a bad thing. You can learn something new each time you set up a microphone. On the other hand, if you avoid using the microphone, you'll never learn how to do it properly. The moral of that story is that if you want to record with a microphone but lack experience, go for it and gain the experience! After all, you can't learn to play a new song without honking out a few stinker notes along the way. And you can't master proper micing technique without learning from mistakes you make along that path either.

> **NOTE**
>
> Since microphone selection and technique is really outside the basic scope of this book, I'm going to leave any detailed discussion or specific recommendations for the experts. You can find tons of information online and in other books.

Microphone Selection

As discussed back in Chapter 6, microphone quality and selection play an important role. A good, sturdy dynamic microphone (like the ubiquitous Shure SM57 or SM58) is probably your best choice for an affordable mic that gives good results. Both of those microphones retail for somewhere around $100. Naturally, the more you're willing to pay, the more specialized and higher-quality microphone you can get, but lots of those two Sure microphone models are used in professional studios and stages all over the world.

Because the microphone you use to record your instrument strongly influences the recorded sound you achieve, I suggest conducting proper research on microphone selection. If you're going to buy a microphone for this purpose, don't just take the advice of the first buddy you talk to or the first website you find. Do the research, and get the most out of your purchase.

Microphone Placement

Microphone technique—particularly mic placement—once again plays a critical role in the character of the sound you'll achieve on your recording. Try all kinds of placement options. Set the microphone close to the amp's speaker and see how it sounds there. If there is more than one speaker cone in the cabinet, try it in front of one, then the other. Try pointing it to a space directly between two speaker cones.

Try different angles of the microphone in relation to the amp speaker. Point it straight on, and then angle it one way and the other. Try positioning the mic to the side, or maybe to the back of the amplifier to see what kind of sound you get in those positions.

Now move the mic different distances away from the amplifier. You'll be surprised how different an amp can sound with the mic 3 feet away instead of 3 inches away.

Add another microphone to the setup and give them different placement. Then combine their recordings in your DAW to see if you can find a combination that works for you.

In short, unless you have lots of experience micing your amplifier, you'll be well served spending a good deal of time experimenting with mic placement.

Amplifier Placement

Where you place your amplifier can also impact the sound you record. For instance, if you're recording with a quiet amplifier sound, room reflections may play a role in the sound you achieve. A loud amp tends to overpower the room reflections to a large extent, so location may not be as much of an issue if you're playing loud.

However, if your amp is very loud, you have a different placement issue to consider. If you're in the same room as the amp, you may not be able to monitor the sound adequately through your headphones. (Obviously, using your studio monitors would be out of the question since their output would be recorded back onto the microphone.)

If you simply must record with the amplifier turned up to 11 to get *your sound*, it's a good idea to put the amplifier in a different room. The more isolated the sound from the amp room is to your *control room* (a fancy term for where you're sitting while working with the DAW), the better you'll be able to hear through your monitoring system as opposed to hearing the amp itself. Remember, just because the amp sounds great doesn't mean that the recording is going to sound that way. You need to be able to monitor the recording so that you get a sense of what *it* sounds like as opposed to what the *amp* sounds like.

Recording Without a Microphone

Amp emulation creates sounds that mimic those made by guitar and other amplifiers. And they do so incredibly well. You can connect amp emulators directly to your computer to transfer the sound to your DAW while keeping the listening volume low. This completely eliminates the need for the microphone selection and placement techniques that we've just finished discussing. And, of course, that means it also eliminates all the issues associated with microphone recording. For the home studio, this technology is invaluable.

In addition, amp emulators give you a much greater range of possibilities than does microphone recording. How so? Well, if you're like most musicians, you have an amplifier for your instrument. You might even have two or three. But even if you have 10 amplifiers, you still can't match the flexibility of an amp emulator because the typical amp emulator mimics a huge array of different amps, speaker cabinets, and effects (reverb, echo, chorus, and so on). You can mix and match amps and cabinets for unique combinations and sounds. For instance, would you like to play your guitar through a Fender Twin Reverb amp but a Vox speaker cabinet? That could be a problem with real equipment, but it's no problem for any decent amp emulator.

Granted, this is emulation technology we're talking about. So it's not the real thing. To a purist, the difference could be noticeable—*maybe*. But for me, the problems this technology solves and the opportunities it provides for working quickly and efficiently outweigh my purist obsessions by a wide, wide margin. In fact, I haven't set up a real amp for recording since I bought my first amp emulator. I do all my recording through amp emulators now. In truth, it's not too much of a stretch to say that I have to credit my Johnson J-Station amp emulator for getting me back into the "studio" and getting my songs recorded once again after several years of recording inactivity.

A PIONEER IN EMULATION TECHNOLOGY

Funny how things work sometimes, isn't it? Months before I had conceived the idea of this book, I had a chance meeting with a pioneer in emulation technology. As I sat alone at the breakfast bar in Tiffy's Restaurant in Anaheim, California one morning before last winter's NAMM conference, another gentleman sat down beside me and struck up a conversation. It didn't take long for me to realize that this guy knew technical stuff that was way beyond me, and I soon fell into doing a lot more listening than talking.

The guy talked about digital audio, dynamic range, microphone technique, tube amplifier technology, and more. His name is Aspen Pittman, and he's the CEO and founder of Groove Tubes. After we both finished, he invited me to stop by his booth later at the show, which I did.

When I walked up to the Groove Tube booth, he was sitting in conversation with another guy, but he saw me and said, "I'd like to introduce you to Buck Dharma of Blue Öyster Cult." Well, that was kind of cool. We talked for a bit, and I went on my way.

Months later as I was writing this book, I thought about Mr. Pittman again and dropped him an email. I told him what I was doing and he wrote back, "By the way; did I mention that I invented speaker emulation technology? We used it to record Buck Dharma's lead guitar on [the smash Blue Öyster Cult hit single] *Don't Fear the Reaper*." With speaker emulation technology, you can run your regular guitar amp but bypass its speaker and use emulation instead for direct recording.

If I'd have known who I was talking to, I could have asked a whole lot more questions! If you want to know more about speaker emulation and all the other great products that Groove Tubes makes, check out their website at www.groovetubes.com.

Funny how things work sometimes, isn't it?

Hardware Amp Emulators

Hardware amp emulators are little boxes that literally take the place of your guitar amp in the studio setup. They have a number of knobs on them, some of which are basically the same as what you'd find on a real amp and others that aren't.

These boxes may be small, but they are feature rich. They contain digital amp emulation technology that enables you to dial up almost any amp sound imaginable and create some that have never been dreamed up before.

There are many different models and makers of amp emulators. I have two different ones. My first was the Johnson J-Station that I mentioned earlier. I also own the king of the heap, a PODxt from Line 6. Figure 8.1 shows both of these amp emulators.

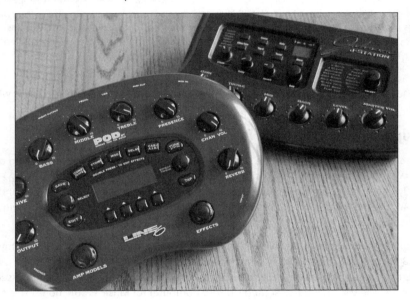

Figure 8.1

The Johnson J-Station and the Line 6 PODxt are two great guitar amp emulators that I use.

NOTE

Johnson amplification no longer makes the J-Station. Still, I mention the unit because (at least as of this writing) information and support for the J-Station still exists at the Johnson website (www.johnson-amp.com). So if you come across a used one, I wouldn't hesitate to pick it up if you can get a good price. I think I paid about $150 for mine new about five years ago, so that should give you some idea of what a fair price would be for a used one today.

Both of these units serve up great sound. The PODxt seems more full-featured and robust and has a better user interface. The controls and LED readout on the PODxt make its features easily accessible right from the unit. This makes it useful not only for recording but for playing live because you can use it as a preamp and effects box for your rig.

The J-Station has a deep features list, too, but it's a little harder to get to all of them from the hardware controls. However, both units come with a software component that you can load onto your computer. When you connect them to your computer (via our old friend MIDI), you can use the more intuitive software interface to control all of the unit's features.

NOTE

Both the J-Station and the PODxt enable you to communicate with your DAW via MIDI. (Remember; I told you that MIDI was a useful tool to understand!) They also both support an external pedal/switch board connection that you can use to control certain parameters of the units by stepping on switches or pedals, much like regular stomp boxes. You can use this stomp board to kick your distortion on and off at different times during your song or control the wha-wha effect much as you would with a regular wha pedal.

Still, if you just want to plug in, dial in a sound, and play your guitar, you can do that easily with either unit.

Setting Up the PODxt to Record a Track

I'm going to use my PODxt to record one of my guitar parts on the song I've been working on so that I can walk you through setting up and using an amp emulator. Though the controls on my J-Station are certainly different from those on my PODxt, once the signal leaves the unit's outputs and come into my DAW, the techniques I use to record them are identical. The same is true for you with any amp emulator you choose.

The PODxt has a USB output on the back that enables me to connect it directly to one of my computer's USB ports. It also comes with its own ASIO drivers. In other words, after I install the drivers, my PODxt acts not only as a guitar amp emulator but as an audio interface device. (We discussed audio interfaces extensively in Chapter 3, "Setting Up Your Computer for Music Production.") This gives me a digital path back to my computer and DAW, which saves me the step of converting the PODxt's digital output to analog to send it out the line outputs and then back to digital when it gets to my computer. This also avoids the potential for resulting noise.

A SPECIALIZED AUDIO INTERFACE

Although the PODxt can serve as your audio interface, it is limited in that regard in that it has only one 1/4-inch input jack. Line 6 makes several other amp emulators/audio interfaces that include XLR jacks (the jacks used by professional microphones) so you can also use them for recording vocals or other acoustic sources. For example, the company's TonePort line features both 1/4-inch and XLR input jacks. The TonePort line uses software amp emulation as opposed to the hardware circuitry that the PODxt uses. We'll talk more about software amp emulators a bit later.

Remember, you can also use the PODxt for live performance because it does all its emulation inside the hardware's circuitry. However, the TonePort line can be useful because you could conceivably use a TonePort as your sole audio interface.

I suggest that if you're on a tight budget, look into the TonePort line since the price of entry is lower than a PODxt. But if you want the best quality and can afford to spend more, or if you intend to use your amp emulator on stage as well as in the studio, look to the PODxt. Just remember that you'll need to buy that and a more robust audio interface that includes XLR inputs.

If you've installed your PODxt's drivers, connected it via the USB connection, and turned it on, you're ready to record. In ACID Pro, choose Options, Preferences and click the Audio Device tab. Click the Audio Device Type drop-down list. Figure 8.2 shows my Audio Device Type list; you can see that it now lists the ASIO PODxt drivers. Choose those drivers from the list, and click OK to close the Preferences dialog box.

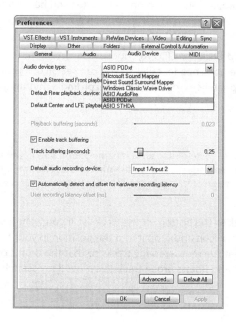

Figure 8.2

Choose the ASIO PODxt drivers from the Audio Device Type list to use your PODxt as your computer's audio interface while you record your guitar parts.

Since you're now using the PODxt as your audio interface, you'll have to monitor the audio through that device. The easiest way to do this is to plug into the PODxt's headphone jack, but you could also connect your studio monitors to the PODxt's left and right output jacks and listen through those.

NOTE

You don't have to make your PODxt act as an audio interface device if you don't want to. Instead, you can simply plug the right and left outputs of the PODxt into two inputs of your audio interface and record the signal coming from those. Just keep in mind that when you do this, you're introducing an extra digital-to-analog conversion coming out of the PODxt and then another analog-to-digital conversion going into your computer. As you learned in Chapter 3, these conversion steps can potentially add noise to your recordings.

In reality, the PODxt's DA/AD converters are probably high enough in quality that they don't add appreciable noise. The same hopefully holds true for your audio interface. So, maybe you don't need to worry too much about it. But nonetheless, if you want to skip the conversions altogether, set up the PODxt as an audio interface device via its USB connection.

Play your project just to make sure you can hear it through the PODxt. If you've got everything set up correctly, you can play the project, play along on your guitar, and hear both in the headphones.

Recording Your Track

Now let's get ready to record. Back In ACID Pro, choose Insert, Audio Track to add the track you're going to record to. Make the track header taller so you can see all of its controls, and in the scribble strip, name the track appropriately. In my case, I'll be recording a rhythm guitar part, so I'll call the track Rhythm Electric.

TIP

For a number of reasons, it's helpful to always name your tracks in the scribble strip. One of the main reasons is that when you record onto the track, ACID Pro automatically appends the track's name onto the name of the recorded file. That helps you keep your files straight.

ACID Pro adds the new track to the bottom of the track list. If you want it somewhere else in the list, drag it by the numbered track icon and drop it into the position in your track list that works for you. You can see in Figure 8.3 that I've reordered my tracks so that the drums come first, then my new (still empty) rhythm guitar track, and Brian's organ track. I've moved my scratch vocal and guitar tracks to the bottom of the list.

TIP

Personally, I get kind of particular about the order of the tracks in my projects; I like to have certain tracks in specific positions. That may seem like a picky detail, but it really helps from project to project to know exactly where in the track list you'll find each particular instrument track. This is especially true as you add more and more tracks to your projects. The less time you have to spend searching the list for a track, the sooner you can get on with your work.

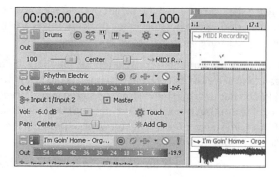

Figure 8.3

Arrange the tracks in your project in an order that makes it easy for you to find the track you want to work on.

I don't want my scratch guitar track to influence my playing while I'm recording my new track, yet I don't want to remove it from my project either since it can serve as a valuable reference. Since ACID Pro can support unlimited tracks, there's no real reason that I have to remove the scratch track just yet (although I may want to later when I'm sure I no longer need it).

To leave the scratch track in your project but not have it influence you while you play your new part, you'll have to take its audio out of your headphone mix. We'll talk much more extensively about mixing techniques later in Chapter 10, "Mixing Your Song," but in reality the mixing process pretty much starts as soon as you start accumulating tracks. In this case, we'll use a mixing tool called *track mute* to remove the track's audio output from the mix while keeping the track in the project.

If you need to, scroll down in the track list until you can see the scratch guitar track on your timeline. Each track header has a Mute button. Click the Mute button for the scratch track. As you can see in Figure 8.4, ACID Pro uses a dark shading to indicate that the track has been muted. Play your project and notice that even though the track is still in your project, you can no longer hear what's on it.

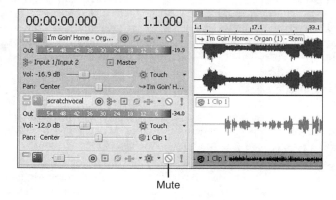

Mute

Figure 8.4

The scratch guitar track in my project (Track 5) has been muted and its track height minimized.

You can also see in Figure 8.4 that I've adjusted the height of the track to be as small as possible so that it takes up the least amount of space possible in my track list. This is another technique that you'll appreciate as your project's track list grows larger and larger.

Now you're ready to record. Click the Arm for Record button for your new rhythm guitar track. Make the track taller if you need to to see all of its controls. Click the Record Input button and choose ASIO PODxt from the list. The PODxt has only one input, but it's a stereo input, so you have to choose whether you want to record the output of one of the channels or both. Some of the effects that you can apply through the PODxt are stereo effects, so if you want to preserve the stereo nature of those effects, choose Input 1/Input 2 from the list.

Keep in mind that recording a stereo file takes up twice the storage space as recording a mono file. Thus, if hard disc storage space is running low and you can't free up more space or buy more, you might want to sacrifice the stereo effects in the interest of keeping the size of your recorded files down.

You won't need ACID Pro to supply input monitoring for this track since you're monitoring it through the PODxt, so leave the input monitoring mode set to off.

Now play your guitar and check the level of the track's input meter. Make the input as loud as possible. (If you're using the PODxt like I am, you control the level sent to your DAW with the PODxt's Chan Vol knob.) Remember not to let the input meter clip. If clipping occurs, lower the input level until the clipping stops. If you need a refresher on the issue of digital clipping, refer to Chapter 5, "Creating Your Guide Tracks."

Now you're ready to roll. Grab your guitar (make sure to tune it using your amp emulator's built-in tuner!), click the Record button in ACID Pro, and play along. When you're done recording, click the Stop button.

CONTROLLING GUITAR HUM

As you probably know, lots of electric and electronic things can cause an annoying hum or buzz in your electric guitar—particularly if your guitar uses single-coil pickups. Your computer's cathode ray tube (CRT) monitor can be one of the worst culprits. You can minimize the hum by facing your guitar in various directions, but if you just can't get rid of it (or at least minimize it) no matter which way you face, you might try turning off your CRT while you record. Just use your CRT's power button to turn it off.

Doing so makes it impossible to see where your mouse is on the screen and thus makes it pretty darned hard to find the Record button when you want to start recording. You can get around this by setting your metronome countoff to two or even four measures. That way you can start recording, and while the metronome is running through its countoff, you have time to switch your CRT off and still get set to play. (You can refresh your memory on the use of the metronome in Chapter 5.)

However, if (like Scott and I did when we recorded our MIDI drums for "I'm Goin' Home") you decided not to record to a metronome, having the countoff may throw your timing off. In that case, leave the metronome countoff disengaged, turn your CRT off, and use the keyboard shortcut Ctrl+R to start Recording. When you're done recording, use the spacebar to stop recording. Then you can hit your CRT's power button to turn it back on.

When you stop recording, the Recorded Files dialog comes up, as you can see in Figure 8.5. Notice that the filename that ACID Pro gives the new file contains both the name of the project and the name of the track that was recorded onto. You can rename the file if you want to, or just click Done to accept the name ACID Pro gives it.

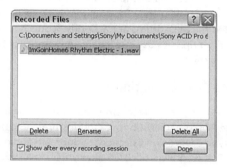

Figure 8.5

The Recorded Files dialog box enables you to make some decisions about the file you just recorded, including whether you want to rename it.

The track now contains an event that holds the waveform of the file you just created. Notice that this event actually has two waveforms. This indicates that you've recorded a stereo file. Notice that every ACID Pro audio track can hold stereo files, mono files, and even a mixture of the two. Play the project to listen to your performance. In Chapter 9, "Recording Things That Require Microphones," we'll talk about your options if you're not totally happy with your performance. For now, let's say you're happy with what you've just recorded. Click the Arm for Record button for your new track to disarm it. To listen to my song with the new rhythm guitar part in it, play the file ImGoinHome_newRhythmGuit from the Chapter 08 folder on the companion disc.

KNOWING YOUR PARTS

Some musicians will have the parts they want to play figured out before they ever sit down to record. That's a commendable talent, but it doesn't have to be the only way to work. Another approach is to sit down with your scratch tracks recorded and your guitar (or instrument of choice) in hand. Play the scratch tracks, and then start playing along on your guitar. Eventually, something resembling a guitar part begins to form. When it gets close enough to something that you think you might want to keep, start recording.

That's pretty much the way I work most of the time. Because you don't have the part solidified, you're really using your DAW as a scratch pad. Just throw down ideas, keep the ones you like, and ditch the others.

In my projects it's not at all unusual to have my final take be the 30th take or even higher. I'll have to admit that some of those takes had to be redone because I didn't like the way I played something (read that: I made a playing mistake), but most of those extra takes are a result of experimentation during the process of developing a part.

One of the great things about using a DAW is that you have unlimited tracks and you never have to worry about the tape wearing out as you record and play it over and over again. That means you can experiment all you want and never have to worry that your final audio quality will be compromised.

Software Amp Emulators

Although I really love my PODxt and my Johnson J-Station, hardware amp emulators are not the only option. I also make extensive use of software amp emulation. For me, the advantage to using software emulators basically boils down to convenience. Especially if you're taking your recording setup on the road (like I did when I recorded the MIDI drums at my buddy Scott's house), it's nice to have one less piece of gear to lug along and set up. Let's use a software amp emulator to record another part. I'll record a lead guitar part for my song.

Setting Up Your Software Amp Emulation

Because you're not using the PODxt for this recording, you'll need to switch back to your other audio device (if you switched to the PODxt earlier). Choose Options, Preferences and click the Audio Device tab. From the Audio Device Type drop-down list, choose your main audio device's ASIO drivers. I'll switch back to my AudioFire 8 ASIO drivers. Click OK. Now you'll do all your audio monitoring through your main audio device again.

For software amp emulation, we turn back to the virtual studio technology (VST) that we first talked about when we discovered the power of Soft Synths in Chapter 7. In this case, however, we won't be using VST instruments (VSTi). Instead, we'll use another form of VST, the VST audio plug-in.

YOUR DAW AND AUDIO PLUG-INS

Any good DAW software will probably support two types of audio plug-in that you can utilize for advance digital signal processing (DSP) tasks: DirectX technology and VST. This is great news, because it means that your DAW can use any of the myriad DSP plug-ins available on the market today. ACID Pro has many DirectX plug-ins included with the software's installation and can support other plug-ins of both DirectX and VST.

As you gain experience with your DAW, you'll discover new ways to use DSP, and you'll be extremely grateful that you can use these plug-ins over and over again in the same project without having to go out and buy the plug-in again, like you used to have to with hardware signal processing units.

You'll utilize both DirectX and VST plug-ins throughout the remainder of this book not only in this chapter but in Chapter 10 and Chapter 11, "Mastering Your Song," so it will really pay off to learn how to use them now.

Several software manufactures sell VST software amp emulators. I'm going to use the one that ships with ACID Pro 7, the Guitar Combo VST plug-in from Native Instruments, but you can use the techniques I show here with any VST amp emulator.

First, just like the VSTi Soft Synths that we used earlier, you'll need to install the VST plug-in on your system. Then use the Plug-In Manager as discussed in Chapter 7 to make sure ACID Pro can locate your VST plug-ins.

Setting Up ACID Pro to Use Your Software Amp Emulator

You're going to need another track to hold the lead guitar, so choose Insert, Audio Track. Name the track, and reposition it as we discussed earlier in this chapter. I've positioned mine under the rhythm guitar track I just recorded.

Arm the track for recording, and route its input device setting to the input on your audio interface that you've plugged your guitar into. Since you're no longer monitoring your guitar through your amp emulator, click the Record Input button and choose Input Monitor Mode: On from the drop-down list. You can now hear your guitar.

Now, let's run it through a VST amp emulator. Every audio track in your ACID Pro project has an effects chain. You can run up to 32 effects plug-ins on this chain, so you can see that you have quite a bit of DSP power on every track. VST amp emulators work as part of this chain.

To add a plug-in, click the Track FX button on the track header for your lead guitar track. You can see the Track FX button in Figure 8.6.

Figure 8.6

You access the track's effects chain with the Track FX button.

This opens the Audio Plug-In window. The window contains one plug-in already: the Track EQ plug-in, which you can see in Figure 8.7. The Track EQ plug-in (EQ stands for equalization) gives you a tool to use in manipulating the frequencies of the audio on this track. We'll talk more about EQs in Chapter 11. For now, just leave the settings of this EQ as they are.

NOTE

Because EQ is such a common plug-in to apply to a track, ACID Pro adds the plug-in for you automatically. This saves you the step of having to add it yourself. If you don't want EQ on your track, you can remove the plug-in from the chain. But, in reality, you don't need to worry about it. The default settings have no effect whatsoever on the track's audio, so you can leave the plug-in in the chain and just ignore it. Don't worry; it doesn't make any demands on your computer's processing power unless you change its settings.

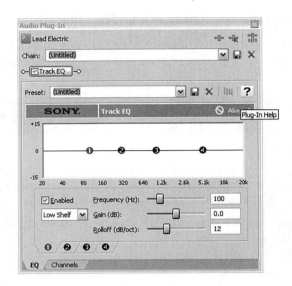

Figure 8.7
The Audio Plug-In window shows the Track EQ plug-in that exists on every audio track.

As I said, you can add up to 32 effects to the chain for each track, and in this case you're going to add your VST amp emulator as one of those effects. To do so, click the Edit Chain button in the Audio Plug-In window. This opens the Plug-In Chooser window. In the list at the left side of the window, click the VST folder icon. The contents of the folder appear on the right, and you see the VST amp emulators there.

I'm going to try the Plexi Combo VST first. Select that from the list at the right, and click the Add button to add that effect to the chain. Figure 8.8 shows my Plug-In Chooser window with the VST now in the effects chain at the top. Click the OK button to close the Plug-In Chooser window.

When the Plug-In Chooser window closes, the Audio Plug-In window changes to show the interface for the amp emulator VST that you've added to the chain. Figure 8.9 shows the VST's interface.

One nice thing about software guitar amp emulators is that it can be easy to choose preset sounds. Click the Preset List drop-down arrow to scroll through a list of preset sounds. Choose a different sound and play your guitar. Try all the presets until you find one you like. You can also click the Show/Hide Preset List button to see the entire list at a glance. (Drag the bottom edge of the Audio Plug-Ins window if you need to make it bigger to see the entire list.)

Plug-in Chain

VST Amp Emulator Plug-in

Available VST Plug-ins

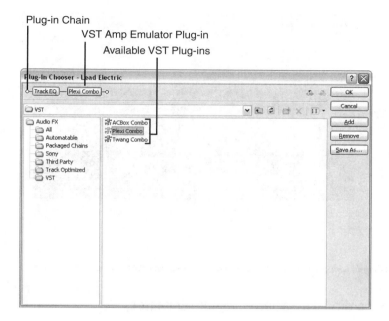

Figure 8.8

Your VST amp emulators appear in the list of VST plug-ins.

Figure 8.9

The guitar amp emulator plug-in's interface looks like the front of a classic guitar amplifier.

If you can't find the exact sound you want in the preset list, use the knobs and switches to dial in just what you're looking for. When you find the sound you want, you can either leave the Audio Plug-In window open (either floating or docked in the window docking area) or close it. Figure 8.10 shows that I've docked mine in the window docking area so that I can quickly make any necessary adjustments.

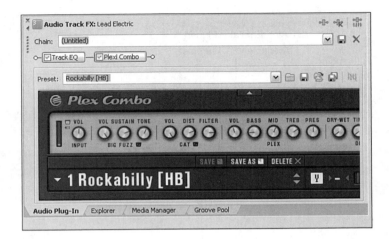

Figure 8.10

Dock the Audio Plug-In window in the window docking area to keep it accessible but out of the way.

Results of Recording with a Software Amp Emulator

With the Audio Plug-In window out of the way, you're ready to record. Click the Record button and play your part. When you're done, click the Stop button.

Another cool thing about using a VST software amp emulator relates to the way ACID Pro (and maybe your DAW) records the signal. You've added the amp emulator to the audio effects chain for the track. When you play, you hear the effects of the plug-in. But interestingly, the plug-in is part of the *playback* signal flow and not the *recording* signal flow. So the recording is actually dry (meaning it has no effects on it). The effects are added during playback.

That means that you can listen to the dry guitar track you recorded and hear what it sounds like without the VST amp emulation. If you don't still have the Audio Track-FX window open, click the Track FX button for the lead guitar track to reopen it. Notice that the plug-in chain across the top contains the Track EQ and the amp emulation plug-in. Each of these has a green check in its check box, indicating that the plug-in is active. Deselect the check box for the amp emulation VST. This bypasses the plug-in. Play your project to hear how the guitar track sounds dry.

What's even cooler is that you can change the guitar sound to see if you can find something you like better. Select the VST amp emulator's check box again to reactivate the plug-in and play the project. As it plays, select different presets from the amp emulators preset list. Make changes to the knobs and controls in the amp emulator. As you do all of this, you hear the changes in real time. Keep experimenting until you find the sound you like.

TIP

As you add more tracks to your project, you might find that it doesn't play back during recording without the occasional glitch or stutter. That only has to happen once to ruin a good take, and it's always frustrating. If this happens to you, try increasing the buffer size in your audio device's software settings. Increase the buffer size in small increments to find the lowest setting that gives you solid simultaneous playback and record. If you set the buffer too high, you'll probably start to experience unacceptable latency where you hear the sounds you make considerably later than you make them. You can't record well that way either!

To hear the lead part I came up with for my song, play the file ImGoinHome_TwoGuitars.wav from the Chapter 08 folder on the companion disc.

SWITCHING SOUNDS IN THE MIDDLE OF A TRACK

You might notice when you listen to my lead guitar track that I use two different tones on it. One of the tones is dirtier (more distorted) than the other. That brings up the question, "How do I change the tone on my amp emulator when I'm playing?" If you were playing through your amp, you'd just hit your foot switch when you wanted the distortion to kick in, but if the amp emulator is supplying the distortion, how can you do that?

Well, there are a few techniques you can use. First, I already mentioned earlier in this chapter that amp emulators often feature optional pedal boards you can use to control the parameter settings of the emulator just as you do with your real amp and foot switches.

Another strategy is to just run a clean sound out of your emulator and then use all your outboard foot pedals to add the effects you want.

If neither of these is an option, you can fake it. Since you have unlimited tracks, record onto two separate tracks: one with the effect you want and one without.

Finally, if you're using a software emulator, you can do what I did with my lead track. First, record the entire track with one tone. Then right-click the track header for the track you recorded and choose Duplicate Track from the pop-up menu. This duplicates everything on the track, including the event you just recorded and the amp emulator VST. Change the settings on the duplicate track's VST to the sound you want, and then delete the portions of the events on each track that you don't want. (You can use the same split and edit techniques you learned in Chapter 7.) When you're done, you'll have an alternating pattern where the first track plays a section with one sound and the second track plays different sections with the other sound.

Tricky. And it points out a strength of software amp emulators because, as I mentioned earlier, you can change your sounds after the fact if you want to.

Recording Your Bass

You can use many of the same techniques for recording your bass as those we've just discussed for recording guitars. You can find amp emulators that have been developed specifically to emulate bass amps. Some emulators give you both guitar and bass sounds. For instance, my Johnson J-Station has at least two bass amp models along with all the guitar amp models. If you're looking to achieve a specific sound that you know you can get from a certain bass rig, a bass-oriented amp emulator is probably the way for you to go.

However, I've never seen any reason why I can't run my bass through my PODxt just to see what I can come up with. You might want to check your emulator's documentation to verify that it won't suffer damage if you run a bass through it, but I've never seen anything to indicate that it would.

If you don't want to run through an amp emulator, you can buy Direct Input (DI) boxes to boost the signal of your bass so that you can record directly. Also, many audio interfaces feature at least one or two instrument-level inputs. These inputs are made specifically to boost the weak signal from a guitar or bass so that you can record directly into the audio interface without first going through a DI or amp emulator. I often record my bass parts this way.

Now that you know how to add effects to the track effects chain, you can add EQ, track compression, and any other effect that you have on your system to shape the sound of the bass to your liking. (We'll talk more about these effects in Chapters 10 and 11.)

The procedure for actually recording the bass (once you've decided how you want to get the sound into your DAW) is exactly the same as that you followed earlier for recording your guitars. Namely, insert a new track, arm it for recording, route it to the audio interface input into which you've connected the instrument, and click the Record button.

I used my J-station amp emulator to record the bass for my track. To hear my track with the bass line I recorded, play the file ImGoinHome_Bass.wav from the Chapter 08 folder on the companion disc.

Recording Keyboard Audio

We discussed using MIDI to create keyboard tracks in Chapter 7. But you don't have to use MIDI to record your keyboard parts. You can also record with a microphone in front of your keyboard's speakers (or in front of the keyboard itself if it's an acoustic instrument like a piano). If your keyboard has line outputs, you can connect those outputs directly to the inputs of your audio interface. Most electronic keyboards have stereo line outputs, so you'll connect those to two line inputs of your audio interface.

CAUTION

Make sure to see whether your keyboard outputs serve up line level or instrument level. If they are line level, don't plug them into the same instrument-level inputs that you used for your bass. They could overpower the more sensitive instrument-level inputs and cause damage to your audio interface. Always make sure to match your line-level outputs to line-level inputs on your audio interface and instrument-level outputs to instrument-level inputs on your audio interface.

After you've plugged it all in, the procedure for recording the tracks in your DAW is again the same as the one you learned for recording your guitars earlier in this chapter. If your keyboard does have stereo outputs and you've plugged both of them into your audio interface, choose the appropriate stereo pair of inputs when you're setting up your input routing so that you record a stereo track.

TIP

Lots of keyboardists are discovering the wonders of amp emulation. They're running their keyboard outputs through emulators and applying guitar amp sounds to them. You can achieve lots of interesting sounds and effects by recording your keyboards this way. Give it a try and see what you can come up with.

Studio Log

Amplifier emulation technology is one of the most important components of the modern digital home recording setup. Amp emulation makes it possible to get those big, fat, rich, and nasty guitar sounds that used to be attainable only through lots and lots of volume. But they also give you access to smooth jazzy tones, spacey swirling sounds, and any other sound you can conceive.

The built-in amp and speaker cabinet models that these units come with, along with the variety of effects pedals and stomp box emulations, make these (along with MIDI) perhaps the most versatile pieces of equipment in your studio. Without amp emulation technology, access to so many different amps and cabinets and the sounds they produce has never been remotely affordable.

Amp emulators come in either hardware or software configurations. And some come in a combination of hardware and software that enables you to use your amp emulator as a high-quality audio interface.

While most amp emulation targets the guitar player, many manufacturers also include models created specifically for bass players who want to emulate popular bass rigs. Keyboardists, too, are utilizing amp emulation to achieve both classic and innovative new sounds.

9

Recording Things That Require Microphones

In this chapter, we talk more about recording techniques such as multiple takes and punch-in recording. We'll discuss recording vocals with a live mic and talk a bit more about some of the challenges that arise whenever you turn a microphone on in your recording space and how to overcome them.

As I walk you through recording the vocals for the song I've been working on throughout this book, you'll learn how to handle the fact that you don't always get it right the first time. But just because you've made a mistake in one part of your recording doesn't mean you have to throw the whole thing out and start again. Instead, you'll want to know how to fix the bad part while keeping the good parts—a technique known as *punch-in recording*. You'll learn a couple of different punch-in recording techniques in this chapter.

Getting Ready to Record Vocals

I'm focusing here on recording vocals mainly because 1) that's what I've got left to do on my song and 2) you'll most likely need to record vocals for your music, too. However, what we talk about here really can apply to recording pretty much anything that you can't record any other way. For instance, if your song requires an acoustic guitar and you don't have a nice electronic pickup that yields a sound you're happy with, you're going to have to record it with a microphone. You can apply what you learn here to that task, too.

NOTE

Of course, micing techniques like selection and placement (which we've talked about at various times throughout the past few chapters) are naturally going to differ depending on what you're recording. I've never recorded an acoustic harp or a tuba, but I'm confident in saying that the mic one would use and the placement of that mic will be quite different between the two! In other words, you'll have to do a little extra research to find out just how to mic the instrument you'll be working with.

INSTRUMENTALS ARE COOL!

If your situation just won't allow for recording with a microphone, don't give up hope on recording music! A few years ago, I found myself in a situation where I couldn't make anything but the most modest noise at the times I could carve out for recording. But I was determined to get a project done. So I set about recording an electric-guitar-driven instrumental just to put some of these (then new to me) recording techniques to the test.

After recording one instrumental song, I was inspired to keep going. I ended up recording a CD's worth of instrumentals. Sort of like the surf instrumentals of the 1960s, but not quite. I called them "Hot-Rod" instrumentals and gave them all muscle-car-themed titles. Okay, maybe it sounds corny to you, maybe it doesn't. But the point is, I had a great time, ended up with a good body of work, and learned a lot about these recording techniques.

Vocals are fun, that's true. But you don't have to have them to make great music. If your situation doesn't allow for recording vocals, stretch your instrumental creativity and see what you can produce. Just be prepared for one of the most common reactions I received: "Cool Song. When are you going to put the words in it?" Sigh…

Blocking Out Audio Reflections

We talked quite a bit about the challenges involved with microphone recording in Chapter 2, "Setting Up Your Recording Studio Space," so I'm not going to go over much of that information again. However, there are a couple of tips I want to share with you that I didn't mention there.

You might not be able to find a space in which you can line the walls with diffusion and sound absorption panels. But you'll somehow have to deal with those audio reflections coming back to your microphone. One thing you can do is to build a temporary sound booth. It sounds more official than it really has to be.

Just find some sound-absorbing materials (like the ones we talked about in Chapter 2) and find a way to build a temporary structure around your microphone. For instance, you could hang a heavy blanket from a door frame, sticking tacks through it and then into the top of the door frame where no one will see the holes you leave behind. Hang another heavy blanket over the door itself. (Again, try sticking the tacks in the top of the door to hide the holes, use a couple of clamps to hold it, or just hang enough over the other side of the door that it doesn't fall.) Close the door partially, and you've created an angle lined with sound absorption.

Place your microphone in the angle so that you'll be singing into the corner of the blanket "walls" and not directly at the face of either of them, like I've done in Figure 9.1. Now when you sing, the blankets will stop much of the audio reflection that would have occurred if you'd sung in a room with blank walls.

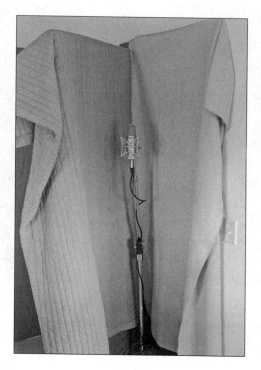

Figure 9.1

It's either a bad decorating scheme or one of Buster's crazy temporary sound booths!

Perfect solution? Clearly not. But it's definitely a creative way to make a bad situation a little bit better.

Here's another idea that might work for you. Find a few sound-absorbing panels (professional panels or even just a few squares of foam rubber) and create a small box around your microphone. Again, it doesn't have to be elaborate; it just has to be something that you can sing into that will soak up the sound and stop those nasty audio reflections. And it doesn't necessarily need to be closed on all sides to be effective. The point is, just build an absorbing barrier between those walls and your microphone. Figure 9.2 shows an example of what I'm talking about.

Figure 9.2

I've used foam panels to create a simple sound barrier that stops a surprising amount of audio reflections from getting into my recordings.

These are just two ideas that might work. The point is, look around your room and figure out how you're going to put your microphone into a "dead" space where the audio reflections don't overpower your recording.

TIP

Before you go to all the trouble of deadening the audio reflections in your space, listen to your room, as we discussed in Chapter 2. Maybe you'll get lucky and find yourself a room in which the reflections *add to* the quality of your recordings rather than *detract from* it. Bathrooms often give great reverb sounds because of all the highly reflective surfaces. You'll have to be the judge of whether that reverb works for your recording—or if you can tolerate singing next to that shower you haven't scrubbed for far too long!

Taming the Plosives

Some of the sounds you make when you speak are more aggressive than others. For instance, you make the sound of the letter *m* with a nice, gentle humming. On the other hand, you make *p* and *b* sounds by building up breath behind your closed lips and letting that air out in a sudden burst. Such sounds are known as *plosives*, as in explosive, because the air comes exploding out of your lips to make the sound. When you sing, the plosives are even more aggressive.

So what? Well, when those sudden bursts of air hit your microphone, they can create an unpleasant popping sound that gets recorded to your vocal track. You can combat the noise made by your plosives in a couple of different ways.

First, you can keep more distance between your mouth and the microphone. This is often difficult to do, because you generally want to be consistent about how far off the mic you are. If you vary your distance too much during a recording, you may end up with uneven volume levels throughout your song, and that makes your job more difficult when you reach the mixing stage (which we'll talk about in Chapter 10, "Mixing Your Song").

Also, the farther you are from the microphone, the louder you'll have to turn up the input of the microphone to get a good recording volume. And, of course, the louder you turn up the microphone, the more audio it picks up. This includes not only the desirable audio (your voice), but also the undesirable audio like the room reflections, refrigerator hum, and dog barking across the street.

So while you don't want to be so close that you cause your plosives to make the mic pop, you don't want to be too far away either.

THE PROXIMITY EFFECT

Your distance from the mic will also affect the sound of your recorded voice. In general, the closer you are to the microphone, the more bass heavy the resulting recording will be. It's called the *proximity effect*. It's not necessarily bad that your voice would sound more bass heavy, but it is something to keep in mind.

Distance can also make a difference when you're recording instruments because the sound doesn't come from just one place on an instrument. Instead, it sort of emanates from all parts of the instrument (some instruments more than others). Therefore, if you get too close, you may focus too narrowly on one part of the instrument and thus miss out on some of its subtleties.

You can see then why it's important to experiment with mic placement.

To help with the problem of plosives, you can use a pop screen. A *pop screen* is a thin piece of material that you'll sing through. It's not thick enough to affect or muffle the sound of your voice, but it's thick enough to disperse those bursts of air that explode from your lips as you're singing.

Some pop screens attach directly over the end of the microphone. These, however, are generally less effective than freestanding pop screens.

Naturally, you can buy commercially manufactured freestanding pop screens like the one in Figure 9.3. These are nice because they come with a handy clamp that you can use to attach them to your microphone stand. The clamp is then attached to an arm (often a flexible gooseneck arm) that holds the pop screen on the other end. The arm enables you to position the screen between your face and your microphone.

Figure 9.3
Commercially manufactured pop screens look tidy and attach conveniently to your microphone stand.

You can also make your own pop screen, and it'll work just as effectively. Just fashion a frame (a wire hanger bent into a rough circle or square works great) and stretch a piece of nylon stocking over it tightly. Use safety pins or some other fastener to hold the nylon stocking in place. Then devise some method of holding your homemade pop screen between you and your mic, and you're all set.

TIP

A large darning hoop makes a great frame to hold the nylon stocking in place. If you have one on hand, you can use that. However, before you buy one, check the price of a commercial pop screen, because it might not be a whole lot more expensive. I recently picked up a perfectly serviceable pop screen with a flexible goose neck and a clamp that I can use to secure the pop screen to my mic stand. I paid about $20.

Another nice thing about using a pop screen is that you can use it to maintain a consistent distance between your mouth and mic. Don't place the pop screen right next to the microphone, because that will likely defeat its purpose. Leave a few inches of space between the two so that the air blast has time to disperse before it hits the microphone.

Choosing the Microphone

The microphone you use to record your vocals has a huge impact on the perceived quality of your recordings. Because your vocals are naturally a focal point of the song for the listener, you have to make them shine. Therefore, if you have a little extra to spend on your gear, this is not a bad place to spend it.

But, of course, not all of us have that little extra to spend, so what do you do? Well, you can't go too far wrong with a Shure SM58 dynamic microphone. It seems like just about every band in the world has at least one of these workhorses, and they aren't all that expensive. (You can get them new for $100 or less if you watch the sales.) If you can afford only one microphone, take a serious look at the SM58 because it's durable, dependable, and versatile. And it sounds good to great for a variety of instruments and vocals.

CAN I REALLY USE MY SM58 FOR STUDIO VOCALS?

You might have noticed over the past few chapters that the Shure SM58 microphone keeps popping up as a recommendation. Almost everyone uses an SM58 for live vocals on stage at one time or another in their careers. They're great for live vocals. But can they really be acceptable for studio work?

Some might scoff at the idea and insist that you need a much more high-end microphone. Although I've never been in the studio with either of them, I've read more than once that both Mick Jagger and Bono have used SM58s in studio for their vocals. Clearly, those are two guys who can afford any microphone they want—two of each, in fact! Yet, they've chosen to use the 58. I guess they must know something about it. So, I don't care what the big-shot engineers at your town's hippest studio say; go ahead and use your SM58 for studio vocals. Tell 'em Bono said it was okay!

Of course, if you can spend a little more, you can find a variety of high-quality microphones that are designed specifically for studio vocal recording. I've been happy with RØDE microphones. This Australian company makes great-sounding mics that aren't excessively expensive. For vocals, I've used the RØDE NT-1A condenser mic, and I think it sounds great. I also have a Shure KSM44 condenser mic. It's a beautiful, rich-sounding microphone, though it's a bit on the high end of my budget (so I treat it gingerly!).

For recording the vocals on *I'm Going Home*, I decided to use the RØDE NT-1A so that you could hear what it sounds like. You can pick up one of these for around $225, and of course they also work great for things other than vocals. For example, try it on an acoustic guitar or cello. If you can afford to spend a little more than the $100 that an SM58 costs, the NT-1A is a great choice.

Ready, Set, Record!

We already discussed the basics of setting up to record a couple of times (most notably in Chapter 5, "Creating Your Guide Tracks." I'll just review the setup here so that we can get onto other helpful techniques.

TIP

You'll have a difficult time following this section if you haven't mastered the basic recording topics that I presented in Chapter 5. If you don't know those techniques yet, you'll be well served to revisit that chapter before you proceed with this one.

NOTE

The techniques we'll use in this section apply equally well to recording instruments as they do to recording vocals. You can also use them whether you're recording with a live microphone or any of the nonmicrophone recording techniques we've discussed.

Setting Up a Track for Recording in ACID Pro

First, connect your microphone to your audio interface. As we discussed in Chapter 5, my AudioFire 8 audio interface has two inputs on the front that can accept an XLR cable plugged into a professional microphone. The interface also has a trim knob for both of these inputs. Connect your microphone to one of the inputs on your audio interface.

In ACID Pro, choose Insert, Audio Track to add a new track to your project. Name the track (in the scribble strip) LeadVocal, and position the track where you want it in the track list. Click the LeadVocal track's Arm for Record button, and route its input to the jack that you've plugged the microphone into on your audio interface. Make noise into the microphone, and adjust the input level so that you have a nice strong signal without clipping.

NOTE

Don't forget that some microphones require an external power source. If this describes your microphone and your audio interface can supply phantom power, turn that on. If you don't have phantom power, you'll have to put a battery into your microphone to supply the power.

If your audio interface supplies input monitoring, turn that off. We'll let ACID Pro do the input monitoring. In the vocal track, click the Record Input button and choose Input Monitor Mode: On from the menu, as shown in Figure 9.4.

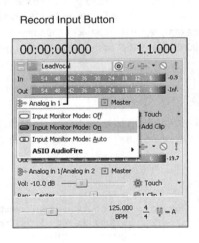

Record Input Button

Figure 9.4

Turn ACID Pro's input monitoring function on for the vocal track.

With ACID Pro's input monitoring on, you can add audio effects to the track's chain and listen to yourself sing with these effects applied to your voice. For instance, I like to add a reverb effect to the chain so that when I hear myself sing, it sounds like I'm in a bigger, more reflective room. This sounds more inspiring than listening to a completely dry vocal and helps me get into it more.

You learned how to add effects to a track in Chapter 8, "Recording Electric Keyboards, Guitars, and Basses," when you added the VST amp emulation plug-in to your guitar track. You use the same techniques to add a different plug-in to your vocal track (although you might find some interesting results if you ran your vocals through your amp emulator plug-in, too!). As you learned in that discussion, the effect you add does not get recorded into the file. Instead, the effect is applied at the playback stage. That means that you don't have to worry so much about what reverb you put on your track while you're recording, because you can always change it later (which you could do at the mixing stage, discussed in Chapter 10).

To add the reverb to your track, click the lead vocal track's Track FX button. In the Audio Plug-In window, click the Edit Chain button to open the Plug-In Chooser. Click the Sony folder in the list on the left, and choose the Reverb plug-in from the list on the right.

Or if you have other audio plug-ins that you'd rather use, choose one of those. For instance, on my computer, I've installed the Izotope Mastering plug-ins that ship with Sony Sound Forge 9 (which we'll use to master your project in Chapter 11, "Mastering Your Song"). Since those plug-ins were developed as DirectX plug-ins, they work in ACID Pro as well as Sound Forge, because both applications support the DirectX plug-in architecture. (We talked about DirectX technology in Chapter 8.) I want to use the Mastering Reverb plug-in from the Izotope package.

To use it, click the Third Party folder from the list on the left. Then select the Mastering Reverb plug-in from the list on the right, and click the Add button. Click OK to close the Plug-In Chooser. The Izotope Mastering Reverb plug-in now appears in the Audio Plug-in window, and you can set the parameters you want. Choose the Big Hall Audience preset, as in Figure 9.5.

Now when you speak or sing into your microphone, you can hear the reverb, and it sounds like you're in a large auditorium. If that preset doesn't inspire you to sing with more feeling and conviction, try other presets until you find one that does. Or adjust the individual controls to shape the exact reverb that works for you.

Recording

Before you start recording, you're going to want to mute the scratch vocal track so you don't hear it while you're singing the new track. Scroll down in the ACID Pro timeline and click the Mute button for the scratch vocal track. Like you did with the scratch guitar track before you recorded your new guitar tracks in Chapter 8, make the scratch vocal track's height as short as possible so that it takes up the least amount of room in your project that it can.

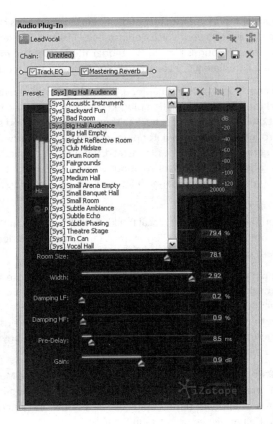

Figure 9.5

You can choose a preset to quickly set the parameters of your reverb plug-in.

USING YOUR DAW TO DEVELOP YOUR VOCAL PARTS

I mentioned in Chapter 8 when we discussed recording with amplifier emulators that you can use your DAW as a scratch pad on which to work out ideas until you develop a concrete part for your song. Here's another place where you can do that.

Although you probably have your lead vocal melody finalized (or very close to it anyway), you might not have the harmony lines figured out yet. Setting your DAW up to record while you experiment with harmonies is a great development tool—particularly if developing harmonies is not exactly your strong suit.

I once read (I think it was on the liner notes for the reissue of the album *Pet Sounds*) that the great creative genius behind the Beach Boys, Brian Wilson, would show up at the studio with everyone's vocal parts in his head. He'd tell the first guy, "Sing this…" then turn to the second Beach Boy and say, "You sing this…" and on down the line until everyone knew his part. They'd roll the tape and everyone would sing what Wilson had told them to. When they played it back—violà!—it would all come together like it was the most natural thing you could imagine.

Now, if you have that talent, I'll attempt to hold my jealousy in check long enough to congratulate you. But if you're more like me and you have to work things out, record them, and play them back to hear if they work the way you want them to, your DAW can really be a helpful partner in that process.

Now scroll back up to the lead vocal track that you want to record into. When you're ready to sing, click the Record button and sing along with your project. Click the Stop button when you're done, rename the file if you want to, and save it.

Then play the project back and listen to your recording. The reverb may be too much when you're listening back, so go back to the Audio Plug-In window. (If you already closed it, click the Track FX button for the lead vocal track.) Remember, you didn't actually record the reverb into the track, so you can change it to something you like better. Let's remove the reverb all together. To remove it, make sure it's selected in the chain (if you can see the reverb's interface, you know it's selected), and click the Remove Selected Plug-In button. Then close the Audio Plug-In window.

DOUBLING YOUR VOCALS

One time-tested recording technique is to double your vocals. In other words, add another track to your project and sing the lead vocals again so that you end up with two tracks of lead vocal in your project. This adds a depth and different feel to your vocals.

It can be difficult to pull this effect off nicely. You have to be quite familiar with the song and its melody and phrasing so that you can sing it the same way both times. If you're off, it'll sound ragged, and it'll be obvious that you doubled the vocal. Of course, you can't possibly sing it exactly the same twice, but if you're tight and you really know the melody, you can get close. It's that situation (you can sing it close to exactly the same, but never really exactly) that creates the fullness that the technique brings to your vocal tracks. If you pull it off effectively, many fans will not even realize that you doubled it.

I'm not sure this technique is as popular as it once was, but if you listen carefully to the songs on the radio, I'll bet you'll notice it sooner or later.

When you're happy with your lead vocal track (or tracks, if you doubled the vocal) you can repeat the process on one or more new tracks as you layer in your harmony and backup vocals. And because you have unlimited tracks, you can use as many as you want to. So don't be afraid to double those harmony tracks to add fullness to them too!

Punch-In Recording

If you're like most of us, you'll make some mistakes while you're singing (or playing an instrument) that you're not going to be happy with and will want to fix them. But it may be a small section of the song, and you'd really rather not go back and record the whole thing over again.

Digital audio and your digital audio workstation (DAW) are absolutely custom made for solving this kind of problem. You can easily create a new recording during the section you want to change without affecting the rest of the song. This technique is commonly referred to as *punch-in recording*.

WHY THE TERM *PUNCH-IN* RECORDING?

Even though with your DAW you don't do things the same way they're done in an analog recording setup, we still use plenty of the terminology that developed with analog systems. The term *punch-in* is an example.

On an analog system, if a musician wants to record over just a specific phrase of the song while keeping the material both before and after the phrase, the recording engineer is key to successfully pulling off the task.

After communicating with each other so that both the musician and the engineer are crystal clear on where the punch-in and punch-out points are, everyone gets ready. The engineer rolls the tape back a bit to provide some preroll (a term I define a little later) and plays the song back. The musician plays (or sings) along with the already recorded material to get into the groove and when the tape reaches the decided upon punch-in point, the engineer "punches" the record button, thus kicking the tape deck into record mode. The process must be exact, and the engineer's timing has to be as good as the musician's or the punch-in might end up being noticeable in the final recording.

The punch-in point usually is chosen so that it corresponds to something like a snare hit or other loud sound that could mask any possible clicking or popping that might be recorded as a result of the tape deck jumping suddenly into record mode. The punch-out point has to be chosen with equal care to mask any noise there, too.

Although with your DAW you don't have to worry about the machine making noise as you punch the record button, I still often mask my punch points with a snare hit or other noise. Old habits die hard.

To see how punch-in recording works, let's say there's a phrase in your song where you hit a bad note or sang the wrong lyric. First, isolate that phrase in the timeline. Determine where you want to start recording the new phrase (the punch-in point). Click the lead vocal event at that punch-in point to both select the event and place your cursor there. Remember, if you can't place the cursor at the exact location you want because it snaps to the nearest ruler mark, use your mouse wheel or up-arrow key to zoom into your project until a ruler mark appears acceptably close to where you want to place the cursor.

Then choose Edit, Split. This cuts (or splits) the event into two separate events. The split happens only to the selected event at the cursor location. Click to place your cursor later in the second of the two events where you want to stop recording (the punch-out point) and split the event again. Now you have three events on the timeline, and the middle event holds the phrase that you want to sing over. Click that middle event to select it. In Figure 9.6, you can see what my timeline looks like after making these splits.

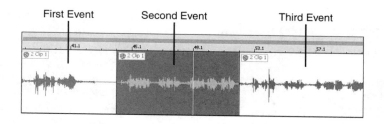

Figure 9.6

Split the event in the timeline into three separate events, isolating the phrase you want to record over in its own event. Then click that event to select it.

Now, with the event that holds the phrase you want to record again selected and the track still armed for recording, you can record again. When you do, ACID Pro replaces the audio in the selected event with the new audio you record. First, though, give yourself a little preroll so you have time to get your bearings after you start recording and before you have to start singing the phrase again.

NOTE

The term *preroll* refers to a portion of the music just before the punch-in point that you listen to without recording over so that you can get in the groove with the song. If you placed your cursor at exactly the punch-in point and tried to start recording, you wouldn't have a lock on the tempo or a feel for the rhythm. So, you'll give yourself a bit of preroll to listen to before the punch-in starts.

In the same way, post roll is a portion of the music that you listen to after the recording punch-out point.

To give yourself preroll, you'll have to place your cursor in front of the selected event. As you've seen, though, if you click in the timeline before the selected event starts, you'll not only move the cursor, but you'll deselect the currently selected event and select the one you click on. For the punch-in to work, you have to have the event you want to record over selected, so you can't click earlier in the timeline to move the cursor.

Way back in Chapter 4, "An Introduction to ACID Pro Fundamentals," you learned that to go to a specific point in your project, you can double-click the Measures and Beats time display, type a new value into the field, and press Enter on your keyboard. The cursor jumps to that location without affecting the event selection.

Now get ready to sing again and click the Record button. The project starts playing, and you can hear the lead vocal track. However, ACID Pro doesn't start recording until the playback cursor reaches the selected event. When it does, sing the phrase, and ACID Pro records it into the event. When you've finished the phrase, stop recording.

REVEALING EXTRA RECORDED MATERIAL

When I say, "ACID Pro doesn't start recording until the playback cursor reaches the selected event," I'm not telling the exact truth. In reality, ACID Pro begins recording immediately when you click the Record button and continues recording until you click the Stop button even if the cursor has passed the selected event. It's just that in your project, only the audio in the selected event gets replaced.

This means that if you start singing during your preroll time (which is a good way to get into the groove of the song before you reach the phrase you really want to replace, thus making your punch-in sound seamless and natural) and keep singing after the cursor passes the selected event, you will have recorded that extra material as well as the phrase you really wanted to replace.

It's good to realize that, because it's not uncommon for the singer to decide, "Wow, I really liked the way I sang that line leading into the phrase I was intending to replace better than the original recording." Well, even though that section didn't get placed into your project, it did get recorded. So you can still use it if you want to.

All you have to do is trim the right edge of existing event (the one that occurs before the originally selected event) back to the left to trim off the original recording. Then fill the hole in your project by trimming the left edge of the originally selected event back to the left to reveal the new recording.

Figure 9.7 shows my project after I finish recording this punch-in. Notice that the labels in the events show that the new punch-in recording has a different number than the first recording.

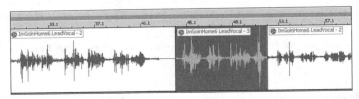

Figure 9.7
After the punch-in, the clips used in the events show different names to indicate that they are not the same recording.

Multiple Take Punch-In Recording

Occasionally, you encounter a phrase or section that you're having a lot of trouble singing or playing well. For times like these, you can use ACID Pro's looped playback feature to help you record as many takes as you need to get the part right. You used Loop Playback mode in Chapter 4, when you looped your project to play while you searched for other files to add to it. You can use the same Loop Playback technique while recording.

Let's say that you've got a passage that you have trouble singing the way you want to. Just as you did in the previous section when you recorded a punch-in, isolate that passage by splitting the event into several events so that one of the events holds the troublesome passage. Select the event that you want to record over.

Now set the gray loop region bar so that it includes the selected event as well as an adequate amount of preroll and perhaps some postroll, too. Click the Loop Playback button to put ACID Pro into Loop Playback mode. (Notice that this turns the loop region bar blue.) Figure 9.8 shows my project with the event selected and the loop region encompassing it with a bit of preroll and postroll.

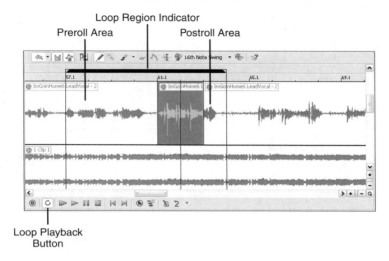

Figure 9.8

The loop region bar encompasses the selected event along with some preroll and postroll and indicates that the project is in Loop Playback mode.

Now, with the track armed for recording, click the Record button. The project plays through the loop region and returns to the beginning to play again. Each time the cursor enters the selected event, it records a new take into the event. Sing the phrase over each time, and keep doing so until you get it right. When you get a performance you're happy with, click the Stop button.

Right-click the event. From the pop-up menu, choose Event Clip. In the cascading menu in Figure 9.9, you see all the clips you've recorded for the track, including the original recording, the punch-in recording you did earlier, and as many takes as you just recorded with the loop punch-in method. Select any of the clips you just recorded, and play the project to hear how it sounds.

The project will continue to play since it is in Loop Playback mode. Each time it plays through the selected event, choose a different clip from the list to hear how that one sounds. When you find the one you like best, click the Stop button, and click the Loop Playback button to take ACID Pro out of Loop Playback mode. Finally, click the Arm for Record button for the track to disable Arm-for-Record mode.

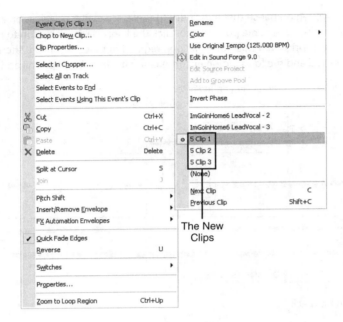

Figure 9.9
The track now contains several clips, including the new ones you recorded with the loop punch-in method.

NOTE

I've finished recording the vocals for my project. In fact, the recording process is complete now. I've recorded the lead vocal and some harmony vocals. To hear my song at this point, play the file ImGoinHome_complete.wav from the Chapter 09 folder on the companion disc.

Now I'm ready to move on to the mixing stage in Chapter 10.

Studio Log

Recording vocals and anything else that requires a microphone presents the most difficult challenges for the home recording studio setup. This is especially true if you have to be conscious of making too much noise at certain times.

If you can't outfit your studio space with a full complement of sound absorption devices, you may be able to at least cut down on the audio reflections that reach your microphone by fashioning something similar to the makeshift vocal "booths" that this chapter discusses.

You also need to give proper attention to your choice of studio vocal microphones. There are many options out there, and you'll want to do some research to find the best one you can afford. If you can't afford much, the Shure SM58 is a great choice, because it's inexpensive while being useful for recording many things in addition to vocals. And for the money, it sounds great.

After you've set up your recording booth and microphone, you can use a couple of different punch-in recording techniques to get that perfect take. The single punch-in technique works perfectly when you're capable of a better performance and you just want to replace something that you flubbed. The Loop Playback punch-in method works great when you need to sing or play a passage over and over until you get it right. You can record take after take until you're finally satisfied with your performance.

With this chapter, we've wrapped up the recording process and are ready to move on to mixing and mastering in the next two chapters.

10

Mixing Your Song

Now that the recording process is complete and you've recorded all the parts you want in your song, it's time to turn our attention to making it sound as good as possible. There are two stages to this process. In this chapter, we'll discuss the first of those: the mixing process. In Chapter 11, "Mastering Your Song," we'll talk about the other stage (mastering the music).

The mixing stage is critical to making great-sounding music. Your goal in mixing your music is not only to bring out the best of each sound in the project, but to blend the overall sound of the piece as a whole.

If you do your job right, few people (aside from someone who's focused on mixing) will notice your mix. They'll just know that the song sounds great. By the same token, few fans will hear a bad mix and say, "Wow, that's a fantastic song! Too bad the mix doesn't do it justice." They're much more likely to say simply, "I don't like that song."

In that regard, mixing is a bit of a thankless job. Since the fans won't be telling you what an accomplished mix engineer you are, you'll have to find the rewards of your hard mixing work in the fact that they're digging the music.

No book can adequately teach you top-notch mixing skills; only experience and determination will give you the chops you need to call yourself a good audio mix engineer. But I can teach you the tools you'll use and some of the procedures I've developed for myself over my many mixing projects. Once you have these tools and techniques in your arsenal, you'll be able to start applying them to your mixes. As you do more and more mixing, you'll refine your art so that soon no one will be noticing your sublime mixes either!

IN THIS CHAPTER

- Deciding whether to mix your own or hire help
- Working with the mixing console
- Mixing MIDI drum tracks
- Creating a submix
- Discovering creative editing solutions
- Digital processing

To Mix or Not to Mix

Well, that's not really the question. You will definitely have to mix your project. The real question is whether to do it yourself, hire a pro with a decked-out studio to do it for you, or some combination of the two, where you take your project to a studio that has a nice room and work with the studio's engineer to create your mix.

> **NOTE**
>
> What is *mixing*? Simply stated, it's the process of blending all the sounds in your project so that they combine to create a pleasing overall sound.

If you don't have experience mixing, or if your home studio setup just can't give you a critical listening environment, you might really want to hire someone to help—or perhaps rent a studio space to mix in.

Of course, if you don't have the money to hire a room and engineer—and that's where most of us find ourselves—you'll be doing the job yourself in your home studio. There's a chance you can get one of your more experienced friends to help, but mixing an entire project of 10 or so songs is a huge undertaking and a lot to ask as a favor from a buddy. Still, you can try! You might find someone with a moderate amount of experience who'd be willing to help you on your project for nothing more than the experience gained in doing the mix and credits on the CD sleeve. (I've been known to donate my time to mix for friends knowing that the experience I gain on their projects will make the next mix I do for my own project that much better.)

> **TIP**
>
> Don't take the decision about how to handle your mixing process too lightly. I encourage you to try on your own; you'll learn with every mistake, and you'll get better with every mix. Just keep in mind that if your project is critical—you intend to try for radio play or sell CDs from the stage and your website—then a bad mix can ruin your chances of anyone bothering to listen. In that case, it may pay in the long run to have a pro help now. Of course, that's often not feasible. But don't worry; you can learn to create great mixes. It just takes experience. If you're doing your own mixes for a critical project, make sure you're ruthless in checking the mix out on different playback systems. Also, seek the advice of other musicians and listeners whose opinions you value.

If you're going to do your own mixing and your studio space isn't all that conducive to good listening (and mixing), don't skimp when it comes time to buy headphones. Buy good, high-end, professional-quality headphones. Naturally, they'll cost more, but you're depending on them, and they'll make all the difference in your mix. I prefer to use enclosed headphones that block out much of the sound from the room so I can really concentrate on the music.

Lots of engineers wouldn't be caught dead mixing in headphones, but generally, those are the ones who have access to really nice rooms and systems. I know from experience that you can create good mixes in the cans (headphones), but you'll have to take some extra care to make sure those mixes sound good *outside* the headphones, too.

You should always test your mix on several sound systems (your car, the stereo in the living room, your neighbor's boom box, and so on) to verify that it sounds good no matter where you play it. Otherwise, you run the risk of creating a mix that sounds wonderful to you on your studio monitors or headphones but not so stunning anywhere else. This is especially true if you do your mixes in headphones.

The Mixing Process

ACID Pro provides various tools specifically for mixing. When is the right time to use these tools? You've already used several of them at different times earlier in the book, but I didn't necessarily point them out as mixing tools when I discussed them.

For example, in Chapter 8, "Recording Electric Keyboards, Guitars, and Basses," you muted your scratch guitar track so that you wouldn't be listening to it when you recorded your new track. The Mute button is a mixing tool. You also used Soft Synth buses during our discussion in Chapter 7, "Utilizing MIDI in Your Projects." Those Soft Synth buses are themselves mixing tools that contain many other mixing tools. When you adjusted the volume of individual events to create dynamics in your drum tracks in Chapter 6, "Creating Drum Tracks," you were using mixing tools.

The point I'm making here is that although I've purposely held off on discussing mixing until this chapter, mixing is in reality an ongoing process that literally starts when you add the first track to your project and doesn't end until you decide you're happy with the way the project sounds.

As I've been working on my project, I've been performing little mixing functions here and there that I didn't tell you about. For example, the track headers in your project are full of mixing tools, including a volume fader that enables you to turn the volume of a track's audio up or down. That's perhaps the most basic mixing function. You turn the guitar down so that you can more effectively hear the vocal. Or you turn the kick drum up so that it sounds more even with the snare.

Look at Figure 10.1. You can see that I've set the volume differently for the three visible tracks. These hasty volume adjustments serve as a *rough mix*—meaning a mix that you don't spend much time on. I made the adjustments without too much thought to more effectively hear each track while working on the project and so that you could hear each when you played the sample files.

While it's true that this type of mixing is ongoing, there does come a point in your project when the recording is done and you can turn your attention fully to the mixing process as opposed to doing the little quick-fix mixing adjustments that you do throughout the recording process. This is what engineers refer to as the *mixing stage*.

Volume Settings

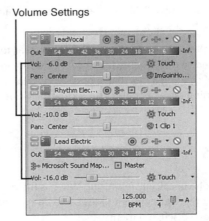

Figure 10.1

The three tracks have already been mixed somewhat because I've set the volume differently for each.

GIVE YOUR EARS A REST

Here we're jumping right from the recording process into the mixing stage. In reality, it's critical that you give your ears a rest before attempting to create a mix. You can conceivably be tracking (recording your tracks) for hours, especially if you find it easy to get lost in your music like lots of musicians do.

Hopefully you're being smart about how loud you're listening to your music as you work (my mantra: I love music far too much to go deaf listening to it!), but regardless of volume levels, you will eventually suffer from ear fatigue. Your ears get tired just like any other part of your body, and when they do, they stop working as effectively as they can when they're fresh.

If you really want to create your best possible mix, walk away from the project for a good long while. A day or maybe even a week is not too long. When you come back with a fresh mind and fresh ears, you'll be in a much better position to create a professional-quality mix.

The mixing stage is where the mixing process becomes the focus. You can start with whatever mix you have created along the way to this stage, which is most often how I approach the task. Other engineers like to start from scratch by setting everything to some desired start setting (like all tracks at a volume of *–Inf.*, for example) and then making adjustments from there.

NOTE

In digital audio, a volume level of *–Inf.* (minus infinity) means no audio. A volume level of 0.0dB (dB stands for *decibels*—a measure of the volume of a sound) means no change in volume. Thus, a file on a track that has its volume set to 0.0dB plays at its natural level of loudness. The ear perceives a doubling in the loudness of a sound for every 6dB boost in the volume (or a halving of the loudness for each 6dB cut in the volume).

The Mixing Environment

As I've mentioned, you can find mixing tools all over the place in your ACID Pro interface. But essentially there are two main areas that hold mixing tools—the track header area and the mixing console.

> **NOTE**
>
> The mixing console contains every control that the track headers contain and more. Typically, you'll do your mixing using a combination of the two areas.

Track Headers

You might have already realized that much of the purpose of the track header for each track is to house various mixing tools. So, the track header area is one place where you will spend a lot of time mixing. I reach for the tools in the track header area whenever I need to make a quick adjustment to a track while I'm in the recording process or when I want to temporarily solo or mute a track.

I also tend to use the tools in the track headers more frequently when I'm working on a computer system that has only one computer monitor since the track headers take up less space than the mixing console and they don't cover the timeline like the mixing console can if you undock it (as we'll discuss shortly).

However, mixing with the track header tools may not seem as natural as those in the mixing console, especially if you have lots of experience working with hardware mixers.

The ACID Pro Mixing Console

ACID Pro's main mixing environment is the Mixing Console window. The mixing console has been designed to mimic a hardware mixer. It gives you all kinds of power over routing your audio, adjusting track and bus volume, adding digital signal processing (DSP), and more.

The mixing console is docked in the window docking area by default. But like other dockable windows, you can tear it out of the window docking area and let if float freely anywhere on your screen.

To undock it, drag it by the six vertical dots just below its upper-left corner. When you drag it far enough away from the window docking area, a title bar appears at the top, which indicates that the window is now free floating. Release the mouse button. Then resize the mixing console so that it takes up your entire computer screen.

The mixing console is the most useful when you maximize it like this to give it as much space as possible because it has a lot of controls on it. The more of those controls you can see at one glance without having to scroll to uncover objects, the faster and more efficiently you'll work with the mixing console. Figure 10.2 shows the mixing console maximized to occupy my entire screen.

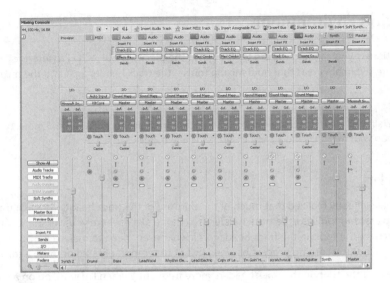

Figure 10.2

Maximize the mixing console so you can see as much of it as possible at a time.

TIP

It really helps to have a second computer monitor attached to your system. This way you can devote one of the monitors to the mixing console and still see your timeline and other tools on the other monitor.

If you have a large number of tracks in your project, the mixing console might look a bit overwhelming—not unlike the experience of walking into a professional studio and seeing a 96-channel hardware mixing console and wondering, "How in the world can anyone ever make sense of that?"

But, just like that hardware console, it becomes easier to digest and understand the ACID Pro mixing console when you realize that it can easily be broken down into manageable pieces. Although it holds many controls, those controls are logically grouped into sections for each track and bus in your project. For example, each track has a Volume fader, a Solo button, an audio meter, and so on. The controls for a track or bus are arranged in a tall, narrow stack called a *channel strip* or simply a *channel*. Each channel is identified by a colored square at the top. Track channels have colors and numbers that correspond to the colors and numbers in their track headers. The controls in a track channel also correspond to the controls in a track header so that if you change the Volume fader in the track's mixing console channel, the change is also reflected in the track header.

SOFTWARE VERSUS HARDWARE

One advantage (of many!) that your software mixing console has over a hardware console is that a hardware console has a fixed number of channels. Those channels are there whether you need them or not; if you need more than your hardware console has, you're out of luck. ACID Pro's mixing console, on the other hand, always gives you exactly the number of channels you need based on the number of tracks and buses you have in your project. That way you'll never have to look at more channels than you need, and you'll never have to worry about running short.

Another advantage is that you don't have to walk 10 feet to reach the Master bus channel at the right end of the console if you happen to be working on the track 1 channel at the left end of the console!

Now that you've been introduced to the mixing environments, let's get busy mixing the song so that you can learn the mixing tools.

Setting Up the MIDI Drum Track for Mixing

Because we recorded our drum track as a single MIDI file, mixing that track is a little different from mixing the other tracks in the project. For now, dock the mixing console to its original position in the window docking area.

You might have noticed when you listened to the ImGoinHome_Complete.wav file in the Chapter 09 folder on the companion disc (which you did at the end of Chapter 9, "Recording Things That Require Microphones") that you can't hear the kick drum in the mix too well. You may have noticed other problems with the drum mix, too.

Look at Figure 10.3, where I've maximized the MIDI track height so you see only that track. Notice that all the drum sounds are represented as notes in dedicated note lanes on the single MIDI track. Although the MIDI track header has a Volume fader, individual faders do not exist for the various drum notes in the track. Therefore, you can't simply turn up the kick drum track by adjusting a fader.

NOTE

In fact, some soft synths might not accept commands from the MIDI track's Volume, Pan, and other controls. If that's the case, the adjustments you make on the track header are simply ignored.

So you're going to need to come up with a method that you can use to mix the drum sounds inside the MIDI drum track. I'll talk about three approaches you can use.

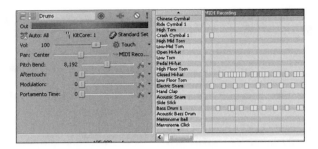

Figure 10.3
There are no individual Volume faders for each note lane on the MIDI drum track.

Adjusting MIDI Note Velocities

One way to mix the various drum sounds is to adjust the velocity setting of the MIDI notes. You worked with note velocity in Chapter 7. We'll expand on the techniques you learned there to mix your drum sounds.

Naturally, if you had to adjust every MIDI note velocity one by one, you'd have a huge, monotonous job in front of you. Fortunately, you don't have to take that approach!

Let's start with the kick drum.

TIP

It's often quite helpful when you're mixing and trying to concentrate on a certain group of sounds (like the drums in this discussion) to solo the sounds. In this case, solo the drum track so that you're hearing only the drums in the mix. That way you can create a mix between the drum sounds that you can later fold into the overall mix as a group.

Just looking at the project now, you can't get a sense for the velocities of the notes. If you're not already in Inline MIDI Editing mode, choose Options, Enable Inline MIDI Editing. Choose View, Show Inline MIDI Editing, Note-On Velocities. As you can see in Figure 10.4, velocity indicators (the vertical lines with diamond tops) have been added to the timeline.

Although these velocity indicators tend to clutter up the MIDI track, you'll find them extremely helpful. If two MIDI notes fall at or close to the same time, you can't easily tell by looking which velocity indicator goes with which note. For example, in Figure 10.4, you see two velocity indicators at exactly beat 5.1, and you can't tell by looking what drum sound each corresponds to.

However, just click one of the diamonds. This selects not only the velocity indicator, but also the note that it corresponds to. It also plays the drum sound associated with that note so you can easily identify what sound goes with what indicator. Click on various diamonds until you find one that corresponds to a kick drum sound.

Now that you have a kick drum note selected, right-click it and choose Select All on Note from the pop-up menu. This selects every kick drum note in the MIDI track as well as their corresponding velocity indicators. You can now easily distinguish them from the velocity indicators for other drum sounds, as you can see in Figure 10.5.

MIDI Note Velocity Indicators

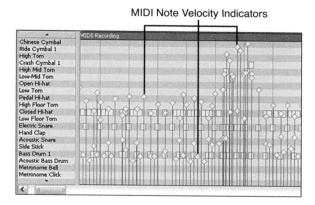

Figure 10.4

Velocity indicators give you a sense of the velocities of the various MIDI notes in your project.

MIDI Note Velocities

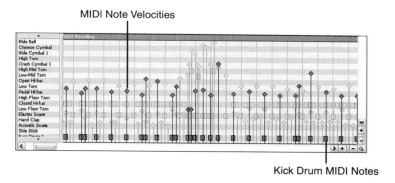

Kick Drum MIDI Notes

Figure 10.5

Once you've selected all the notes of one drum sound, it's easy to distinguish their velocity indicators from those of other drum sounds.

Zoom out of your project so that you can see the entire thing. You can now look to see how much variation there is in the velocities of the kick drum notes. Figure 10.6 shows a pretty wide variation in my kick drum notes.

Point to the diamond head of the kick drum velocity indicator that appears to be the highest. The information field below the lower-right corner of the timeline shows you the velocity value for that indicator. In my project, the highest velocity is 114, and several notes have a velocity in a range close to that value. But the majority of the kick drum velocities are in the range of 65. This causes a problem in my mix because the variation is just too great.

I know I want to raise the volume of my kick drum overall, but I can see that with this amount of variation, I can raise it only so much before the loudest notes hit the MIDI value ceiling. (Recall from Chapter 7 that MIDI can have a value ranging from 0 to 127.) So I need to narrow that variation a bit.

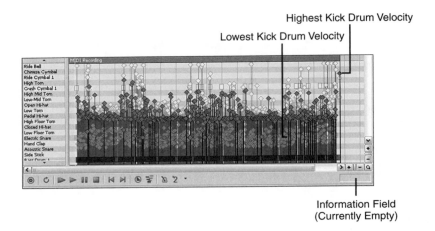

Figure 10.6
The variation in the heights of the kick drum velocity indicators shows that some kick drum hits are much louder than others.

The velocity indicators give you an easy way to do this. You can drag the diamonds on the velocity indicators up and down to change the velocity value for the associated note. Drag the velocity indicator of any of the selected kick drum notes up slightly. Since all kick drum notes are selected, dragging one up drags the others up as well.

Now find a note whose velocity is around 80. This is higher than the average note velocity but considerably lower than the highest. Drag that note's velocity indicator up. As you continue up, the higher notes hit the ceiling of 127 and can go no higher. Drag the note up until it, too, hits the ceiling.

Figure 10.7 shows that this has raised all the lower-velocity notes to a much higher velocity. In the process, you've made the notes that originally had proportionally higher velocities fall much more in line with the average note's velocity. This has removed some of the dynamic volume differences from the kick drum, so you'll want to make sure that sounds okay. If it doesn't, click the Undo button and try again, this time closing down the volume gap a little bit less by dragging a velocity diamond for a note that has a higher velocity to begin with (say, around 90).

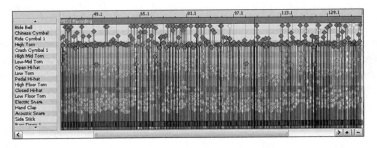

Figure 10.7
The differences in velocity have been narrowed. The average kick drum note velocity is now much higher.

When you're done, play your project to hear what it sounds like. You can use the same technique to narrow the gap between any of the other drum sounds. Then, when you've got the gaps narrowed to what you want, use the multiselection technique to raise or lower the various pieces of the drum kit to create a good mix between them.

TIP

Now is also a logical time to make any adjustments to the timing of the drum hits. One of the great things about working with MIDI is that if the timing is off on a hit, say a snare shot, you can easily move it to where it should be. Remember to hold the Shift key as you move the MIDI note if you want to prevent it from snapping to the ruler marks.

Creating Audio Tracks from the MIDI Drum Sounds

The method we discussed for mixing your MIDI drums works reasonably well if all you want to mix is the volume of the drum sounds. But it doesn't work at all if you want to change the panning of the cymbal or add DSP to the snare. One way to give yourself total flexibility to really mix the MIDI drums is to render audio files from each drum sound. We briefly discussed rendering a file in Chapter 7, when we talked about creating an MP3 file to send to a partner for long-distance collaboration.

We can use the same technique here. Essentially you'll isolate the sounds on the MIDI drum track one by one and create a new audio file that you'll add to your project.

CAUTION

Make sure you're totally happy with the drum track before you render it out as pieces of separate audio. Once it's audio, you won't be able to change the position of a note or other aspects that are easy to adjust in MIDI without going back to the MIDI track, making the change, and rendering it as audio again.

First, use the techniques you learned in the previous section to raise the velocity of each drum sound as high as possible while maintaining some of the dynamics between individual instances of that same sound.

In the mixing console, scroll over until you can see the Synth bus that holds the drum soft synth that your project uses. Double-click the number icon for the Synth bus to open the Soft Synth Properties dialog box. Recall that I'm using the KitCore soft synth. Play the project and watch the soft synth's interface in the Soft Synth Properties dialog. The synth should give some indication of what drum sound is playing when. For example, as you see in Figure 10.8, KitCore uses a yellow light that flashes each time a sound plays.

Start with the kick drum. When you identify (with the yellow light) which of KitCore's drum sounds plays when the MIDI sends it a kick drum note, click the Solo button for that sound in the KitCore interface.

Indicator Lights

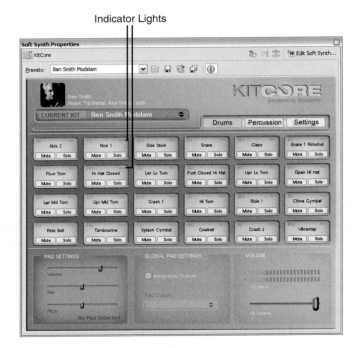

Figure 10.8

The yellow lights indicate the drum sound as it plays according to the MIDI information on your track.

Scroll over in the mixing console if you have to so that you can see the Soft Synth bus. As the project plays, you see the Synth's audio level on the bus' meter. Remember, you don't want your audio to clip as we discussed in Chapter 5, "Creating Your Guide Tracks," but you do want to make the audio for the file you're about to create as loud as possible without clipping.

If the kick drum audio is causing the Soft Synth meter to clip, lower the synth bus Volume fader. If the audio is not clipping, raise the bus' volume until the meter peaks between −1 and 0.

If you don't still have the MIDI drum track soloed, click the Solo button for that track in the track header. Now the only sound you hear in your project is the kick drum. When you render the project to an audio file, the resulting file will contain just the kick drum audio.

In ACID Pro, choose Tools, Render to New Track. In the Render to New Track dialog box, shown in Figure 10.9, select a location to save the file into, name the file KickDrum, and select Wave (Microsoft) (*.wav) from the Save As Type drop-down list. Choose 44,100Hz, 16 Bit, Mono, PCM from the Template drop-down list, and click the Save button. (We'll discuss these choices in more detail in Chapter 12, "Delivering Your Music.")

Figure 10.9

Use the Render to New Track dialog box to define the parameters of the new file you're about to create.

TIP

The name you give the file here will become the name of the new track in your project, so it makes sense to name it something useful. Also, some Synths create stereo sounds. If you choose to render a mono file, you'll lose the stereo effect of the Synth. In this case that's okay with me, because I prefer to place the sounds in the stereo field the way I want them. But for other sounds (like Brian's organ part, for example), I want to use the original stereo sound. In those cases, I'd render a stereo file instead.

After a minute or so when the render process completes, a new track appears at the bottom of your project. The track's clip list holds the kick drum audio that you generated from the MIDI through the drum Soft Synth, but the track does not yet have an event in it for the new audio, so let's add it.

First, drag the new track (which appears now at the bottom of the track list) to a place in the list that suits your working style. I've dragged my new track to sit right beneath the MIDI drum track. You might also make the track taller so you can access its controls more effectively.

Unsolo and then mute the MIDI drum track. Then start at the beginning of the KickDrum audio track and draw an event from the beginning of the project to the end. You see the waveform for the kick drum audio file fill the event.

TIP

To quickly paint an event that holds the entire file into your project, click the Paint Tool button in the toolbar. Then hold the Ctrl key and click at the beginning of the track you want to paint into. The entire file is added instantly, and you don't need to paint it manually. When you're done, click the Draw Tool button to return to the Draw tool.

Now repeat that same process for every drum sound in the MIDI drum track. When you're done, you'll have multiple tracks of drum audio, and each of those will hold one piece of the drum kit, as you can see in Figure 10.10.

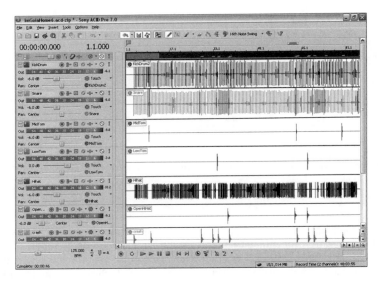

Figure 10.10
Once you've created a new track for each drum sound on the MIDI track, you have a multiple-audio-track drum section.

Mute the original MIDI drum track and minimize its height. You could delete the MIDI track at this point since you don't need it anymore (because all the drums are on separate audio tracks now), but it doesn't hurt anything to leave it in the project, and it may come in handy. For example, if you decide later that you need to make an adjustment to the timing of a drum hit, you can go back to the MIDI track, make the correction, and render that instrument as a new, corrected track.

TIP

Notice that in Figure 10.10, you can't see the window docking area (or any of the windows it holds). I've hidden it temporarily so that I can see more tracks on my timeline. To hide the window docking area, press the F11 key on your computer keyboard. Press F11 again to bring the window docking area back into view.

Breaking the MIDI Drums into Multiple MIDI Outputs

Another approach to gaining individual mixing control of the MIDI track is possible only if the Soft Synth you're using features multiple outputs. The KitCore Soft Synth that I'm using does, so let's walk through breaking the drum sounds into separate outputs.

In the mixing console, scroll over until you can see the Synth bus that holds the KitCore Soft Synth. Double-click the Synth bus' heading to open the KitCore interface in the Soft Synth Properties dialog box (if you don't already have it open).

Click the sound pad for the kick drum sound. (For my drums, this happens to be pad 36.) In the Global Pad Settings area, select the Assignable Outputs button, shown in Figure 10.11. The button turns yellow when it's active.

Figure 10.11
Select the Assignable Outputs button to activate assignable outputs for the selected pad.

Click the Assignable Outputs drop-down list. As you see in Figure 10.12, KitCore has 24 outputs, the last eight of which are mono outputs. Since I want to control the panning (the placement in the stereo field) of my drum sounds, I'm going to use the mono outputs. I happen to have nine drum sounds, so there aren't enough mono outputs for me to use.

Choose the first available mono output (output 17) for the kick drum, and assign the rest of your sounds to other outputs. If you have more than eight drum sounds in your kit, you'll have to use stereo outputs for some of them. I'm going to leave the ride cymbal bell hit in my project routed to the main output since it only occurs once in the song.

You'll need to be able to see all these extra outputs to work with them. You can make them visible in the mixing console. Close the Soft Synth Properties dialog box (or dock it out of the way in the window docking area).

Right-click the Synth bus' header bar and choose Insert/Remove KitCore Outputs from the pop-up menu. From the cascading menu (shown in Figure 10.13), select the first used output from the list. A new Synth bus appears in the mixer window. Repeat the process for all the outputs you've used.

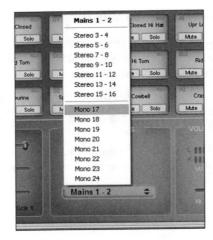

Figure 10.12

KitCore has 24 outputs through which you can route your drum sounds.

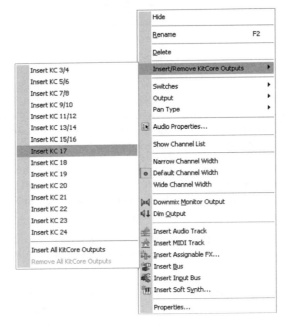

Figure 10.13

Insert a new Synth bus for each of the KitCore outputs you've used.

After you've inserted all your buses, they appear in the mixing console, as shown in Figure 10.14. These individual Synth buses contain all the controls you need for mixing the drum sounds individually. (We'll talk about those controls later in this chapter.) Play your project, and notice that you see the audio meters for all these new buses react to the drum sounds.

CAUTION

If you routed all the sounds away from KitCore's main output, you won't see meter activity in the original Synth bus. You might be tempted to delete it from your project since you won't be using it, but remember that all the other outputs depend on the main output. If you delete the main, you'll delete all the outputs you just added. It won't hurt anything to have it in your project even if you're not routing sound to it.

Figure 10.14
The mixing console now holds a new bus for each KitCore output that you inserted.

If you don't like the order of the Synth buses for all your drum outputs (or any other channel in the mixer for that matter), you can change them. Most engineers have a specific order that they want things in (for example, kick drum first, snare next, toms after that from high to low, hi-hat, and so on).

For example, since I left the ride bell sound routed to the main outputs bus (which currently is the farthest of the Synth buses to the left), it's out of place according to the way I like to arrange things. To reorder the channels in the mixer, drag a channel by its heading. As you drag it right or left, a dark insertion bar appears between other channels to indicate the position the channel will be dropped at if you release the mouse button. When the position bar is where you want to place the channel, release the mouse button. The channel moves to the new position.

TIP

Whenever you click a channel to select or move it, aim for the channel number at the top. That way you won't inadvertently click any of the controls in the channel and change a setting.

It'll be helpful to name each of the drum bus channels so that you know which is which while you're working. Each channel in the mixing console has a scribble strip (like those you've seen on tracks throughout this book). Double-click the scribble strip for the channel to which you've routed the kick drum, type KickDrum, and press the Enter key. Rename all your other drum channels, too.

> **NOTE**
>
> When you change the position of a track channel (as opposed to a bus channel), the track's position in the track header list changes so that its position in the track list matches its position in the mixing console.

Mixing

Now that you've got your MIDI drums broken out either as rendered audio files or separate MIDI output buses, you can get serious about mixing your tune. Again, people have their own methods, and there's no one right way to go about creating a mix. But I can share a few of the tips and techniques I use to make mixing easier for me.

Creating Submixes

When you have a lot of tracks in your project, it can be a real challenge even to know where to start with a mix. There's just so much going on that it's difficult to get a handle on all of it.

To help combat that feeling of being overwhelmed, I like to break down my projects into smaller pieces of related material. The drums are a perfect example. Instead of trying to find just the right volume and panning for each piece of the drum kit in relation to every other track in the project, I find it easier to start by finding the right volume of each piece of the drum kit in relation to just the other pieces of the drum kit. Creating a mix like this is called creating a *submix*.

The mixing console gives you great flexibility to create submixes. Since you're going to be working extensively with the mixing console during the mix process, undock it and let it float above the ACID Pro timeline. Double-click the mixing console's title bar to maximize it to fill your entire screen.

MAXIMIZING THE MIXING CONSOLE ON A ONE-SCREEN COMPUTER SYSTEM

If you have two computer monitors, maximize the mixing console on one of them and use the other for the timeline. If you have only one screen, you can maximize the mixing console on it. Remember that your computer's spacebar starts and stops playback, and the Enter key starts and pauses playback. This is true even if you can't see the timeline because the mixing console is in the way. This makes it easy to control playback when you're working with the mixing console maximized on a single screen.

Not all windows behave this way. Sometimes if a window has focus, it intercepts the Spacebar command, and your project will not play. You can click the timeline to give focus back to it and then use the spacebar to play. Or you can press Ctrl+Spacebar or the F12 key. These commands start playback regardless of what window currently has focus.

My first step is to make the mixing console easier to look at while I'm working on my drum mix. Since all the mixing is going to be done with the Synth buses that you added, there's no need to look at all the channels for the guitar, vocal, and other tracks.

You can use the mixing console's Show/Hide buttons, which you see in Figure 10.15, to view exactly the channels you need to see as you're working. When you hover over the Audio Tracks button, the ToolTip reads, "Hide All Audio Tracks." Click the button, and the audio track channels disappear.

Figure 10.15

Use the Show/Hide buttons to create the exact view in the mixing console that gives you the tools you need.

Play the project. Even though you can't see the track channels in the mixing console, you still hear their output. But it'll be easier to create your drum submix without all the other tracks playing.

To accomplish that, we'll insert another bus into the project. Click the Insert Bus button. A new bus channel labeled Bus A appears in the mixing console next to the Master bus channel. Use the scribble strip for this new channel to name it Drum Submix, as I have in Figure 10.16.

TIP

You can add up to 26 additional audio buses to your project. If you don't see the extra bus you added, check to make sure that the Audio Buses Show/Hide button is in Show mode.

Each channel in the mixing console has an output routing button that you can use to specify where the audio output of the channel should go. In Figure 10.16, you can see that all the Synth channels currently route to the Master bus. You want to send each of them to the new Drum Submix bus instead. To do that, click the Output button for each Synth track and select Drum Submix from the drop-down list.

New Bus

Scribble Strip

Figure 10.16

I've added a new bus to my project and labeled its channel strip Drum Submix.

Now play your project You hear all the tracks in your project. Because you want to hear just the drum submix, click the Solo button for the Drum Submix bus. Since all the drum sounds are routed to this bus, soloing the bus enables you to hear them without any of the other tracks in your mix. Notice that the Drum Submix's Output button is set to Master, which indicates that the audio from this bus is routed to the Master bus.

CREATING AN ALTERNATE MIX

Creating a submix is a great use for extra buses in ACID Pro, but it's not the only use. You can also use an extra bus to feed an alternate mix to a second set of studio monitors or, more likely, to headphones.

For example, say you've invited a singer to come in and help you on your song. You've got her set up to record her part, but she complains that the piano part is too loud in the mix and is making it difficult for her to keep to her melody. She asks you to bring the piano down in the mix, and while you're at it, bring the acoustic guitar up, remove the lead guitar altogether, drop the snare a little, and bring up the bass.

If you're feeding the singer the same mix you're listening to (that is, the main mix), you'll have to change your mix to give her what she wants. As I mentioned, mixing is really an ongoing function, and you may be reasonably happy with the mix you've started, so the thought of changing it for the singer hurts a little bit.

Instead of changing the main mix, set up another bus and create a mix specifically for your singer. To do it, click the Insert Bus button to insert the new bus into the mixing console. Name the bus Headphone Mix.

Click the Output button for the new bus. The outputs of your audio device (in addition to all the other buses in your project except for Synth buses) appear in the pop-up list. Select the output pair from the audio interface into which you've connected the inputs of a headphone distribution amplifier. (Of course, the singer's headphones are connected to one of the amp's outputs.)

Then click the Channel Send button in the Send section of any channel in the mixing console (you might have to undock the mixing console to see the Send section if it's docked and there's not enough room to show it) and choose Headphone Mix from the drop-down list. This shows the Send control for every channel in your project, which includes a level fader just beneath the Channel Send button. Adjust the Channel Send level fader to create the perfect mix for your singer to listen to as she sings.

Now, as the singer records her part, you can continue to tweak your master mix all you want, and it won't affect what she hears since she's listening to the alternate headphone mix through the new bus.

Creating Your Mix

Now that you've got your routing set up, you can get to mixing. You've set up a sub mix for the drums, and that's where I like to start with my mix. The sub mix enables you to isolate the drums so you can work on that mix without the other tracks influencing your mixing decisions. You did this a moment ago when you clicked the Solo button for the Drum Submix bus.

With the project playing, you can now adjust the volume and panning of each channel of the KitCore drum synth. Even though the Drum Mix bus is soloed, you can still solo and mute individual Synth buses if you need to. For example, if you want to remove the Hi-Hat channel temporarily from the mix, click the Mute button for it. If you want to hear just the snare drum, click the Solo button for the Snare channel.

CAUTION

Make sure you keep your eye on the output meters for each channel as you adjust the volume so that you don't create clipping. You also need to watch the meters for both the Drum Submix bus and the Master bus to ensure that the cumulative volume of all the drum channels isn't causing either of those to clip.

Notice that every channel in the mixing console contains an Insert FX section. You can click the button in this section if you want to add an effect to a channel. So if you want to add compression to the snare drum, click the Insert FX button for the Snare channel and follow the menu hierarchy to find the plug-in you want to use.

NOTE

A detailed discussion of the plug-ins you would use while creating a mix goes well beyond the scope of this book. It's my intention to show you how to access the tools that enable you to create a mix. You'll want to do further study on the techniques and strategies used for mixing, including when and how to use various effects like EQ, compression, and noise gating. Chapter 11 contains high-level descriptions of some plug-ins that can be used in mixing as well as mastering.

Click the Audio Tracks Show/Hide button to show the audio tracks for a moment. Notice that audio tracks already have a plug-in added to the Insert FX section. In fact, that's the same plug-in (the Track EQ plug-in) that you see in the Track FX chain for every audio track, as we discussed in Chapter 8.

This points out again that the mixing console contains controls that duplicate the controls in the track headers. The Mute button on a track channel mutes the track just as if you'd clicked the Mute button in the track header for that track. You can do all your mixing right here in the mixing console, or you can do track mixing entirely in the track header area. In reality, you'll probably use a combination of both tools.

USE AUDIO EFFECTS TASTEFULLY

It would not be unusual if you're new to mixing for you to go overboard with audio effects on your project. Lots of us (yours truly included) have fallen victim to the seduction of adding tons of reverb and echo to tracks just because we can. There's an old joke that you can always tell when an engineer has a new effect in his arsenal because suddenly every mix he creates is awash in that effect.

Well, now that you're working in a DAW, you have tons of new effects. You shouldn't be shy about experimenting with them, but the trick is to use them subtly. In general (special effect situations aside), if you do your job well at the recording stage, you shouldn't have to add too much by way of effects at the mixing stage. Think of effects as the spices, not the meal—just a touch of EQ here and a taste of reverb there with a dash of compression sprinkled in where it's needed.

Fix It in the Mix

You've probably heard someone say, "We'll fix it in the mix" a time or two in your career. In fact, the phrase has become sort of a cliché and joke. But it's no joke that your DAW makes it possible to solve problems that could otherwise detract from the quality of your song. And the mixing stage is often where you do some of your most critical listening and thus are likely to catch problems that may have gone unnoticed up to that point. Or it may be the point where you decide to fix a problem you noticed earlier in the process.

For example, my song begins with a chugging rhythm guitar that sort of provides a count-in for the rest of the instruments. At some point I realized that I wasn't happy with the way that intro sounds. It sounds stiff and without soul to me. You may have something similar in your song.

If you do find something you're not completely happy with, you can, of course, go back and record it over. In the best of all worlds, that's what you'd probably do. But in reality, you have to "stick a fork in it" at some point and move on with the project. Otherwise, your project may drag on indefinitely.

So you begin to look for creative ways to solve the problem. If you can find something that works, no one will ever know the problem was there, and you may come up with a treatment that you never would have thought of otherwise.

Creative Editing

Back to my song. I decided to try a couple of things and see if I could salvage that chugging guitar intro. First I thought I'd try a fade-out effect. Let's create such an effect.

Figure 10.17 shows my guitar tracks. After you get some experience, you'll be able to tell a lot from the waveforms in your project. For example, I can tell just by looking at the height of the waveforms in track 4 that I recorded my rhythm guitar track a little quietly. The peak indicator shows the loudest level the audio on the track reached when I last played the project. You can see that I have a long way to go before I'm in danger of clipping on this track. (Remember, clipping occurs above 0.0dB.)

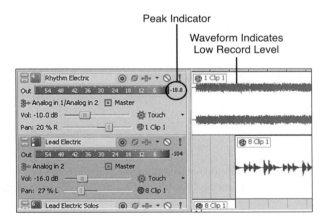

Figure 10.17

The waveforms for the rhythm guitar track show that the track could have been recorded at a higher input level.

I want my tracks to be as loud as they can be before I start mixing so that I don't run into trouble trying to get the volume I need out of them. So let's fix that problem with the track first.

Right-click the event for the track in the timeline and choose Event Clip, Normalize from the menus. The process of normalization basically increases the loudest volume peak of the file to a specific level (which you set in the Audio tab of the Preferences dialog box) and raises the rest of the file's volume in proportion.

Now, back to the fade-out effect we talked about. Each track in your project has objects called *envelopes* that you can use to automate your mix. Automating the mix means that you define an action (like increasing the volume of a track at a specified time) that takes place automatically while the project plays. We'll add a volume envelope to the rhythm guitar track that will cause its volume to fade out and then come back up abruptly when the rest of the instruments kick in.

Right-click the track header for the track and choose Insert/Remove Envelopes, Volume from the pop-up menu. This adds the blue envelope line that now runs through the track.

You can drag the envelope up and down. As you do, a readout shows you how you're affecting the volume for the track. Notice the point at the beginning of the envelope. Right-click that point and choose Set to 0.0dB from the pop-up menu. Recall that a setting of 0.0dB means that you're not changing the volume of the track at all.

You can add additional points to the envelope to break it into smaller segments and then adjust those segments to create fades. To add a point, right-click the line where you want the point and choose Add Point from the pop-up menu.

Figure 10.18 shows the envelope I've added at the beginning of my rhythm guitar track. It creates the fade-out effect that I've used to mask the playing I wasn't happy with during the short intro. You can see that the waveform is much higher now as a result of the normalization step.

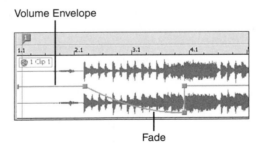

Figure 10.18

A volume envelope automates the volume of the audio on track 4.

To hear the beginning of my song with this new volume envelope in place, play the file ImGoingHome_FadeOutIntro.wav from the Chapter 10 folder on the companion disc.

I wasn't exactly sold on that effect, so next I thought maybe some sort of reversed audio effect would work. I decided to have reverse guitar playing right up to the point where the band kicks in and then put the guitar back to normal.

To do this, click the event in the track you're working on to select it, and place the cursor right at the point when the other instruments come in. Choose Edit, Split to split the event into two separate events. Then select the event you want to play in reverse, and press U on your keyboard. This reverses the selected event.

Now listen to the project. The file may not work just the way you want it in the reversed section; you may need to adjust its timing a bit. To do that, hold the Alt key and drag the waveform inside the event. This slips the waveform without moving the event. Try a few different positions until you find one that works for you.

Figure 10.19 shows my project after I've split the first section out and reversed it. An arrow inside the reversed event indicates that the file in the event will play backward. Notice that I've also included a volume envelope to add to the effect. To hear what this sounds like, play the file ImGoinHome_reverseIntro.wav from the Chapter 10 folder on the companion disc.

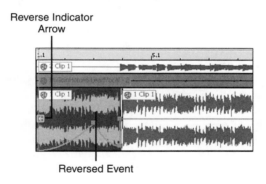

Reverse Indicator Arrow

Reversed Event

Figure 10.19

I've split the intro of the rhythm guitar track into a separate event and reversed it.

Finally, I thought I'd like to hear what it sounds like without a rhythm guitar intro so that all the instruments just start together. To do this, I just deleted the first event (the one I had reversed earlier). Figure 10.20 shows what that looks like. To hear this version, play the ImGoinHome_NoRhythmIntro.wav file from the Chapter 10 folder on the companion disc.

After trying all these things, I still had trouble deciding which way to go. So I saved each version as an MP3 file (like we discussed in Chapter 7) and emailed them to a couple friends to get their opinions. In the end, I decided I wasn't happy with any of these options. In fact, the entire track had fallen out of favor with me by now, so I grabbed a different guitar, dialed in a different sound on my amp emulator, and recorded a new version of the track. That's the version I ended up using. Still, even though you might not end up using any of these editing tricks to salvage your original track, it's great to know that the tools are at your disposal and ready for you to use in experimentation.

The introduction has been removed.

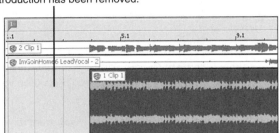

Figure 10.20

I've simply deleted the portion of the rhythm guitar part that holds the lead-in.

AN EXAMPLE OF AN EDIT THAT I DID USE IN THE FINAL MIX

Although I ended up not using the editing techniques I describe in the case of my guitar intro, I did use creative editing elsewhere in my project. For example, coming out of the solo, everyone drops out a little early and it seemed like the bottom just sort of fell out of the song for a moment before the next verse.

To fix that problem, I copied a small section of muted guitar strumming from a different part of the project and dropped it into the hole. Then, I split out the last sustaining note of the keyboard part so that the note occupied its own event on the timeline. I moved that event a little later in the timeline and extended the original event to match it. This had the effect of stretching that last note so that it now lasts exactly as long as I want it to.

You can hear the before and after of this process if you want to. Listen again to the file ImGoinHome_Complete.wav from the Chapter 09 folder on the companion disc. The solo ends at around the 3:00 mark. Notice how the mix gets very empty at that point.

Then, listen to the file ImGoinHome_Mixed.wav from the Chapter 10 folder on the companion disc. Note how in this final mixed version of the song, I've filled the hole in the phrase between the end of the solo and the following verse as I described above.

One more note on this subject. I didn't notice this problem between the solo and the next verse. Luckily, I sent my mix to Brian (my keyboardist friend from Chapter 7), and he's the one who pointed it out. That just serves to underscore my earlier point about running your mixes by other objective ears whose opinion you value. Just this little detail improves the song greatly in my opinion. And I would have missed it if Brian hadn't have pointed it out. Of course, once he mentioned it, it hit me like a hammer every time I heard it and I wondered how in the world I could have missed something so obvious. Sometimes you just get too close to your project to hear it objectively. It's times like those that you need another set of ears.

You can use the same envelope automation technique that we've discussed here to accomplish many different things in your project. For example, if you want a guitar solo to start in the left speaker and then sweep across the stereo field until it ends up in the right speaker, you can add a Pan envelope to the track, add a couple of points to the envelope line, and position them to create the effect you're after.

You can also automate certain aspects of the buses in your project, including the Master bus. To see how this works, let's say that you want your song to repeat and fade to the end. Instead of using separate volume envelopes to fade the audio from each track individually, you can add a volume envelope to the Master bus and create a fade there that affects the output of the whole project.

First, choose View, Show Bus Tracks to reveal tracks in the timeline for every bus in your project. These bus tracks now appear at the bottom of the timeline in a new section. Drag the bar that separates the regular timeline area from the bus tracks upward to make the bus tracks area taller so you can see more bus tracks. Use the scrollbar for the bus tracks section of the timeline to scroll until you can see the Master bus track in the track list.

> ### NOTE
>
> As you scroll through the list of bus tracks, notice that you have a bus track for every bus in your project, including each Soft Synth bus. This means that if you want to automate the audio generated by any of those Soft Synth buses, you can do so here in the bus tracks area of the timeline.

Right-click the Master bus icon in the track header for the Master bus and choose Insert/Remove Envelope, Volume from the cascading menu. The same blue envelope line that you saw in the track earlier now appears in the Master bus track. Use the same techniques you learned earlier to add points to the line. You'll only need two points to create a simple fade. Drag the second of the two to the bottom of the track, as I have in Figure 10.21, and you've got your fade-out ending.

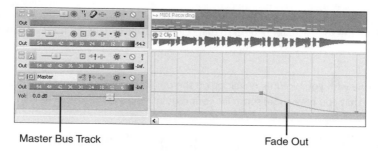

Master Bus Track   Fade Out

Figure 10.21

Add two points to the envelope line, and drag the second of the two to the bottom to create your fade-out ending.

You can change the shape of the curve between any two points on your envelope line. To do that, right-click the first of the two points in the curve and select the curve shape that you want from the pop-up menu, as shown in Figure 10.22.

When you first change the shape of a curve, you may not immediately hear the difference it makes in your song, but eventually you'll come across a situation where one shape just somehow sounds better to you than the other shapes.

Figure 10.22
You've got six different fade shape options to choose from for every curve on your envelope line.

TIP

It isn't a bad idea to add an automation envelope to the Master bus track even if you don't want to create a fade-out for the entire project. For example, I'll often use an envelope on the Master bus to cut the volume at the beginning of the project (between when recording started and the song actually begins) so that I eliminate any extraneous noise like humming guitars and the drummer's count in.

When you're done with your volume envelope on the bus track, choose View, Show Bus Tracks again to hide them so that you have more room for your regular tracks in the visible timeline area.

Adding Audio Effects and Digital Signal Processing

Modern music is full of digital signal processing (DSP), which happens at pretty much every stage of the recording process. This is the audio engineer's chance to put his or her mark on the recording. Of course, if you're doing the job yourself, it's just an extension of the creative process you're undertaking. Let's take a look at some of the issues involved with adding DSP to your project.

Adding DSP at the Recording Stage

Many times you'll add DSP well before you ever get to the mixing stage. For example, think about your electric guitar tracks and how you (or your guitar player) shape the guitar's sound. You run it through stomp boxes and pedals and whatever else to give it your sound.

You might add compression, echo, reverb, chorus, flange, phase, tremolo, and more to any track that you record. As I mentioned earlier, it's easy to go overboard with DSP. There's an art to using it properly and tastefully—even at the recording stage.

Adding DSP at the Mixing and Mastering Stages

You can also add DSP at the mixing stage. This is where you'll typically use subtle adjustments to make things sound better. For example, you might add a touch of EQ on a vocal track to bring out the richness of the singer's voice a little bit. Or you might apply compression to your overall drum mix to punch it up a bit. All the effects you apply here will, of course, be in addition to the effects you applied while recording. So you can see that it is indeed easy to go too far.

In Chapter 11, you'll see that DSP plays a starring role in the mastering stage, too. We'll talk in just a little more detail about what some of the audio effects are and how you might use them to improve your recordings.

A distinction that might help is that when you apply DSP at the mixing stage, you'll typically be doing fine surgery on a specific track in your project. For example, you might be applying a slap-back echo to the lead vocal. In the mastering stage, you'll typically be doing that surgery on the whole body of the song. You might notch up a frequency with an EQ just to give the high end of the entire mix a little shimmer.

Use DSP Judiciously

Just remember that it all adds up. My general thought on the topic of DSP is the less the better. The more DSP you pile onto your recording, the less natural and organic it will sound. Now, of course, lots of musical styles call for heavy processing as part of the sound, and if that's what you're going for, you have all kinds of tools to use. But if you're looking for a more natural sound, less DSP is usually better. That's where all the techniques we've discussed for controlling the sound of your room, getting proper record input levels, and choosing the right instrument, amplifier sound, and microphone for the situation can really help.

Remember, garbage in/garbage out. If your initial recording is substandard, you are *not* likely to be able to fix it in the mix. Small fixes like those we've discussed here are one thing. But trying to salvage a poorly recorded track by piling DSP onto it is another thing altogether. It just won't work.

NOTE

If you want to hear my song's final mix, play the file ImGoinHome_Mixed.wav from the Chapter 10 folder on the companion disc.

Studio Log

The mixing stage is one of the most challenging aspects of making high-quality recordings. As a home recording musician, you may have to learn some new skills as you step into this process. You may have to learn to listen to music in an entirely different way than you ever have before.

You might want to hire someone with experience and a high-quality room to work with you on your mixes. But you can gain a lot of satisfaction from learning to create nice mixes yourself. If you are going to do your own mixing and you don't have a quality space in which to do the job, spend the extra money it takes to buy a high-quality set of headphones. But make sure to evaluate your mix on several other listening systems to verify that the mix that sounds so wonderful in your headphones also sounds wonderful on any other system.

Mixing is really an ongoing process that starts as soon as you lay down your first track. Every time you tweak the volume of a track, solo or mute a track, or add a new bus and route related tracks to it, you're mixing your project. Your DAW gives you lots of mixing tools to work with while you're recording or evaluating a newly recorded track.

But eventually you'll enter into the mixing stage, where you devote all your attention and energy to creating a pleasing mix. Make sure you give your ears a rest before you jump into the mixing stage because ear fatigue equals substandard mix.

In this chapter, you learned several mixing techniques. You learned how to break your MIDI drum track into separate, totally controllable outputs so that you could then control each drum sound individually. You learned to create a submix that takes the daunting task of blending all your project's tracks and sounds together and breaks it into manageable pieces of related tracks that you can mix separately and then fold into the overall mix with the submix bus' controls.

We also discussed "fixing it in the mix" and showed a few examples of where it's appropriate to use mixing tools to solve problems. However, we also talked about making sure that you make quality recordings going in, because no matter how good you are at mixing, it's always better to do it right at the recording stage than try to fix mistakes at the mixing stage.

Mixing is critical to your project's success. I enjoy the mixing process almost as much as the recording part of the job. If you're going to do your own mixes, you'll have to take a positive approach to it. Don't look at it as a burden or something you dread, because if you do, you won't do a good job with it. Accept it as a vital part of your art, and then challenge yourself to master that art. If you can't—or just plain don't want to—put the time and effort in that a good mix requires, hire someone to do it for you. If you're going to put out music that sounds professional, you don't have a choice; you have to have a quality mix.

11

Mastering Your Song

In Chapter 10, "Mixing Your Song," we turned our attention from the recording process and began the process of making it all sound as good as possible. A quality mix is critical to the process. In this chapter, we discuss another stage of the process that is just as critical but typically far less understood and often neglected.

It's difficult to describe what *mastering* is other than to say it's the process of putting the finishing touches on your recording. People describe mastering as "putting the sheen on the mix," "making the song sparkle," and "giving the music that extra punch," along with other such nontangible descriptions. What you're actually trying to accomplish with the mastering process is highly subjective. It's something you can't necessarily describe, but you know it when you hear it.

A superb mix of a great recording might sound a bit dull and somewhat lifeless next to the same recording and mix after it's been properly mastered. If you've ever been excited about a mix you've done until you've heard it played next to a commercially produced CD and noticed how dull, lifeless, and flat it seemed in comparison, you have a pretty solid idea of what difference a proper mastering job makes on even the best mix.

In practical terms, mastering is the process of using digital signal processing (DSP) to improve the quality of the recording. That's what I'll concentrate on in this chapter: the practical side of mastering. We'll talk about the tools you use and the process you follow to master your music. But as with Chapter 10, I'm going to have to leave the *art* of mastering to trial and error as well as further research because no book can teach you that aspect of the process.

IN THIS CHAPTER

- Decide whether to master yourself or hire a pro

- Discuss the mastering environment and tools

- Learn about mastering digital signal processing tools

- Set up a mastering session in Sony Sound Forge

To Master or Not to Master

I posed a similar question at the beginning of Chapter 10. The question is actually a little more relevant here than it was there because, although you can never skip the mixing process, there are cases where you can get away with not mastering your recordings.

> **NOTE**
>
> Technically, this chapter deals with the process of *premastering*, meaning getting your song ready for the true mastering process, which involves sequencing it for the CD, level matching, creating the final files, and so on. We'll talk about much of that in Chapter 12, "Delivering Your Music." But the term *mastering* is often used for what we're talking about here, so I'll stick with it.

For example, if you're creating a demo recording for your band mates to learn one of your new tunes, you could skip the mastering process, but you'll still have to mix it, even if only roughly.

However, if you're creating your recordings for sale on your website or CD and you skip the mastering step, you'll relegate yourself to the realm of amateurism and will never move into pro-sounding territory. When you're trying to sell your music, you naturally want it to sound as professional as possible, so *you cannot skip the mastering stage*!

Even more so than with mixing, it might make sense to send your project to a professional mastering engineer who can use his experience and high-quality room and gear to do the job for you. Keep in mind that even the top pro mixing engineers typically hand over the mastering on a project to a mastering engineer. At the pro level, you're likely to find engineers who specialize in either mixing or mastering but don't hold themselves out as the expert in both.

A pro mastering studio is typically set up differently from the room that a mix is created in. While the pros might create the mix in the same room that they recorded the tracks in, they are not likely to use that same room and equipment to do the mastering.

I guess the point is that mastering is a highly specialized and detailed operation. Let's face it; you probably don't have much of a chance with the facilities and gear you have (not to mention your experience) to do the same quality mastering job as someone who can boast a large body of mastering work and has the high-quality equipment and room to work with. Naturally it'll cost you more, but you should give serious consideration to hiring an experienced mastering pro to get the most possible out of your recording project.

Okay; now that we've had that discussion, let's get back to reality. The reality is that you and I will probably find it difficult to part with the kind of scratch that a pro mastering engineer is able to demand. And the cheaper the mastering engineer comes, the less chance that he's going to give you something that you can't achieve yourself. So for the rest of this chapter, let's get on with doing the job ourselves. You might not be able to match what the pros could give you, but you can improve the sound quality of your recording dramatically.

Your Mastering Environment

Let's break the mastering environment into two parts: the room in which the mastering will take place and the software you'll use to do the job. I already mentioned that a pro mastering studio is likely quite different from a tracking or mixing studio. You and I probably can't swing that. After all, you've probably fought for the limited space you have devoted to your musical projects and it's unlikely you can grab more. It's even more unlikely that you can outfit two different spaces so that you have one dialed in for tracking and mixing and the other for mastering. So in this section we'll talk about how to make your space serve all those purposes.

We'll also discuss the software you'll use to do the mastering job. You might use your DAW software, but a more specialized audio editing application might be a better choice. We'll address that issue here too.

Your Mastering Studio

We've touched on your studio space so many times now that I'm probably beginning to sound like a broken record. Naturally, you need the best acoustic space you can put together to master in. All the topics of extraneous noises, room reflections, and so on are just as relevant here as they were in the recording and mixing stages. Again, if you can't put together a space that works well, you'll have to do your mastering in headphones.

ANOTHER OF THOSE USELESS ARGUMENTS

Go to any online forum that deals with mixing and mastering and ask what headphones you should buy to do the job. You'll get tons of responses, and I can almost guarantee that an argument will break out about whether you should ever mix and master in the cans. Lots of well-intentioned people will lecture you about how you should never trust headphones for your mixes or your mastering jobs. They'll offer up all sorts of good reasons to support this position.

Then some poor fellow will chime in and report how he always does his work in headphones and his results get rave reviews. The others will pick him apart no matter what he says or who comes to his aid.

All this is just plain idiotic because it doesn't answer the relevant question: What headphones should I buy to do my mixing and mastering? Whether headphones are the optimal environment in which to do the work is a totally meaningless side distraction. After all, who among us wouldn't own a great pair of reference monitors (or multiple pairs) and use those if we could? The point is, some of us just can't work with monitors. Remember, we're trying to get our work done without disturbing the neighbors or waking the kids. And we don't have the greatest listening environment in which to work, either. For some of us (this includes me, by the way) headphones are really the only viable option. So forget about the argument and let's get back to the relevant question: What headphones should I buy?

Well, the answer to that question is (naturally) first and foremost a matter of budget. How much can you afford to spend? If you have in the neighborhood of $300 to $500 U.S. to spend, you can get amazing sound quality from headphones made by companies such as Sennheiser, Grado, Denon,

AKG, Sony, Beyer Dynamic, and others. It's a simple equation, really: The less you have to spend, the less amazing sound you can expect to get. But that should not stop you! Do some research. Get the best-sounding headphones you can afford, and get to work. If you can't afford the best now, hopefully someday your situation will improve and you can upgrade later.

The key is, become intimately familiar with the characteristics of your headphones. Get to know their qualities and quirks and you'll soon learn to adjust for those in your work. And remember, always, always, *always*, check your mixes and mastered songs on as many different sound systems as you can and against reference music that you're very familiar with. That's your insurance policy against creating music that sounds great in your headphones but nowhere else.

That presents many challenges, but they're not insurmountable. Get the best headphones you can afford, and then get to know them well. After you work with them for a while, you'll start to develop a sense of their character. For example, you'll begin to recognize that perhaps your phones are a little light on the bottom, and you'll start to compensate for that by adding less bass frequencies to your recording than might sound perfect in the headphones.

In Chapter 2, "Setting Up Your Recording Studio Space," I talked about getting to know the sound of your room. If you're recording, mixing, and mastering in headphones, those phones are your "room," and you need to spend just as much time getting to know the sound of that room as you would if you were monitoring through studio monitors.

Take some time to play some of your favorite recordings while you just sit and listen to them through your studio monitors or headphones. Find recordings that have the production quality you wish you could achieve, and use them for reference when you're mastering your music.

MANAGE YOUR VOLUME LEVEL

When you're listening to your reference music as well as working on your own music, pay close attention to your listening volume. First of all, there's the obvious reason for doing so—you don't want to damage your hearing with music that's too loud. But there are other good reasons for managing your volume level. I talked about ear fatigue in Chapter 10, and that's relevant here, too. If your ears are tired, they'll be far less effective for the mastering task.

Also, the tendency is to listen at loud volumes because it makes the music sound powerful. But it's important to listen at low volumes, too, because things may sound quite different (aside from the volume issue) that way. You'll be surprised at how problems with your mixing and mastering present themselves at low volume levels in ways they do not at high levels.

You might logically think that higher volume will make problems easier to hear, and surely that's true to some extent. But although it might seem counterintuitive, higher volume can also mask problems that can present themselves at more moderate and even very low volume levels. The point is, listen to your project both soft and loud and at lots of volume levels in between. When you're happy with the way it sounds at all different volume levels, you're on to something good!

And by the way, this concept also applies to the mixing stage.

Your Software Environment

The music software that you do your mastering in is less critical than the DSP that you use. I'm fortunate enough to have a choice of applications that I can use to host my mastering tasks. I've used Sound Forge from Sony Creative Software on past projects, and I would consider that my desired tool. Sound Forge is designed specifically to work with file formats that are already mixed—like a stereo-mixed file of your project. But I've also done mastering right in ACID Pro. Because both tools support identical audio plug-ins, I can apply the same DSP regardless of which application I use.

Sound Forge provides some tools that ACID Pro does not. For example, Sound Forge features a spectrum analysis tool that makes it possible to evaluate the frequencies of your project for clues to problems that might exist. Or you can use the tool to compare the sound spectrum of your music to that of your reference music. That might give you some clues as to what you need to do to make your project sound more like your reference project.

Another plus to purchasing Sound Forge is that the current version (version 9 at the time I write this) comes bundled with four high-quality mastering plug-in tools from Izotope. Because I have Sound Forge, I also have these tools. Furthermore, because a good DAW supports the same DirectX and VST plug-in architecture that Sound Forge does, you can use those mastering plug-ins whether you're working in something like Sound Forge or your DAW.

One advantage to doing your mastering work in your DAW is that you can easily go back and adjust your mix if you need to. If you're mastering in something like Sound Forge, you need to render a mixed file (like we did when we created a file to send to our collaborators) and bring that into the application for mastering. Although this is arguably the proper way to approach the task, I have found it beneficial in the past to have instant access to my mixing tools during the mastering process, so sometimes I like to master inside my DAW. Others would tell you to keep the processes separate, and there's validity to that, too. First get things recorded properly. Then mix it well. Finally, master what you've mixed. That's probably the best way to do things, but sometimes I'm a rebel.

NOTE

Perhaps the best reason not to do your mastering in the same project that you've done your recording and mixing in has to do with computer resources. It might be a lot to ask your computer to not only process all the mastering DSP you're about to apply, but also to mix the track and perform the mixing DSP at the same time. Your computer just might not be able to keep up with these demands on processing power. If that's the case, you may have no choice but to render out a stereo file of your song and then bring it into a mixed file-editing application like Sound Forge to master it.

Your Mastering Tools

As I mentioned, the main tools you'll reach for when mastering your projects are the DSP plug-ins that help you refine the sound of the mix and finalize your song. I mentioned the Izotope mastering plug-ins that ship with Sound Forge 9. These give us a good base for discussing DSP at the mastering stage. If you don't have the Izotope mastering plug-ins that I discuss here, your DAW probably includes similar plug-ins of its own. In addition, you can find several plug-in vendors who sell DSP tools intended specifically for mastering music.

TIP

Even though the Izotope plug-ins that I discuss here are intended for mastering, there's no reason you can't use them at the mix stage. For example, recall that when we talked about recording the vocals in Chapter 9, "Recording Things That Require Microphones," we applied the mastering reverb to the vocal track upon input monitoring. That gave the vocals a sense of space while you monitored them as you sang.

Equalization

We've talked a little about equalization (EQ) in a couple of other places throughout this book. An EQ plug-in enables you to adjust the volume of specific frequencies in your song without affecting other frequencies. This is not unlike your home stereo system, which has a simple EQ built into it in the form of Bass, Mid, and High knobs that enable you to shape the sound a little bit.

Unlike that simple EQ, a good EQ plug-in enables you to adjust specific frequency ranges and change those ranges according to what your song needs. For example, instead of a control that affects simply "bass" as your stereo's EQ does, an EQ plug-in gives you the power to define exactly what frequency is affected, along with how much the frequencies around that target frequency are affected.

Figure 11.1 shows the interface of the Izotope Mastering EQ plug-in. The red line indicates the shape of the equalization you've applied to your song. The flat shape indicates that I haven't yet made any EQ adjustments.

NOTE

Different types of EQs have different interfaces and controls. For example, you may be familiar with graphic equalizers that have controls for specific frequencies. The frequency bandwidth is determined by the number of band controls a graphic EQ features and cannot be changed the way it can be with the Izotope EQ shown in Figure 11.1.

The green Xs on the line are the tools with which you set the parameters of the EQ. (You can also enter exact numbers in the table below the graph, but usually you'll start by adjusting things with the Xs.) Each X, called a *filter*, can be adjusted completely independently of the others. Notice that under the Enable column of the table, the four "band" filters are selected. These correspond to the Xs in the graph.

The table below the graph area gives the current values of each filter. Notice that the filter consists of a target frequency measured in Hertz (Hz), a level of volume change measured in decibels (dB), and a bandwidth, which we'll talk about shortly (Q/slope).

Band 2 Filter   Band 4 Filter
Band 1 Filter | Band 3 Filter

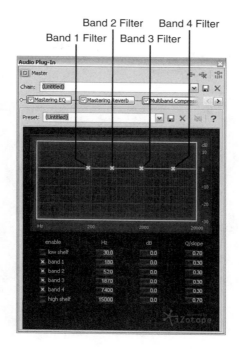

Figure 11.1

An EQ gives me the power to target frequencies and raise or attenuate the volume of those frequencies to shape the sound.

You can enable two additional filters: the Low Shelf and High Shelf filters. Select those check boxes to enable them. Now let's see how the EQ works.

First, play your project. Beneath the red, a waveform appears, which is the EQ's version of the spectrum analysis tool that I mentioned earlier. You can use it to get a sense of the loudest frequencies in your song. You can see in Figure 11.2 that volumes of the low-end frequencies are generally higher than the high-end frequencies. That information may give you some clues as to which frequencies you might want to adjust. (Of course, you can't master by what you *see*; you have to rely on what you *hear*.)

As your project plays, drag the Band 3 filter control (the filters are numbered from left to right) all the way down. Figure 11.3 shows that this creates an inverted bell-shaped dip in the line. That bell shape is the hallmark of a band filter; in a moment you'll see how that differs from a shelf filter. You can readily hear how this dip, sometimes called a *notch*, affects the sound of your file as it attenuates (turns down) the volume of the target frequency.

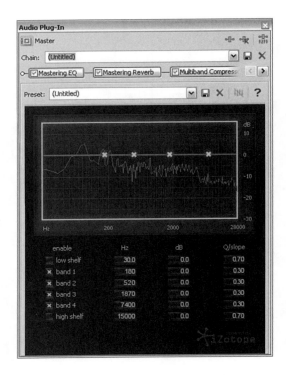

Figure 11.2
The spectrum graph shows that the low frequencies (on the left end of the graph) are considerably louder than the high-end frequencies.

You can use the Q/slope setting to adjust the width of the notch you've created. Drag one of the two angles that appear around the filter control toward the X to make the notch narrower. The narrower you make the notch, the smaller the range of frequencies that are affected by the filter. So if you identify one problem frequency, you can make the notch narrow and pull the volume down to "notch it out."

Now double-click the filter control to reset it.

A shelf filter creates a different effect. Instead of using it to notch out a particular frequency, you use it to raise or attenuate all frequencies above (or below if you're using the low shelf) a specified frequency.

For example, drag the high-shelf filter up and move it to the left so you can see the result more clearly. You can see in Figure 11.4 that this creates a slope upward, but notice that it never comes back down the way it did when you used the band filter a moment ago. Double-click the filter control to reset it.

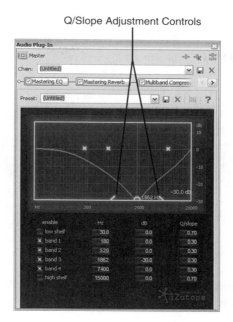

Figure 11.3

When you adjust a band filter, you create a dip (or bump) in the EQ line.

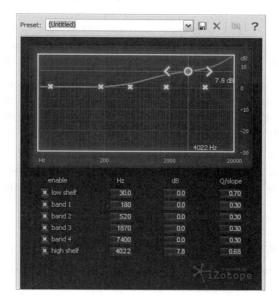

Figure 11.4

A shelf filter raises or lowers the target frequency and every frequency beyond it.

EQUALIZATION: THE SUBTRACTIVE ART

The guy who first taught me how to mix sound a few years back shared a piece of wisdom that has stuck with me all these years. He called equalization a "subtractive art." By this he meant that instead of turning up the frequency you think needs a boost, first try turning down other frequencies. This makes logical sense because it prevents you from turning a frequency up so much that it begins to distort.

In practice, I've found it difficult to hold to this technique—it just feels so much more intuitive to turn up the frequency you want to hear more of. But I still keep his words in mind and try to live by them. In any event, if you find that you're raising any particular filter by more than 6dB, stop and think about what you're doing and whether you can attenuate different frequencies to solve the problem you're addressing.

Keep your eye on all the relevant volume meters to make sure that the adjustments you're making with the Mastering EQ do not cause your project output to clip.

Reverb

We talked about natural reverb when we discussed controlling audio reflections in your studio back in Chapter 2. Back then (and several times since) I stressed the importance of eliminating, or at least controlling, room reflections. So it may then seem counterintuitive to use a plug-in that puts reverberation back into your mix, yet that's exactly what the Mastering Reverb plug-in (and others like it) does.

The thing to remember is that reverb in and of itself is not a bad thing—as long as you have control over it. Reverb adds a sense of depth and space to the mix. It can make it seem more natural, warmer, and more alive. It can put you in a "room" and change your mix to sound like it was recorded in a closet or a stadium. Of course, it can be—and has often been—grossly overused, and then it causes more harm to the song than good. But if you use it tactfully, you'll enhance your mixes with it.

In all likelihood, you'll have added some reverb to your project already. (You probably have added EQ already as well.) For example, you'll often add reverb at the mixing stage. Maybe you added some reverb to your vocals to give them more depth. And most electric guitar players add some reverb at their amp (or amp emulator) as part of their guitar sound.

Even though you've added reverb at these earlier stages, you may still want a touch here at the mastering stage. When you add reverb to the entire mix (as opposed to individual tracks like you probably would when mixing), you can use it to tie the whole project together. Sometimes when you get to the mastering stage, it sounds like the various pieces of the project are a little disconnected—like they weren't recorded together in the same space, which in reality they probably weren't! A touch of reverb at the mastering stage can pull everything back into the same space and make it sound—or perhaps more accurately, *feel*—more unified and cohesive.

Figure 11.5 shows the interface for the Izotope Mastering Reverb plug-in. The graph area at the top shows a spectral analysis of the audio coming into the plug-in. (You'll only see the bars of the graph if you're playing your project.) The controls at the bottom enable you to adjust the characteristics of the reverb.

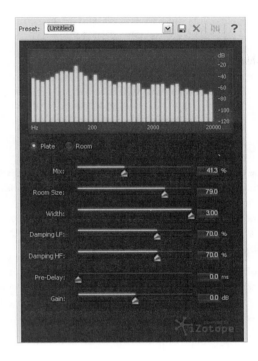

Figure 11.5

You can add a touch of mastering reverb to your project to pull it together and make it sound a bit more cohesive.

You can choose either the Plate or Room radio buttons. Plate reverb is more synthetic and artificial sounding, while room reverb uses more of a natural room simulation sound.

The Mix control enables you to adjust how much reverb sound and how much unaffected sound you use. If you set this to 0%, you won't hear reverb, while if you set it to 100%, you won't hear any of the original (unaffected) sound.

TIP

You can use the sliders to adjust the settings of the reverb plug-in or double-click the current value and type an exact value into the field.

The Room Size setting dictates how long the reverb will last before it dies away, while the Width setting controls the stereo spread of the reverb. The Dampening LF (low frequencies) and Dampening HF (high frequencies) controls define the brightness of the reverb effect for the associated frequency range. The Pre-Delay setting dictates the time between the original sound and the occurrence of the reverb. Finally, the Gain control adjusts the output gain of the plug-in. You might use that to compensate for any volume changes that occurred as a result of changes you made to the mix setting.

TIP

At the mastering stage, you'll probably want reverb to be a subtle effect. In fact, you might want it to be something that your listeners don't even consciously notice. Just add a touch to pull the mix together (unless you're after some sort of special effect, like making your song sound like a live recording of a stadium concert). The effect may well be something you don't even notice yourself unless you toggle it off and on and listen for the difference.

Multiband Compression

Audio compression may be one of the least understood (or most misunderstood) techniques you'll use. That's because, though it's easy enough to tell someone technically what's happening, it's extremely difficult to explain or even demonstrate how to do it properly. Conversations where one engineer tries to explain compression to another, less experienced engineer typically end by the first engineer sort of throwing up her hands and saying something to the effect of, "Well, I can't explain how I know when it's right; I just know!"

I'll try to give you an idea of what a compressor does, but you really owe it to yourself to study the topic more thoroughly because, used properly, compression is one of the most powerful tools you have available for making your music sound professional. Unfortunately, used improperly, it's one of the most dangerous tools and can easily brand your music as, well, not so pro.

A compressor plug-in can be single band or multiband. Because a multiband compressor is essentially just four single-band compressors each assigned to a specific range of frequencies, I'll talk in terms of a single-band compressor, and then later we'll apply what we discuss to each of the separate bands on the Izotope multiband compressor.

In simple terms, a compressor listens for audio that exceeds a specified volume level and automatically turns it down by a specified amount. A common analogy is that it's as if you were sitting there watching the level meters and riding the volume fader turning the volume down and up as necessary to keep the overall output volume within a certain range. Essentially what this does is limit the dynamic range of the audio so that the quiet portions of the audio are closer in volume to the loud portions. This makes the overall volume sound louder because you can turn the audio up as a whole; the loudest portions have been attenuated to be closer to the quieter portions.

A compressor normally has five settings. You can see these in Figure 11.6.

The *threshold* setting determines the volume level above which the audio will be affected by the rest of the settings in the compressor. For example, a threshold setting of –12.5dB means that the audio will not be affected by the compressor until it gets louder than –12.5dB. If the audio never exceeds the threshold, it is never affected by the compressor. In the analogy I used of your riding the fader, the threshold is that level where you begin to turn the volume down because it's gotten too loud.

Figure 11.6

A compressor normally features threshold, gain, ratio, attack, and release controls.

After you attenuate the loudest volumes (those that rise above the threshold setting), you can use the *gain* control to raise the volume of the compressor's total output. Keep an eye on your meters to make sure you're not clipping. Also, keep in mind that because you're raising the volume of the quiet parts of the music, you're also raising the volume of any noise in your recording. Things like guitar amp hum or the furnace that kicked in while you were recording are going to be louder along with the quiet parts of the music.

The *ratio* setting determines how much the audio that rises above the threshold will be attenuated. In our analogy, it's how much you turn the volume down when you see it surpass the threshold on the meters. A high ratio means you turn it down more aggressively than a low ratio. The ratio is defined in terms of x:1, such as 2:1 or 10:1. A ratio of 2:1 means that any audio that exceeds the threshold by 2dB will be attenuated so that it ends up exceeding the threshold by only 1dB. Likewise, audio that exceeds the threshold by 4dB will be reduced at the same 2:1 ratio and will end up exceeding the threshold by only 2dB.

Figure 11.7 shows a graph from a compressor plug-in interface that provides a helpful illustration of what's going on. The horizontal axis shows the input volume (the volume before the compressor acts upon it) of the audio in decibels, while the vertical axis shows the output volume (the volume after the compressor attenuates it). A 1:1 ratio setting would not affect the audio, and the graph would follow a perfect 45 degree angle from the lower left to the upper right (the dashed line in Figure 11.7). This graph shows a ratio setting of 3:1, with a threshold of –24dB. You can see that the threshold acts as a hinge point where the line bends and takes on a new slope so that the output volume is now less than the input volume. Note that volume levels that fall below the –24dB threshold remain unaffected by the compressor and are still right on the 1:1 slope.

So the higher the ratio, the more you're squashing the dynamics of the audio (that is, the difference between the softest sound and the loudest). Essentially, you're removing the subtleties of the sound. While you want to be careful doing this to an entire mix (so you probably wouldn't use a high ratio), it can help make an individual sound—like a kick drum, for example—more forceful. Therefore, higher ratios are more appropriate for individual sounds with strong attacks, like drum sounds and bass guitar.

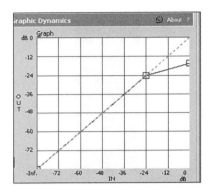

Figure 11.7

The compression graph shows that output volume is less than input volume for any audio that rises above the threshold.

The *attack* setting determines how quickly the compression kicks in after the audio surpasses the threshold. In our analogy, it's the time between when you notice the volume is too loud and when you turn it down. Be careful not to make the attack too short, as this can cause distortion.

The *release* setting dictates how long the compressor remains active after the audio level falls back below the threshold. Again in our analogy, this is how long it takes you to turn the volume back up after it falls below the threshold. A slow release may mean that even though the audio has fallen back below the threshold, the compressor continues to act on it. If you set the release too fast, you might cause what's commonly referred to as *pumping*, where you can actually hear the sound return to its normal volume when the compressor lets go.

NOTE

This discussion of compressor controls is framed in terms of a single-band compressor. You're more likely to use a basic compressor in the mixing stage. For example, the example I give here of applying compression to the kick drum would really be done at the kick drum track level so that it affects just the kick drum and not the entire mix—that's a mixing function. I use this example here mainly to describe how compression operates. You really need to do more studying and experimenting on the art of compression to get a feel for how the different settings affect your audio.

Now that you have a sense of how a basic compressor works, let's turn our attention back to the multiband compressor that works so well when mastering an entire mix. The multiband compressor adds another dimension to the compressor we just talked about—the dimension of multiple bands (surprise!).

You can see in Figure 11.8 that the Izotope multiband compressor has four bands. Notice that each band has its own set of the five compression controls we just talked about. Also notice the white vertical lines in the graph area at the top of the window. These lines are called the *crossover settings*, and they define the width (the frequency range) of each of the four bands.

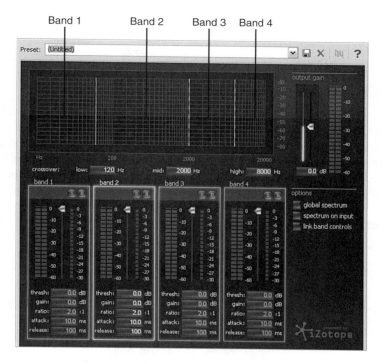

Figure 11.8

The Izotope multiband compressor features four bands with identical compression controls.

The leftmost of the three vertical lines defines the Low crossover frequency. You can see the exact setting of the line in the Low field of the crossover section, between the graph and the compression controls. In Figure 11.8, the Low crossover is set to 120Hz. All frequencies to the left of the Low crossover line fall into Band 1. Everything between the Low crossover line and the Mid line (at 2,000 Hz) falls into Band 2, and so on.

You can use the fact that each band affects a separate frequency range to really shape the sound of your file. For example, the compression settings that help add clarity and punch to your low end (bass, kick drum) of your mix are not going to be the same as the settings you need to add sparkle to the top end. The multiband compressor makes it possible to do both because you can set each band individually to bring out the best of each frequency range in your project.

TIP

In a great generalization, you could say that Band 1 includes your bass guitar and low drum sounds, Band 2 contains your midrange sounds like guitars and vocals, Band 3 contains high-end sounds like cymbals, and Band 4 contains the highest sounds generally referred to as "air."

There is naturally some overlap depending on the character of each instrument (obviously, female vocals occupy a higher frequency range than male); thus, you can change the crossover settings if you need to so you can include the frequencies you want to manipulate. Just drag the white crossover lines left and right or type an exact value into any of the crossover value text fields.

Audio Limiting and Loudness Maximizing

The concept of a limiter is similar to that of a compressor. It also does basically the same thing as a volume maximizer plug-in. The idea is to limit the volume of the loudest audio peaks so that you can raise the volume of quieter audio and thus make the whole file sound louder without clipping. Again, this tool effectively squashes the dynamics of your audio by bringing the loud portions more in line with the quiet portions, and it does so in even a more drastic fashion than a compressor. If you've ever wondered why you just haven't been able to make your mixes seem as loud as those on your favorite rock CD, it's in part because you haven't added a limiter to squeeze the dynamics out of your file the way it's been squeezed out of the music on that CD.

The limiter, shown in Figure 11.9, is a simple enough tool with really just two main controls (and four all together).

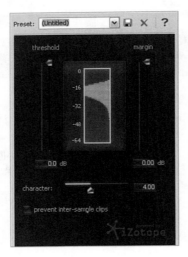

Figure 11.9
The mastering limiter helps you get more perceived volume out of your mix.

When you run audio through the limiter, the graph shows the character of that audio's volume. You can see that the bulk of my audio in the screen shot is at around –16dB.

The *threshold* setting works much like the threshold on a compressor. Any audio that rises above the threshold is altered to match the margin setting.

The *margin* setting dictates the level that the loudest peaks in the file are set to. The lower the threshold setting, the more peaks that will be set to the margin setting. For example, say your audio has one peak at −1dB and another at −3dB. If you set your threshold to −2dB, the −1dB peak will be limited to peaking at the specified margin setting. If you set your threshold level to −5, both the −1 and −3dB peaks will be limited to the margin setting, thus equalizing those two peaks and making the mix seem louder. Unlike a compressor, which uses a ratio to attenuate audio that surpasses the threshold so that louder peaks will remain louder than quieter peaks (although the difference will be diminished), the limiter slams any audio that exceeds the threshold hard to the margin so that the quieter peaks that exceeded the threshold will end up at the same volume as the louder ones that exceeded the threshold. Thus, a limiter is more heavy handed than a compressor.

NOTE

Recall how we discussed narrowing the difference in the volumes of individual MIDI notes in Chapter 10. In that discussion, we raised the velocities for all the kick drum notes whose original velocities were above 85 or so and set all of them to 127. This enabled us to raise the velocities of all other kick drum notes to a higher level. It squeezed the dynamics out of the kick drum track, as the limiter has in this discussion. In essence, back then you were playing the part of a limiter by making the adjustments manually.

The *character* control dictates the harshness with which the limiter conforms audio to the margin setting. A lower setting is more unforgiving, and a higher setting should feel a bit more organic.

If you're going to be setting your margin and threshold aggressively (a margin close to 0dB and a low threshold), you may want to select the Prevent Inter-Sample Clips check box. This prevents clipping that you may not detect in your digital meters but may result later in the conversion back to analog audio (for listening). This option requires a bit more processing power, but it's a little insurance against accidental distortion caused by clipping.

ANOTHER GREAT DEBATE

Producers of modern rock and country music (and, for that matter, producers who are digitally remastering classic recordings) find themselves in a bit of a bind these days. All of this compression and volume limiting that we're talking about as essential aspects of mastering your song are not without problems.

The main problem is that people are constantly comparing the song they're hearing to the one they heard just prior to it. Radio is the biggest culprit here. If you're a record producer trying to make sure your song gets noticed (which you are, by the way!), the sad truth is that the loudest song wins. If your song comes on the radio and the listener perceives it to be quieter than the one he just heard, the natural tendency is to assume that something is wrong with your song.

In an attempt to make their song louder than all the others (or at least *as* loud), producers began compressing and limiting their mixes to extreme levels. As we discussed, this squeezes the loud parts of the song more closely to the level of the quiet parts. These tools destroy the natural dynamic range (the difference between the quiet and loud parts) of the song.

So modern recordings have gotten relentlessly louder. As a result, they've become more fatiguing to listen to and less interesting musically, because the dynamic range of a song is one very important aspect to making the music interesting. Although the dynamic range in a rock song is likely to be narrower to begin with than that of, say, a Beethoven symphony, natural dynamics still exist even in rock. That is, until the producer eggs on the mastering engineer to squeeze it more and more! This is one reason some people hate the sound of digitally remastered classics.

There are a few brave souls in the industry who refuse to give into this madness. They leave the dynamics in their recordings, knowing full well that their song won't be as loud as the ones that play before and after it on the radio. You have to respect them for that decision. Unfortunately, you and I likely don't have the clout to pull that off, and we'll probably have to squeeze dynamic range out of our tunes to make them sound as loud as the next one. Otherwise, no matter how good the music, no matter how good the mix, and no matter how good the mastering, listeners will feel like our tunes don't hold up to the pros. Sad, but true.

Setting Up a Mastering Session

Now that you know a little bit about the tools you might use for mastering your music, let's set up a mastering session and learn how to pull it all together. I mentioned already that I use Sound Forge from Sony Creative Software to master my songs. Sound Forge is a great audio editing tool. Unlike ACID Pro or your DAW, an audio editor typically works with a mixed file—usually a two-channel (stereo) file in the case of the music we're recording. I've talked a couple of times about rendering a mixed file from your DAW, and we'll talk more about it in Chapter 12. For the file you're going to master, you'll want to render into an uncompressed file format (typically WAV for the PC and AIFF for the Macintosh).

When you have the file rendered from your DAW, open your audio editor. In Sound Forge, choose File, Open. Navigate to the file you want to master, and open it. Figure 11.10 shows my song open in Sound Forge.

Now create a chain of effects that holds the plug-ins you want to use during your mastering session. I'll add the four Izotope plug-ins that I discussed earlier. To create the effects chain, click the Preview Plug-In Chain button. This opens the Plug-In Chainer window, which at the moment is empty.

Click the Add Plug-Ins to Chain button to open the Plug-In Chooser (which will look familiar to you from your work in ACID Pro). Click the Third-Party folder in the list at the left. In the list on the right, you see the Izotope mastering plug-ins. Select them one by one, and add them to the effects chain.

TIP

You can experiment with different orders for the plug-ins in the chain, but always place your limiter or volume maximizer last . One possible order is the Mastering EQ, Mastering Reverb, Multiband Compressor, and finally the Mastering Limiter.

Preview Plug-In Chain Button

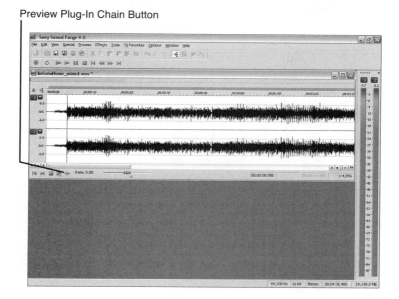

Figure 11.10

I've brought my two-channel mix into Sound Forge, and I'm ready to start mastering.

Work with the effects in your chain starting from the left end of the chain and working your way right. I'll assume you use the same order as I have, so that means you'll start with the Mastering EQ. To concentrate on just the EQ, deselect the Bypass check boxes for all the other effects in the chain to temporarily bypass them, as I've done in Figure 11.11.

Now click the Preview button in the Plug-In Chainer. As you listen to the project, start making adjustments to your EQ settings. When you're happy with your EQ, activate the next plug-in in the chain, and make your adjustments there. Continue one by one until you've reactivated all the plug-ins and made your adjustments.

When you're happy with your mastering adjustments, click the Process Selection button, which applies the parameters of the effects to the file. You will probably see changes in the file's waveform.

When you're finished, save the file and close its window in Sound Forge. You're now ready to move onto the next song, although in reality this may well have been a process that took hours. You should give your ears and your head a rest before working on the next song.

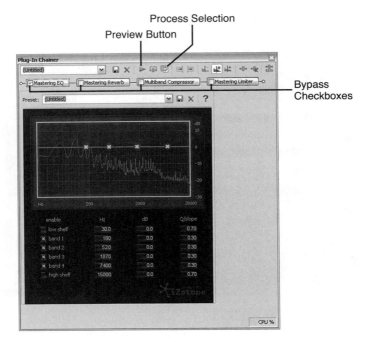

Figure 11.11

The Mastering EQ is the only plug-in that's currently active in the chain.

TIP

Mastering can be a daunting task, especially if you've never done it before. It can feel next to impossible to figure out where to even begin making adjustments. Luckily, each of the plug-ins in your mastering chain has a number of presets. That's where I usually start. Try various presets to see if you like how they make your song sound. If they improve things (even if not completely perfect), you can look at the settings of the preset to learn what adjustments created the sound you like. Then start making further adjustments manually from there. Stick with small changes at first. You'll start getting a handle on what to adjust to solve different problems or achieve specific results.

If you'd like to hear the difference that mastering made to my song, play the file ImGoinHome_ MasterToggle.wav from the Chapter 11 folder on the companion disc. This file starts off with the unmastered version, and after a few seconds I announce that the mastered version is about to be toggled on. Several seconds later I announce the mastering will be toggled off again, and a bit later I toggle the mastering on again (without the announcement). If you want to hear the whole song in its mastered state, play the file ImGoinHome_Mastered.wav from the same folder.

Studio Log

If you want your music to sound professional, mastering is not an option; it's an absolute necessity. In fact, you really need to give serious consideration to investing in an experienced pro to do the job for you.

If you can't afford a pro (it isn't cheap to hire someone who really knows how to do the job right), you'll have to do your best to master your own music. Several plug-in DSP tools aid in the mastering process, including EQ, reverb, multiband compression, limiting or volume maximizing, and others.

Study hard to understand mastering and get a feel for how to approach it. Also, jump right into it so that you can learn as you go through trial and error. Make each mastering job a learning experience that improves the quality of the next job.

Make the best out of your equipment and working environment, but make sure you always check your work on other playback systems and in other playback environments. It's difficult to be objective because by this time you're overly intimate with your song. It will really help for you to put a good deal of space between the mixing process and the mastering process. Take time to get the song out of your head so that when you do sit down to master it, you can come back to it with fresh ears.

12

Delivering Your Music

Finally! This is what it's all been leading up to. In this chapter, we'll talk about the various ways you can deliver your music. You'll learn a little bit more about creating the mixed files for your fans to listen to.

When you have the files you need, you'll master a CD project that you can use to either burn one-off copies of your project from your own computer or send to a CD replication facility to have multiple copies of your CD project manufactured.

We'll also look at a few of the resources that have become available over the past decade for sharing and distributing your music online.

You've learned a lot over the course of this book. This chapter brings it all together so that you can share your music with your friends and fans.

Creating a Mixed File

Before your fans can listen to your music, you have to give it to them in a format that they can play on their home stereo, their computer, or a personal music player. Typically this involves giving them a CD to play on their stereo or providing a file that they can stream or download from your website or some other online location. Before you can do any of that, you have to create a file that takes everything you did in the recording, mixing, and mastering stages and rolls it into one manageable file called a *mixed file*.

We created a mix file in Chapter 7, "Utilizing MIDI in Your Projects," when we emailed an MP3 file to Canada so that Brian could record his keyboard part. I mentioned the concept again when we discussed mixing and mastering in Chapters 10, "Mixing Your Song," and 11, "Mastering Your Song," because you create a mixed file after you're done mixing to bring it into an application like Sound Forge to do your mastering work. Let's take a moment to talk about the process in a little more detail now.

Rendering Your Project

To create a mixed file from ACID Pro, you need to *render* your project. You can think of the rendering process almost like baking the project the way you'd bake a cake. The project contains all the ingredients that make up your music, and you've mixed those ingredients in just the right way to make it all sound perfect. Now you just need to cook it so your fans can enjoy it.

To render your project, choose File, Render As. The Render As dialog box, shown in Figure 12.1, works just like a standard Save dialog box. Here you'll choose a location for storing the file you're about to create, give the file a name, and choose the file format.

Figure 12.1

Specify a save location, filename, and file format for the file you're rendering.

Let's take a closer look at the file format options. Click the Save As Type drop-down list. You can see in Figure 12.2 that you have a number of different options here.

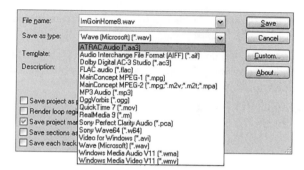

Figure 12.2
You can create files of many different types from your ACID Pro project.

NOTE

If you look closely, you see that several of the options listed in the Save As Type drop-down list are video file formats. We haven't discussed it because it isn't relevant to the topic of this book, but you can import a video file into the ACID Pro timeline. You can then open a video preview window that you can use to watch the video as you create music to go along with it. Finally, you can render the file into one of these video formats with the video and your new music bed. This makes ACID Pro a powerful video scoring tool that you can use to create custom music for videos.

There are several file formats in the list that are particularly relevant to our discussion of delivering your music:

- **Audio Interchange File Format (AIFF) (*.aif)**—An uncompressed, full-quality file format commonly used on applications for the Macintosh operating system. Use this if you're rendering a mixed file to send to a colleague for opening on her Macintosh.

- **FLAC audio (*.flac)**—FLAC stands for Free Lossless Audio Codec. This compression format gives the same audio quality as uncompressed formats, but at a smaller file size. This is becoming more widely supported by various software manufacturers as well as manufacturers of software and hardware playback devices. FLAC is a good choice if you need high-quality audio but want to conserve file storage space.

- **MP3 Audio (*.mp3)**—A lossy compression format that's common for use on websites (typically for downloading) and personal media players.

- **RealMedia 9 (*.rm)**—A lossy compression format that's common for streaming audio from websites.

- **Sony Perfect Clarity Audio (*.pca)**—A lossless compression format that gives the same full quality as an uncompressed file at a compressed file size. Because this is a proprietary Sony format, it is not widely supported by applications manufactured by other companies. Use it only if you know that you'll be opening it inside a Sony Creative Software application like ACID Pro or Sound Forge.

- **Wave (Microsoft) (*.wav)**—An uncompressed, full-quality file format commonly used on applications for the Windows operating system. Use this if you're rendering a mixed file that will be opened in a Windows application.

- **Windows Media Audio V11 (*.wma)**—A lossy compression format that's common for streaming audio from websites.

NOTE

Some of the file formats that your DAW supports are *compressed*. This is a different type of compression than the audio compression we discussed in Chapter 11. This compression is not about dynamic range and audio volume; instead, it's about file size. Compressed file formats use different techniques to make the file size smaller. A *lossy* compression scheme cuts file size at the expense of audio quality. In lossy compression, some of the audio information in the file is actually discarded or degraded to make the file smaller. So with lossy compression, you make the trade-off between file size and audio quality. In lossless compression, the file size is decreased with no loss of audio quality. In general, you can make files with smaller file sizes with lossy compression, but of course, the smaller you make these files, the more audio quality you sacrifice.

You can customize each of these file formats to create exactly the file you need. For example, if you're creating one of the streaming file formats listed previously for streaming from your web server, you probably want a high-quality version (high audio quality requires a faster Internet connection for streaming) as well as a low-quality version (lower audio quality that can be streamed over a slower Internet connection). Click the Template drop-down list to choose common settings for the file type you've selected in the Save As Type drop-down list. You can choose any of these templates for your file. Figure 12.3 shows the list of templates for the MP3 file format.

TIP

If you don't find the settings you want for your file in one of the templates from the Template drop-down list, you can create a file with custom settings. Start by choosing the template that comes closest to the settings you want, and then click the Custom button.

After you've chosen your file format and template, click the Save button, which initiates the rendering process. After the file finishes rendering, you have a mixed file in the location you specified on your computer.

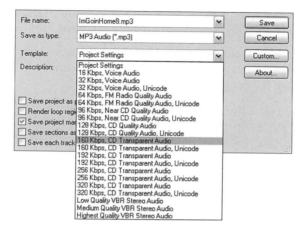

Figure 12.3

ACID Pro provides several templates for different audio quality under the MP3 file type.

RENDERING OPTIONS

There are several check boxes at the bottom of the Render As dialog box that give you a little more control over the rendering process. The two most important ones for our purposes are likely to be the Render Loop Region Only check box and the Save Each Track as a Separate File check box. Often you'll want to render just a portion of your project for review or some other purpose. To do that, set the loop region indicator bar to cover that section before you start the render process. Then select the Render Loop Region Only check box.

If you're collaborating with someone—particularly in the mixing stage—who uses a tool other than ACID Pro, you can render each track in your project individually. Then you can easily import those separate files into your colleague's application. To save each track in your project as a separate audio file, select the Save Each Track as a Separate File check box before you render. Keep in mind that if you also want to create an audio file from any MIDI tracks in your projects, you need to route those tracks to a Soft Synth (as we discussed in Chapter 7).

Batch Rendering

As we'll discuss shortly, you're most likely going to want to render files of multiple formats from a single project. For instance, you'll probably want an uncompressed (or a lossless compression) format for burning your CDs, an MP3 to make available for download from various websites, and perhaps a couple different streaming formats for posting on your website. As you've seen, you can create all these file types from ACID Pro. If you're not using ACID Pro, your DAW almost certainly creates all these formats too.

However, you can see that creating those files one by one from your DAW is a lot of busy work. Sony Sound Forge, which we used in our mastering discussion in Chapter 11, features a helpful tool called the Batch Converter. This tool enables you to set up the application to create all your files regardless of how many different formats or combination of properties you need.

Suppose you've finished mixing your project, rendered out a WAV file, brought that file into Sound Forge, and completed your mastering work. You can save your work on that WAV file, and then you have a mastered file to use for your high-quality audio file purposes.

Because that WAV file is uncompressed and full quality, you can render all the other files you need from it. You set up a batch job in Sound Forge's Batch Converter to do this. With the WAV file still open in Sound Forge, choose Tools, Batch Converter. The Batch Converter window opens, as shown in Figure 12.4.

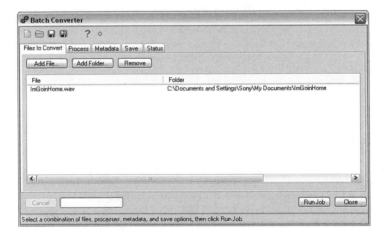

Figure 12.4
The Sound Forge Batch Converter creates multiple files automatically.

The file you currently have open in Sound Forge appears in the list on the Files to Convert tab. Click it to select it from the list.

TIP

You can run the Batch Converter on multiple files simultaneously. Click the Add File button to add one or more new files to the Files to Convert list, or click the Add Folder button to have the Batch Converter operate on every file in the selected folder. For instance, if you have a 10-song project and you've created WAV files for each of the 10 songs, you can add them all to the Files to Convert list and create files of multiple formats from each of those 10 songs in one operation. That can be a huge time saver.

On the Process tab, you can apply a chain of audio effects to the new files you'll be creating. For instance, if you have 20 files that you want to add reverb to, you can add a reverb effect plug-in to the chain and let the Batch Converter apply it to all the files for you.

The Metadata tab gives you a place to add information that will be embedded into the files you create. For instance, if you're creating several files of different formats from one WAV file, you can add the song's title, copyright information, track number, and much more. The Batch Converter embeds that information as *metadata* to the file. The information can then be displayed by certain devices like a personal media player.

You can use the Save tab to indicate the characteristics of the files you want to create. Click the Add Save Options button to open the Save Options dialog box, shown in Figure 12.5.

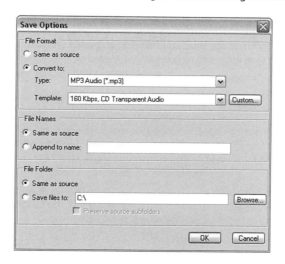

Figure 12.5

Specify your save characteristics in the Save Options dialog box.

Here you can choose from all the same file formats that we saw earlier in the ACID Pro Render As dialog box as well as all the same render templates for each of those formats. You can also specify whether you want the new files to have the same name and be saved into the same folder as the original, or whether you want to create something different. When you've made your choices, click the OK button.

Back on the Save tab of the Batch Converter, the file format you specified appears in the list. If you want to create more than one file format during the batch conversion process, click the Add Save Options button again and specify the characteristics of the next format you want. You can add as many to the list as you need.

The Status tab gives you information about your batch job as it runs. To run the job, click the Run Job button. Once the Batch Converter starts working, you can walk away from your computer and let Sound Forge do the rest of the work for you. When the batch finishes running, you have all the files you want ready to use.

Creating a Master Compact Disc

Naturally, when you're finished with all your recording, mixing, and mastering and you've created the mixed files for all your songs, you'll be anxious to hear them on CD. Whether you want to send your project to a CD replication facility or just burn a copy or two on your computer that you can listen to on another stereo, you'll need to sequence the songs and make sure everything sounds right together.

You can use several applications to create a *Red Book–compliant* CD. For example, Sony Creative software makes at least three applications that are capable of creating CD projects. One of those applications is ACID Pro, and because I've been doing all my work in that application, I'm going to use it to sequence and burn my master CD.

NOTE

A standard dubbed *Red Book* is used to specify the characteristics of audio compact discs. The name Red Book was derived from the simple fact that the book that first laid out the audio CD specifications (in the early 1980s) was bound in a red cover. The specification dictates many things about an audio CD, including a maximum playing time of 74 minutes, a minimum track duration of four seconds, a maximum track number of 99, and so on.

A CD that you intend to send to a CD replication facility *must* adhere to the Red Book standard, or it will more than likely be rejected. Therefore, it's critical that the application you use to burn your project master disc creates Red Book–compliant CDs.

TIP

Although ACID Pro is capable of sequencing and burning a Red book–compliant CD, that function is clearly not the main focus of the application. You may want to look into different applications that have been created specifically for the purpose of sequencing and burning CDs. Sony Creative Software's CD Architect application is an exceptionally good CD authoring and burning tool. Software that has been designed specifically for creating CDs provides much more sophisticated tools for getting the job done. Still, ACID Pro (and possibly your DAW) provides the basic functionality.

Sequencing Your CD

To create your CD in ACID Pro, first click the New button to start a new project. In the Explorer window, navigate to the folder that contains all the songs that you want to include on the CD. Drag the song you want to be the first song on the CD from the Explorer window, and drop it at the beginning of the timeline.

If you created the file in ACID Pro, that file contains tempo information. (ACID Pro embeds that information into the file when you render it.) Recall that you used files that contained tempo information in Chapter 4, "An Introduction to ACID Pro Fundamentals" when you built a project using loop files. The tempo information that's built into those loop files makes it possible for you to change the project tempo and have all the loops conform to it.

A long file (by default, anything over 30 seconds) that contains tempo information is called a *beatmapped* file. Because I created my song in ACID Pro, it contains tempo information and is a beatmapped file. Figure 12.6 shows my mixed WAV file on the timeline. The beatmapper icon next to the filename on the event indicates that the file contains tempo information.

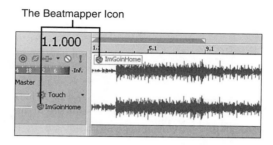

Figure 12.6

A beatmapped file contains tempo information.

CAUTION

It's critical that you pay attention to whether your mixed files are beatmapped and thus contain tempo information. If they do, they will conform to the ACID Project tempo and thus be either sped up or slowed down from the tempos that you recorded them at (unless their tempo just happens to match the project tempo).

Like me, you probably recorded your song at something other than the ACID Pro default project tempo of 120 beats per minute, so you need to tell the application to disregard the tempo information built into the song.

Right-click the event in the timeline and choose Clip Properties from the pop-up menu to open the Clip Properties window. There are a lot of tools and information in the Clip Properties window. For example, the window gives you important details about the file, including tempo information (if it exists). However, other than that information, the only thing that's of interest to us at the moment is the ACID type setting. If your file is a beatmapped file, that will be indicated here. To disregard the file's tempo information (so that it plays at its normal tempo instead of the ACID project tempo), choose One-Shot from the ACID Type drop-down list, as shown in Figure 12.7.

Close the Clip Properties window. The icon in the event on the timeline now indicates that the clip is being treated as a one-shot file instead of a beatmapped file. Now the file will play at its normal tempo.

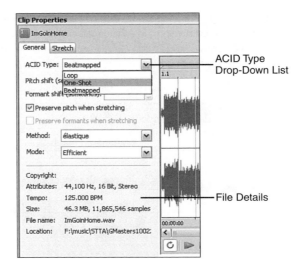

ACID Type
Drop-Down List

File Details

Figure 12.7
Change the ACID Type setting to One-Shot so that the file plays at its normal tempo.

NOTE

If you add a long file to your project that does not contain tempo information, ACID Pro launches the Beatmapper Wizard and asks if you want to have the application estimate the file's tempo. The only purpose for doing so is to make it possible for ACID Pro's project tempo setting to control the tempo of the song. Because you want the file to play at its recorded tempo, you don't need ACID Pro to figure out the tempo. So select the No radio button and click Finish. This adds the file to your project as a one-shot (with no tempo information), which ensures that your song plays at its actual tempo instead of the ACID Pro project tempo.

TIP

ACID Pro always sets the volume for a new track to the setting of the Preview fader in the mixing console window. By default, that fader is set to –6dB. This is important because, as you'll recall from Chapter 11, you used a limiter to bring the volume of your file close to 0.0dB to make it as loud as possible (hopefully without totally destroying the dynamics of the song!) If you leave the new track's volume set to –6dB, you'll end up with a very quiet CD, so set the volume to 0.0dB.

Double-click the track's Volume fader to quickly set the volume to 0.0dB. You'll find that double-clicking most controls in ACID Pro (and Sound Forge) sets the control back to a logical default setting.

Now that you've added the first song to your CD sequencing project, you need to indicate the start of the CD track or cut. Click to place your cursor at the beginning of the event you just added to the timeline. Choose Insert, CD Track Marker. A red CD track marker appears in the ACID Pro marker bar.

The red book standard specifies that there should be two seconds' worth of silence between each CD track. You don't have to stick with this specification if you don't want to (for instance, you might want two songs to overlap on your CD), but let's add the two seconds between the first and second cut on our CD. Place your cursor at the end of the event in the timeline.

The time display shows you the current cursor time. When you added the new CD track marker a moment ago, the time display changed to show Audio CD time. For instance, in Figure 12.8, you can see that my cursor sits in CD track 01 (the number to the left of the plus sign) at the 4:28:07 mark. Select the seconds value (in my song, that's 28), type the number that's two seconds larger (30 for me), and then press the Enter key. The cursor jumps to the new location and now sits two seconds later in the project than the end of the first CD track.

NOTE

When you select the current value in the time display, the display switches from CD track time to the standard hours, minutes, seconds, and milliseconds reading. Therefore, the time value changes as soon as you select it. However, you can still add two seconds to the time readout to move the cursor.

CD Track Number

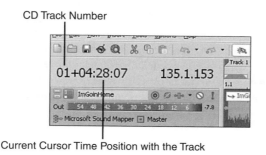

Current Cursor Time Position with the Track

Figure 12.8

The time display shows the CD track and time at the current cursor location.

You know that you want the second CD track to start here, so choose Insert, CD Track Marker to place your second CD track marker at the cursor location.

Now you can drag the second song from the Explorer window to the timeline and place it at the cursor location. Chances are pretty good that the cursor doesn't currently sit right on one of the timeline ruler marks. Because ACID Pro wants to snap events to the ruler marks, this makes it difficult to position the event to start at the cursor. You can hold the Shift key to temporarily override the snapping behavior and then place the event at the cursor. If you want to keep snapping on but would like ACID Pro to use the cursor as a snap object (in addition to the ruler marks), choose Options, Snapping, Grid Only to turn that option off so that now your events snap to the cursor (and project markers).

Use the same techniques to add the rest of your project's songs along with CD track markers to the timeline. Figure 12.9 shows my project with all my CD tracks in place.

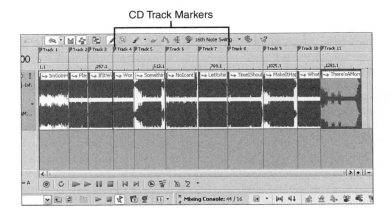

Figure 12.9
Here is a completely sequenced CD project with CD track markers in place.

If you did a good job mastering your songs, they should be pretty consistent as far as volume level goes. However, you can make adjustments here in your CD burning project if you need to. You can start by looking at the waveforms for the various songs in the project. If any one song's waveform looks much different from the others, you can use the techniques you've learned to change the volume of the event that contains that song. Specifically, drag the top of the event down to attenuate the event's volume (as you did when you were building dynamics into the one-shot drum tracks you assembled in Chapter 6, "Creating Drum Tracks"). You can also insert a volume envelope into the track and use it to adjust the volume over specific events, as you did in Chapter 10.

Burning Your CD

When you've finished laying out the order of the songs in your CD project, it's time to burn a copy. You'll use this copy as the master that you can send to a replication facility. Or you may just want to burn CDs one at a time when you need them. Either way, you can burn them right from the ACID Pro timeline.

Choose Tools, Burn Disc-at-Once Audio CD. Figure 12.10 shows the Burn Disc-at-Once Audio CD dialog box.

Naturally, you'll need a CD burner in your computer, and you'll select that burner from the Drive drop-down list. You might want to do a little experimentation with the Speed setting to make sure your computer doesn't have trouble burning at high speeds (particularly if you have a slower processor). Be prepared to waste a blank CD or two while you find the maximum speed your machine is capable of burning at. Or just choose a slower speed to start with. Even if you go down to a speed of only 10x, you'll still burn your project in around five minutes.

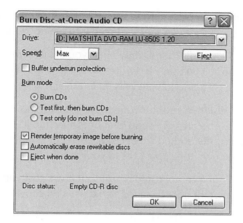

Figure 12.10
Use the Burn Disc-at-Once Audio CD dialog box to set your burning parameters.

> **CAUTION**
>
> Although the Buffer Underrun Protection feature can help your machine keep up to the burn process at higher speeds, it may cause problems with replication facilities. Avoid using it if you're burning a CD that you want to use as a replication master.

The only other setting that isn't fairly self-explanatory is the Render Temporary Image Before Burning check box. Select this to lighten the load on your processor. ACID Pro will do all the rendering of the CD image before starting the actual burn process.

When you're ready (and you have a blank disc in the burner), click the OK button to start the burn process.

Protecting Your Music

Before you put your music out there for the world to hear, make sure you protect yourself from anyone who might try to steal your work. In this section we'll discuss registering the copyrights that you own on your music to help prove that the music is indeed yours. We'll also talk about registering with a performing rights organization that will help you collect any income that you might have coming as a result of your music being used by others.

Registering Your Copyrights

You'll often hear people refer to *copyrighting* creative works. What they really mean is registering the copyrights they already own. In the United States, copyright law dictates that you own a copyright on any song you write the second you finish recording it to a fixed, tangible medium. So, in technical terms, you are protected from anyone claiming to have the rights to your music as soon as you write the lyrics and melody down on a piece of paper or record it to tape or your computer.

In practicality though, it can be very difficult to prove that you actually wrote the song. If the court hears compelling arguments from you that you wrote the song, as well as from someone else who says she wrote it, who the court is going to believe is up in the air.

To avoid such an unfortunate situation, register your copyright with the United States Copyright Office at the Library of Congress before your song ever becomes public—whether it's made public by a recording, public performance, distributed sheet music, or in any other way. If you do so, you have incontrovertible proof that you own the copyrights to your music.

Registering your copyrights is not a complicated matter, but it will cost you a little bit of money. Still, it's just not worth risking a copyright fight to save a few dollars on copyright registration.

To register the copyrights on your songs, go to www.copyright.gov. There you'll find all kinds of information and the forms you need to complete the process.

NOTE

Since I last registered copyrights for my music, the U.S. Copyright Office website has begun accepting electronic copyright registration submissions. Until recently all submissions had to be made via the U.S. mail. I haven't had the opportunity to use the online submission process yet, but it appears to be $10 less expensive ($35 for a collection of as many songs as you want, so it pays to register many songs at the same time) and certainly will be more convenient. I'm looking forward to using online registration for my next batch of songs!

Registering with a Performing Rights Organization

Another wise step to take before you go too far with promoting your music is to become a member of a performing rights organization (PRO). A PRO essentially monitors the public use of your music— radio airplay, use on network television, cable TV, nightclubs, restaurants, and other public uses. They then collect royalties for this use on your behalf and pay you.

Registering your music with a PRO is also another effective way to provide evidence of copyright ownership. After all, if you've registered your music with your PRO before you ever introduce it to the public, it's going to be very difficult for anyone else to prove that they wrote the music before you claim to have done so. It just doesn't make any sense for you not to join a PRO!

There are two major PRO players in the United States: The American Society of Composers, Authors, and Publishers (ASCAP) and Broadcast Music, Inc. (BMI). A third PRO (originally called the Society of European Stage Authors and Composers but now officially named SESAC) also has growing popularity in the United States. I'm a member of BMI.

Visit the websites of these PROs and figure out which one you want to join. Then join and register your songs! Here are the web addresses for each of the PROs I mentioned:

- **ASCAP**—www.ascap.com
- **BMI**—www.bmi.com
- **SESAC**—www.sesac.com

Posting Your Music Online

Part of the excitement for independent artists springs from the vast opportunity we have to have our music heard far and wide by fans who never would have heard it even 10 years ago. The Internet has clearly made it possible to share music with fans all over the world. While this doesn't mean you're guaranteed to become famous after you post your music, it does open the doors to possibilities. In addition to having your own website, there are many opportunities to get your music heard via the Internet—too many for me to do them justice here. But I'll give you an idea of some of the resources that I use, and you can take it from there.

Working with CD Baby

Now that you've burned your master CD, you can send it out to have it replicated. I did a Google search on the term *CD replication* and got 665,000 results, so you ought to be able to find someone to manufacture your CDs for you without too much trouble! Therefore, I won't go into much detail about it here except to say that some facilities offer services beyond simply replicating the CD. For instance, some manufacturers offer graphic art and printing services so that you can get a complete package including discs, j-cards, inserts, jewel cases, and so on from the same vendor. Make sure you do a little homework to find your best deal.

Once you have your CDs duplicated, you're going to have to take some concrete steps to ensure that you don't end up with 850 copies stashed in boxes underneath your bed for the next 10 years. One of the first steps is to get your music in the hands of the folks at CD Baby (www.cdbaby.com) or a similar service.

CD Baby works with independent musicians (like you and me) to warehouse, sell, and ship your CDs. You send an inventory of CDs to them, tell them what price you want to charge, and they do the rest. For their troubles, they keep a set amount of every sale (four U.S. dollars as I write this). The rest comes to you, and you're paid weekly (assuming you've sold anything during the week). CD Baby claims that your CD could be available in over 2,400 retail stores across the United States.

CD Baby will also help you make your music available for download sale from their own site, Apple iTunes, Rhapsody, Napster, eMusic, and other download sites. They'll pay you 91% of the download price (keeping 9% as their cut).

Working a MySpace Music Account

Most of you have heard of MySpace.com. And for various reasons, many of you have resisted joining this (and other) online social networking sites. But now that you're trying to promote your music, it might be time to get involved.

MySpace has a section specifically intended for musicians and bands that is somewhat isolated from the general MySpace population. So if social networking sites are not your thing, you can maintain your music page, stay fairly separated from the general population, and send friend requests only to those people you want to.

That said, MySpace and other social networking sites are great tools for networking and getting your music out there. I know that there are people all over the world who have visited my page and listened to my music. Those are people who probably never would have heard my music otherwise because I'm not currently a touring musician. If you don't already have a MySpace page for your music, you should consider getting one set up as soon as you can and start developing a network of fans and other musicians who might be able to help you promote your music.

TIP

To set up a MySpace Band/Musician page as opposed to a general population page, click the Sign Up tab on the home page and then click the Band/Musician Sign Up Here link in the column at the right of the sign-up page. You'll be taken to a Band/Musician-specific form. That's where you want to enter your information.

After you set up your MySpace Band/Musician page, send me a friend request! I'd love to hear from you and keep in touch so that I can see and hear what you're up to with the techniques you've learned in this book. You can visit me on my page at www.myspace.com/busterfayte. My page is shown in Figure 12.11.

Figure 12.11

Visit me at MySpace and send me a friend request to keep in touch!

Joining ACID Planet

Sony Creative Software maintains a community of musicians and other artists who use their software to create music and video. Visit www.acidplanet.com to get involved. ACID Planet is a good place to connect with other musicians who are using ACID Pro to record their music. You can share ideas and listen to the music other artists are making. You can also set up an account and post your music to receive reviews from others, participate in forums, and so on.

Make sure you check in for the monthly 8 pack (eight free loops that you can download and add to your loop collection) under the Tools menu. There are always a few contests running, and the Mosh voting feature lets you put your songs up against others to see which ones rise to the top as voted on by other members of the ACID Planet community.

To find me on ACID Planet, click the Search link and search for *Buster Fayte*. Figure 12.12 shows my main page at ACID Planet.

Figure 12.12
You can post your songs, videos, lyrics, and more at ACID Planet.

Making Connections at Broadjam

Another great community of musicians exists at www.broadjam.com. The company states, "Broadjam is dedicated solely to the success and support of independent musicians and songwriters." The whole idea behind the site is for musicians to interact with one another to provide help, feedback, and inspiration to each other.

You share all this activity with the connections you make on Broadjam. This means your fans and fellow artists are continually and automatically informed whenever you upload a new song, book a gig, upload a video, or make any other changes to your profile.

After you set up a Broadjam account, you can post your songs and make them available for review by other Broadjam artists. You earn reviews by reviewing other music, so the site really thrives on participation.

Broadjam also runs several song contests each month and keeps many Top 10 charts, which are generated from peer reviews.

The site also puts musicians in touch with people who are looking for music for TV shows, films, and so on (and are willing to pay for using it). You're provided with a list of opportunities, and you can choose the ones that sound most like they're looking for your type of music.

Finally, Broadjam gives you a place where listeners can purchase and download your songs. Each song costs the customer $.99. As the artist, you get $.80 of that.

TIP

At their highest level, the Primo Member, Broadjam offers web hosting. This is a great way to get your personal website up quickly. Basically, you enter your information at Broadjam and choose one of their design templates. Broadjam does all the site design and back end for you if you want them to (although you can also create your own custom design).

You can visit my Broadjam page at www.broadjam.com/busterfayte. Figure 12.13 shows my page.

Figure 12.13

Broadjam is a great place for musicians to provide valuable feedback for one another and discover professional opportunities for placing their music.

The Desktop Music Channel

I've recently discovered the Desktop Music Channel (DMC), and though I don't have much experience with it yet, it looks like something worth keeping an eye on. This clever approach to promotion—found at www.desktopmusicchannnel.com—makes it possible for you take a more active role in what your fans see and hear from you. With it, you put your music and other content right on your fans' computer desktops every time they boot up their PC.

DMC is a combination desktop and server-based software application that your fans install on their Internet-capable PCs. Every time your fans start their computers and make an Internet connection, they receive the latest content you've posted to the server. This content can include music (for streaming or downloading), video, photos, blogs, events calendar, text messages, links of interest, and more. You update that content whenever you want, and the server pushes that new content to your fans' computers.

The application provides several opportunities to generate new revenue and include links to your personal website, music download sites, and anywhere else you have a presence on the Web. DMC offers an interesting and unique opportunity to connect with your most dedicated fans. To keep up on what's going on with me, download my DMC to your computer. I'll use it to share news and information related to both my music and this book. To download it from my website, visit www.busterfayte.com. Or install it from the Chapter 12 folder on the companion disc.

1,000 TRUE FANS

An interesting school of thought that I've seen tossed about in various forms is the concept of *1,000 True Fans*. This idea basically holds that you don't need to have a million fans to make a decent living in the music business. Instead, if you have 1,000 fans who are willing to spend $100 per year on you and your music, you can make a darn good yearly salary.

These dedicated souls are your True Fans. They're the people who come to your concerts every time you hit town, buy all your CDs, pick up a T-shirt and baseball cap with your logo on it at your merchandise table or from your website, and so on.

Now, I'm not saying that it's easy to create 1,000 True Fans, but no matter how you look at it, it's a much less daunting task than building up a fan base of a million! Your True Fans would be the ones who'll be willing to utilize something like the DMC discussed here. And it's they who will make it possible for you to turn your hobby into a revenue stream.

Your Personal Website

MySpace.com and these other resources are important aspects of a successful web presence, but if you're serious about promoting your music, you really have to consider maintaining your own professional website. You can find full-service web hosting for less than $10 U.S. per month. (Remember, Broadjam offers web hosting service with its Primo membership, which might be a good way to go because you get the use of Broadjam and a personal website.)

NOTE

You can find several providers who will host your website at no cost to you. Although free unarguably is a good price, these providers will load your website with advertising that you have no control over. *That's* the price you pay for the web hosting. In my opinion, that price is higher than the 10 bucks a month you can pay for really good hosting that gives you complete control of your site, but you might see it differently.

With a website devoted to your music, you can add any additional content that you feel you want to share with your fans. You can offer downloads, message boards, chats, forums, and so on. Make your website a destination of choice for your fans. Give them the opportunity to feel involved with you and your art. The more they feel part of what you're doing, the more they will support you!

A huge benefit to maintaining your own website is that your web host will be able to provide you with important information, such as detailed visitor statistics. Don't underestimate the benefit of knowing who's visiting your site and what they're looking at and listening to while they're there!

Finally, being seen on MySpace is one thing. But having a professional-looking website puts you in a completely different league. It gives you an air of professionalism that MySpace can't provide. Plenty of your potential fans will have negative feelings toward being involved in a social networking site like MySpace. But those same people won't balk at all about visiting your website.

NOTE

In this section I've listed several online resources I've had some experience with. There are many others out there that you might want to look into. For example, I've recently heard that many people are hot on www.sonicbids.com, but I have no personal experience with it. Take a look around the Web and see what other opportunities are out there. Maybe you'll find one that works better for you than those I've listed here.

Visit me at my website, www.busterfayte.com, to check out the things I'm doing there. Naturally, you'll find information about my music. But you'll also find information related to this book.

Studio Log

In this chapter, you attain the goal you've been working toward throughout the book: getting your music out there for your fans to discover and enjoy. When you create mixed files—the process of rendering—you create the final product. These are the files your fans will listen to, whether from a CD or from one of your web locations.

Independent musicians and artists have the potential to reach around the globe with their music via a multitude of online resources and services. CD Baby, MySpace, ACID Planet, and Broadjam are just a few of the services that I use to promote and sell my music. There are many others, and your professional website is certainly not the least of these!

The Internet isn't going to make you instantly rich and successful with your music; you've still got a lot of hard work ahead of you, and the competition hasn't slacked off any. But any way you look at it, the opportunity for your success is there now like never before.

We've covered a lot of ground over the past 12 chapters. I've laid out a solid plan of action for getting your songs recorded. But I haven't answered every question, and I don't pretend to have the definitive one true way of doing this. If you've had any "I would never do it that way!" moments while reading, that's good! That means you're already on the way to crafting your own system. In the end, recording music is every bit as personal a process as writing it and playing it. One hundred different musicians will have 100 different approaches and 1,000 different techniques.

But you have to start somewhere, and in this book I've given you concrete advice on how to get started. You can—and should—take my methods, techniques, and advice and mold them into a personal system that enables you to create the best recordings you can.

I've left a lot yet to be learned. In some cases I presented the topics, painted broad strokes regarding it, and left the rest for you to learn through further study and experience. That's not so much a challenge as it is encouragement for you to continue your quest for making top-notch recordings and enjoying the process!

Keep in touch. Visit my website and drop me an email at buster@busterfayte.com to give me feedback about what I've discussed here. I'll use that feedback and my website to provide any corrections, clarifications, and other ideas I collect from you and other readers. Think of it as a place where we can all come together and continue to develop our recording techniques.

And finally, let me know where I can find you online too. I'd love to hear the music you make using what you've learned here!

I sincerely appreciate that you took the time to study these techniques with me, and I hope you realize all the success that you seek through your music. Most of all, I hope that what I've taught you here can help you develop and enjoy your art to its fullest extent and to build a catalog of recorded music that will become your legacy.

Choosing Your Audio Interface

IN THIS APPENDIX

- Consider the issues you need to understand before buying your audio interface

- Determine what type of audio interface makes the most sense for you

- Learn the questions you need to ask when shopping for an audio interface

As you've seen, there are many issues to consider when deciding upon an audio interface. This appendix summarizes many of these issues to help you make a decision. Answer the questions posed here, and you'll have a more solid understanding of the issues involved as well as the questions you'll want to ask the salesperson or research online. I don't intend to make the decision for you here; rather, I'll try to guide you as you go through the process so that you can choose the audio interface that works for you and your setup.

How Much Can You Spend?

Like anything else, the more you spend on your audio interface, the more features and better quality components you're likely to get. At a minimum, though, you'll need two mono inputs and two mono outputs. You'll also need a device with decent AD/DA converters. Finally—if you're setting up on a Windows-based PC—it's critical to purchase a device that supports ASIO drivers so that you can avoid nasty latency problems.

How Many Inputs Do You Need?

Think about the procedures you'll be following in your studio. How are you going to record your tracks? If you'll always be recording just one or two input sources at a time, you can get by with minimal inputs—most devices have at least two.

On the other hand, if you'll be recording several inputs at a time (multiple microphones on a drum kit, a horn section, or a choir, for instance), you'll need a device with multiple inputs to handle all the microphones.

Most audio interfaces seem to max out at 10 inputs, so if you'll need more than that, you'll probably need more than one device. Make sure all the devices use the same software drivers, which essentially means that all the devices must be the same make and model. Make sure that the device you decide upon can work in combination like this. For instance, if you buy a FireWire audio interface, make sure that the unit has two FireWire ports so that you can daisy chain more than one device together.

How Many Outputs Do You Need?

Most of us can probably get by with just two mono outputs—one to feed the left monitor and one to feed the right. These outputs feed your monitors either directly or through a mixer/amplifier setup.

However, if you'll be creating surround-sound mixes, you'll need more outputs. (For example, if you're creating a 5.1 mix, you'll need six outputs on your audio device.)

You might also want more outputs to send your audio to an alternate set of monitors. You might want more than one set of monitors in your studio so you can hear your mixes on different speakers or if you have an isolation booth and want to feed the output to monitors in that area of your studio. You might also want to route the audio output to some piece of outboard gear like a compressor or a reverb unit (although your DAW's DSP options make outboard DSP all but unnecessary).

If you want to create alternate headphone mixes and send them to different people in your studio, you'll need extra outputs for that, too.

As you can see, there may be several situations in which you'll want or need extra audio outputs. But again, for most of us, two will do just fine.

What Connectivity Do You Want?

You'll have to decide between PCI, FireWire, or USB. If you don't intend to change your setup often, PCI may work fine for your studio. But, generally, PCI also dictates that you'll be using a mixer in your setup since (at least from what I've seen) PCI cards usually don't offer the input connectivity flexibility that FireWire and USB cards do.

Do You Need to Share Between PCs, or Do You Use a Laptop?

For portability, look toward FireWire and USB since these devices can easily be disconnected from one computer and connected to a different computer (as long as both computers contain the appropriate software drivers).

Remember also that if you're basing your system around a laptop, the PCI option won't work for you without some sort of external gear to hold it. It's much easier to connect a FireWire or USB unit to your laptop since many laptops come with a FireWire port and pretty much all laptops come with a couple of USB ports.

Will You Incorporate a Mixer?

You need to give some thought as to whether you'll need a mixer in your setup. You can find lots of different opinions on this topic! Ultimately, you must consider your unique situation and decide for yourself whether you need or want one. For example, if you have several pieces of electronic gear that you want to run into your audio interface (such as a tape deck or DVD player) you might find it more convenient to use a mixer. You'll have to make the decision before you buy your audio interface because it could have a bearing on which interface you choose.

If you plan to use a mixer in your setup, all you really need on your audio interface are the in and out jacks since the mixer controls everything else. Essentially, your audio interface serves as just a box to connect your mixer to your computer and convert analog signal to digital and back. In this setup, a PCI device that you can install and wire permanently may be exactly what you need.

However, if, like me, you want to eliminate the mixer from your setup, the audio interface you choose will have to take over for the mixer in several areas. For instance, the audio interface must be able to accept XLR inputs and have mic preamps so you can plug your microphone directly into it. You'll want easily accessible input trim controls, too, so that you can adjust the input level from your microphones or instruments.

You might also want output volume controls along with a headphone jack and headphone volume controls. And you'll want all this in an easily accessible location so that you don't have to do gymnastics to make adjustments.

What Input Connectivity Do You Need?

This question is related to the previous question about using a mixer. If you'll be recording straight to your audio interface, make sure it accepts XLR connectors as well as 1/4-inch connectors.

I love being able to go directly into my audio interface with my input devices. If your microphone requires a power source, look for an audio interface that supplies phantom power and features a convenient way to turn that on and off.

It's also great if the device has both 1/4-inch line- and instrument-level inputs. That way you can plug line-level devices such as electronic keyboards and drum machines into the device, but you can also plug instrument-level devices such as your guitar or bass guitar directly into your interface. It enables you to skip buying some sort of direct input box (DI box) for your instrument. This is especially useful if you use guitar or bass amplifier emulation software.

Do You Intend to Use MIDI Gear?

MIDI plays an important role in the type of studio you're setting up. Some MIDI controllers can connect via USB. However, others can't. If yours can't, you'll need MIDI in/out ports. You can purchase separate MIDI interface devices to get your MIDI signals into and out of your computer, but it can be awfully nice to have that capability right in your audio interface.

Do You Want a Specialty Device?

You can make your audio interface pull extra duty if it has additional components such as a MIDI controller keyboard or guitar/bass amp emulation capabilities. You can also buy drum machine–specific devices and devices that combine with mixer controls that interact (via MIDI) with your DAW software.

Such devices can give you extra functionality but can also be a problem because there are more components to go bad. For example, if the keyboard controller portion goes bad, you may find yourself without your audio interface, too.

Do You Need the Device for Field Recording?

Again, portability is the issue. You also might need an audio interface that can be powered through the FireWire connection (and thus off your laptop's battery) if you're in a location that doesn't have accessible power.

Bit Depth and Sampling Rate

Most high-quality cards now support high sampling rates (up to 192Hz) and at bit depths up to at least 24 bit. Make sure the one you purchase supports at a minimum a sampling rate of 44.1Hz and a bit depth of 16. These are the standards for CD-quality audio, and anything below that will give you vastly inferior sound quality.

Recommendation

As you've probably gathered, I'm a big fan of FireWire-based audio interfaces. This technology has made a huge difference in my studio and in my workflow. I've been able to completely eliminate my mixer from the setup because my audio interface handles everything I need a mixer to do. A mixer may provide a bit more flexibility, but I don't miss it enough to overcome the benefits I realize from going without one.

I have 10 inputs on my card and, although I rarely use all of them, it's great to have them when I need them (although, of course, it costs more). I look for something with multiple inputs, including XLR along with line- and instrument-level 1/4-inch input jacks. I have record-level trim controls, a headphone jack, volume controls, and phantom power controls on my device. And all this is easily accessible from the front of the audio interface so I can reach it easily when I need it.

Although I also have 10 outputs on my card, I use only two. Most cards that have multiple inputs have an equal number of outputs. I might not use them now, but it's nice to know that if I want to set up an alternative pair of studio monitors or an alternative headphone mix, I'll be able to do so.

Conclusion

The purchase of your audio interface is one of the most important decisions you have to make in setting up your computer for audio recording. The interface you choose has a direct bearing not only on how easy your setup is to use, but also on the potential quality of the sound you get out of your system.

Because I like the reduction in clutter on my workspace that I get by eliminating my mixer, I have to have a card that can substitute for the mixer in several ways. Even if you do use a mixer, it's not a bad idea to use an audio interface that's as robust and flexible as possible.

So now you know the questions to ask and the features to look for. Hopefully you've answered these questions and now have a good idea of what you need from an audio interface.

Glossary

0.0dB—Used to indicate no attenuation or boost to audio volume in digital audio. Also, the point above which audio begins to clip on input and output.

A

ACID Planet (www.acidplanet.com)—An online community of musicians who use Sony Creative Software tools to create their music.

ACID Pro—Digital audio workstation software from Sony Creative Software that enables you to work with loop-based music, multitrack audio, and MIDI sequencing.

active monitors—Monitors that feature built-in amplification.

alternate mix—A mix that's different from the main mix and that you set up to compare two mixes or (more typically) provide a custom mix for a performer as he listens while recording a new track.

amplifier (amp) emulation—*See* amplifier modeling.

amplifier (amp) modeling—Using digital processing to mimic the sound of actual guitar (or other types of) amplifiers and speaker cabinets.

analog to digital/digital to analog converter (AD/DA)—Equipment that converts analog audio signals into digital signals that a computer can understand and the digital signal from a computer to analog signal that can play through your speakers or headphones.

arming a track—The process of enabling one of your multitrack recorder's tracks to receive incoming audio signal from a microphone or other source to record that audio to the track.

attack—A setting on a compressor, limiter, or other gear that dictates how quickly the effect kicks in once the threshold setting is surpassed.

attenuate—The term you use instead of the phrase *turn the volume down* when you want to sound like an audio engineering guru.

audio interface—A piece of equipment that enables you to send audio into your computer for recording and out of it for listening.

audio reflections—Sound waves bouncing off of objects and surfaces in the room and coming back to your ears (or microphone), thus causing reverberation and echoes.

audio routing—Also known as the audio signal path. The path (physical or software based) that the audio takes through your audio equipment. As a verb, the act of specifying how the audio will travel through the various parts of your system.

Audio Stream Input/Output (ASIO)—Audio driver technology developed by Steinberg that provides low latency and high fidelity.

automation—Setting up your DAW so that one or more parameters (like volume or panning) adjust automatically at specific times during a song according to your instructions. Some hardware mixers can also support automation.

B

band—Apart from the obvious collection of freaks and weirdos that you hang out with to play music, a band is a type of frequency control that covers a range of frequencies above and below the target frequency, thus creating a bell-shaped curve with the target frequency at the highest (or lowest) point in the bell.

batch converter—A tool that enables you to set up multiple render scenarios to run automatically so that you don't have to manually render each file individually.

beatmap—A long file (typically over 30 seconds) that contains tempo information and will thus conform to the ACID Pro project tempo settings.

bleed—Sound from one audio source (like an instrument or vocals) that ends up being recorded by a microphone that was intended to record the sound from a different audio source exclusively.

bouncing—The technique of recording a mix of the audio from several tracks of a multitrack recorder (typically an analog tape machine with a small number of tracks) down to one or two open tracks to free up those original tracks for new recording.

Broadjam (www.broadjam.com)—A community of musicians dedicated solely to the success and support of independent musicians and songwriters.

bus—A hardware or software device that transfers audio from one place to another.

C

CD Baby (www.cdbaby.com)—An online service that warehouses, markets, and sells CDs for independent musicians.

central processing unit (CPU)—The brains of your computer that does all the complex calculations required by whatever it is you're doing in your software.

channel strip (channel)—A grouping of controls in a mixing console.

clip list—A listing of all the clips (audio or MIDI files) that have been added to a track in ACID Pro.

clipping—A phenomenon of digital audio where the audio gets so loud that your software runs out of bits to describe it accurately. When clipping occurs, any audio that happens above the clipping point is discarded, resulting in ugly audio distortion.

compression (audio compression)—A DSP tool that diminishes the dynamic range of the audio according to a specific ratio by attenuating any audio that rises above a certain level (threshold) and thus can make the audio seem louder overall.

compression (file compression)—Technology for saving audio files with a reduced file size. *See also* lossy compression and lossless compression.

crossover settings—Settings that define the limits of a frequency range in a multiband compressor or other DSP that enable you to affect multiple frequency ranges separately.

D

dampening—Creating surfaces in a room that minimize or eliminate audio reflections.

DAW (Digital Audio Workstation)—Can refer specifically to multitrack recording software or more generally to the entire computer system on which you record and edit your audio.

decibels (dB)—A measure of audio volume.

diffusion—Creating surfaces of varying angles in a room that cause sound waves to reflect in many directions instead of in one distinct direction.

Digital Audio Workstation (DAW)—Can refer specifically to multitrack recording software or more generally to the entire computer system on which you record and edit your audio.

Digital Signal Processing (DSP)—Digital equipment (hardware or software) that adds effects and other filters (such as reverb, delay, echo, equalization, and so on) to your audio to change its sound qualities.

Direct Input (DI)—A device that boosts the low signal from an instrument such as a guitar or bass guitar to make that signal stronger for recording purposes, thus enabling you to plug directly into your mixer or audio device inputs without playing through an amplifier.

DirectX—A plug-in standard that enables your digital audio software to communicate with DSP plug-ins.

disc-at-once—A technique of burning a CD from your computer's CD-ROM burner where the entire burning process happens from beginning to end in one session.

Downloadable Sound (DLS)—A file that contains various synthesized or sampled sounds that are used to play back MIDI files.

driver—Software that comes with various pieces of computer hardware so that the hardware can communicate with the computer.

dry audio—Audio that DSP has not affected.

DSP (digital signal processing)—Digital equipment (hardware or software) that adds effects and other filters (such as reverb, delay, echo, equalization, and so on) to your audio to change its sound qualities.

dynamic range—The difference between the quietest sound and the loudest sound.

dynamics—Variations in the overall volume of a sound.

E

ear fatigue—A phenomenon by which your ears perform at less than their peak because you've been listening to music for too long and perhaps too loudly.

envelope—A tool used in some DAW software to create an automated mix.

EQ (equalization or equalizer)—As equalization, this is the act of changing the volume of specific audio frequencies to shape or alter the sound. As equalizer, this refers to the equipment (hardware or software) used to adjust the volume of specific audio frequencies.

equalization (EQ)—The act of changing the volume of specific audio frequencies to shape or alter the sound.

equalizer (EQ)—The hardware or software equipment used to adjust the volume of specific audio frequencies to shape or alter the sound.

event—An object on the ACID Pro timeline that displays the audio waveform of an audio file or MIDI note indicators of the MIDI file associated with it. The position of the event on the timeline dictates exactly when the file will be played.

F

FireWire—Apple's brand name for an interface (officially known as IEEE 1394) used for high-speed data transfer between a computer or other equipment like digital video cameras and audio interfaces. Also known by Sony's brand name for the same interface, i.Link.

fresh ears—A term used to indicate that you've taken a break from listening to music (and other loud noises), specifically the music you're working on, to give your ears a rest.

full duplexing—The ability of an audio interface to play audio while simultaneously recording audio.

G

gain—A setting on a compressor, limiter, or other DSP that enables you to attenuate or boost the output volume of the effect.

H

Hertz (Hz)—A measure of wavelength and thus audio frequency.

I

input monitoring—A feature of some software or hardware gear that enables you to hear (via your speakers) the audio you're sending into your computer.

input or input jack—A connection on your multitrack recorder, audio interface, or other piece of audio gear that accepts a cable carrying the audio signal being sent from another piece of audio equipment (like a microphone).

isolation booth/Iso booth—A room that can be used to separate a live microphone placed inside the room from sounds being made outside the room that you don't want to record with the microphone (or sounds being made inside the room that you don't want to record with a microphone placed outside the room).

Izotope—A manufacturer of high-quality DSP tools.

J

jack—A connection on a piece of audio equipment into which you plug a cable that carries audio signal either into (input jack) or out of (output jack) the equipment.

K

KitCore—A VSTi manufactured by Submersible that features drum sounds.

L

latency—The time it takes an audio signal to pass from the source of the audio, through the audio equipment, and out the speakers to your ears.

limiter—A DSP that attenuates any audio that is louder than a specified level (the threshold) and holds it to that level. This attenuates the loudest peaks, which enables you to raise the overall volume and results in louder sounding audio, but also audio with less dynamic range.

live room—A room that has highly audio reflective surfaces that result in lots of echo or reverberation.

loop—A small section of music that's been edited so precisely that if you play it over and over again without stopping, it plays with perfect musical timing.

loop library—A collection of loops usually sold on CD or DVD.

loop region—An area you define in your DAW that will play repeatedly until you purposely stop playback.

lossless compression—File compression that reduces the file size without sacrificing audio quality.

lossy compression—File compression that reduces the file size but also sacrifices audio quality.

low/high shelf—A type of frequency adjustment in an equalizer where the frequency and every frequency below (low band) or above (high band) is attenuated or boosted never to come back to its original level.

M

margin—The setting on a limiter that specifies the volume that any audio that surpasses the threshold setting will be held to.

master bus—A set of controls in a hardware or software mixer that accepts audio from different sources, combines that audio as your main mix, and sends the combined signal to its next destination (like the outputs of your audio interface).

mastering—The process of applying DSP to improve the sound quality of the recording and to ensure that it sounds even and consistent with other recordings in the same project.

metadata—Nonaudio information such as composer name, copyright details, and so on that can be embedded into an audio file and displayed by various playback devices.

mic—A common abbreviation for the word *microphone*. It can also be used as a verb to refer to the process of setting up a microphone to record sound.

MIDI (Musical Instrument Digital Interface)—A protocol that enables musical equipment, computers, and other equipment to communicate with one another.

MIDI controller—A device that generates MIDI information.

minimum system requirements—A software manufacturer's basic minimum standards in terms of storage space, random access memory (RAM), processor speed, operating system version, and so on that your computer must meet to run the software effectively.

minus infinity (–Inf)—Used to indicate silence in digital audio.

mixed file—A file that's been mixed down from the original multitrack project to a mono, stereo, or multichannel (surround sound) file in a format that can be played on a stereo, computer, personal music player, and so on.

mixing—The process of blending all the sounds in your project so that they combine to create a pleasing overall sound.

mixing console (mixer)—A piece of hardware or software equipment that makes it possible to control the volume and equalization of several separate audio input devices, combine the audio from those sources, and send that signal to the same set of speakers or other device. In ACID Pro, this is the main mixing environment.

mixing stage—The part of the production process when you turn your attention away from recording new tracks and concentrate on creating a final mix of the project as a whole.

multiband compression—*See also* compression (audio compression) and compression (file compression). A compression tool that enables you to specify different compression settings for different frequency ranges.

multitrack—A hardware or software recording device that is capable of recording onto many tracks, thus making it possible to record several sound sources simultaneously (or separately) while keeping the recording of each separate from every other source and then playing back those recordings in perfect synchronization with one another.

mute—A mixing term that means to take a track or bus out of the mix temporarily by preventing its output from routing to the output mix so that you can hear how your mix sounds without it.

MySpace (www.myspace.com)—The most popular online social networking site that features a musician and band section where you can promote your music for free.

N

Native Instruments—A manufacturer of high-quality VSTi and VST plug-ins, including the Guitar Combo amplifier emulation plug-ins.

near-field monitors—Reference monitors that have been designed with an optimal listening distance of between 3 and 5 feet away.

normalization—A DSP step that increases the audio's highest peak to a specified level and boosts all the other audio in the file proportionally, thus making the audio as loud as it can be (or as loud as you want it to be) without clipping.

O

oneshot file—A file that contains a recorded sound that is not intended to repeat and thus contains no tempo information.

output or output jack—A connection that you plug a cable into that carries the audio signal from one piece of equipment (like an audio mixing console) to another (such as your speakers).

overclocking—The potentially dangerous (to your computer) practice of forcing your processor to run at a faster speed than it was designed and tested for. Don't do it!

overdubbing—The process of recording new audio material as you listen to and play along with audio material that you recorded previously.

P

panning—The placement of a sound in the stereo spectrum from left to right.

passive monitors—Monitors that require amplification from an external source.

patch—A preset sound in a synthesizer. Also called a program.

PDS (Portable Digital Studio)—A multitrack recording machine that incorporates—all in one box—many of the component pieces that go into making a multitrack recording setup, such as a mixer and digital signal processing.

peak (audio peak)—The point where an audio waveform reaches its highest point before going back down.

peak indicator—A readout in your DAW or other digital audio software that shows the value of the audio's highest peak. In ACID Pro, if the peak indicator turns red, your audio is clipping.

Peripheral Component Interconnect (PCI)—Technology used for plugging peripheral devices into a computer's motherboard to bring extra functionality to the computer.

phantom power—Power sent by a mixer, audio interface, or other gear to supply a microphone that requires a power source to operate.

Phonautogram—The first device to successfully record audio. Built in 1860 by French inventor Edouard-Leon Scott de Martinville, the device recorded sound as a crude representation of sound waves drawn onto paper that could be read but not heard.

plosive—Consonant sounds made by momentarily holding back the air behind your lips and letting it out explosively.

plug-in—A small software application that works within a host application (like DAW software) and brings extra functionality to the host that it did not originally have.

pop screen—A device used to diffuse the air coming from a vocalist's mouth and minimize the popping sound that can result when a sudden burst of air hits a microphone.

Portable Digital Studio (PDS)—A multitrack recording machine that incorporates—all in one box—many of the component pieces that go into making a multitrack recording setup, such as a mixer, digital signal processing, and so on.

preroll—The portion of audio that plays to enable you to establish the rhythm and timing of the song before you reach the portion you are replacing in a punch-in recording.

processor—Short for *microprocessor* and also referred to as *CPU* (central processing unit). The CPU is the brains of your computer that does all the complex calculations required by whatever it is you're doing in your software.

program—A preset sound in a synthesizer. Also called a patch.

proximity effect—A phenomenon of directional microphones in which the closer the sound source is to the microphone, the louder the low frequencies of the sound are recorded.

pumping—A phenomenon in compression where you can hear the effect of the compressor kicking in and out. Although it can be used to special effect, pumping is generally considered an undesirable end product.

punch-in recording—Recording new material over just a portion of an existing recording to fix a mistake or play something differently over that portion.

R

Random Access Memory (RAM)—The memory available for your computer to use while it runs the operations that your software is asking it to run.

ratio—A specification of how much the audio passing through a compressor will be attenuated once it surpasses the threshold setting.

red book—The specifications to which a CD must adhere to be officially considered an audio CD and thus play properly in audio CD players.

reference monitors—Speakers that have been designed to accurately reproduce audio without coloring it in an attempt to make it sound better.

reference music—Recordings that you are familiar with and that exhibit the kind of production quality that you want to achieve with your music. You can use reference music to become intimate with the sound of your gear and room and as a comparison when you're mixing and mastering your songs.

release—A setting on a compressor, limiter, or other DSP that dictates how quickly the effect will stop acting on the audio once it falls back below the threshold setting.

render—The act of creating a mixed file that can be played by common music playing hardware or software.

replication—The process of having your master CD mass produced.

reverberation/reverb—The effect of many reflections of an initial sound reaching your ears at different times, yet so close together that you cannot distinguish one reflection from the next.

rough mix—A typically hastily prepared mix of all your audio tracks and buses that you create to get a better sense of what the project will sound like either for evaluation purposes or to make it easier to hear certain elements during the recording of other elements.

S

sampler—A device that creates sound by playing back actual recordings (samples) of the instrument it's attempting to imitate.

scribble strip—An area on a mixer (hardware or software) that you can write or type on or in so that you can label a channel for easy identification.

self-powered speakers—Speakers that provide their own amplification.

sequencer—Software that you use to alter and edit MIDI information.

sequencing—The process of altering and editing MIDI information.

signal-to-noise ratio—The ratio of the desired audio signal to the noise that the equipment the audio passes through creates.

snapping—A feature of ACID Pro and other software in which, when you drag an object (like an event edge) close enough to a snap object (by default, ruler marks and other objects by choice), the object jumps, or snaps, to the snap object so you know that it is precisely positioned.

Soft Synth—A software-based synthesizer.

solo—A mixing term that means to silence the output from all tracks and buses other than the one (or ones) you want to hear so that you can hear it alone.

Sony Creative Software—The developers and manufactures of ACID Pro, Sound Forge, and other audio- and video-related software.

spectrum analysis—A tool that provides a visual overview of the frequencies in your project either in an overall average or at a specific time in the song.

split—Dividing an event on the ACID Pro timeline into two separate events that can be moved and otherwise edited independently of one another.

standing waves—A build-up or accentuation of specific audio frequencies that can often occur when two flat surfaces face each other in a room.

streaming—Serving audio (or video) files directly from a web server in real time to the listener (or viewer) so that it can be experienced without waiting for the file to download to the local computer.

submix—A grouping of related tracks or buses (for instance, drum tracks or buses) that you can solo or mute as a group so that you can concentrate on just that group or remove the entire group from the overall mix.

synthesizer (synth)—A device that generates and combines a variety of frequencies to create sound.

T

threshold—A setting on a compressor, limiter, or other DSP that specifies the volume level at which the effect will activate.

track header—The area in the ACID Pro workspace that contains various mixing tools for each track, such as volume, pan, and other controls.

trim control—A knob or fader on a mixer or audio interface that enables you to adjust the volume level of an audio input source.

tuning a room—Analyzing a room for audio reflections and frequency response and controlling the sound through the use of sound dampening, diffusion, and other techniques.

U

uncompressed—A file format that saves the audio without any lossy or lossless compression algorithm.

USB—The common abbreviation for Universal Serial Bus, a high-speed interface connection common with computers and other equipment such as external hard drives and audio interfaces.

V

velocity or MIDI note velocity—A value assigned to a MIDI note that gives the synthesizer instructions regarding the volume of the note.

Virtual Studio Technology (VST)—A specification for integrating software synthesizers and DSP modules into digital audio software.

Virtual Studio Technology Instrument (VSTi)—A software synthesizer or sampler that conforms to the VST specifications.

W

wet audio—Audio that DSP has affected.

window docking area—The area in the ACID Pro workspace where multiple windows can be placed either in their own sections or as tabbed windows beneath other windows in the same section.

X

XLR connector (Cannon connector)—An electrical connection design commonly used in high-end audio equipment, especially professional-level microphones, but also speakers, mixers, and so on.

Index

G - H

I

M

Q - R

S

TUBES, TRANSISTORS, TOLEX AND TWEED.

WELCOME TO GUITAR RIG 3. Imagine having a dream collection of classic amps and effects, all plugged in and ready to go. That's the basic idea behind GUITAR RIG 3, a hardware/software system featuring the world's best models of 12 legendary amps, 23 guitar and bass cabinets, 4 rotary speakers, 9 mics, and 44 effects. So you can tweak, record and recall your perfect custom tone, whenever and wherever. GUITAR RIG 3 is also the only system with a rugged floor controller that doubles as a high-quality audio interface – letting you plug your guitar or bass right in to your Mac or PC.

Dreaming of tubes, transistors, tolex and tweed?
Visit **www.native-instruments.com**

NI NATIVE INSTRUME

THE FUTURE OF SOUND